To Graham, with thanks

Contents

Acknowledgements

First of all, I acknowledge with considerable gratitude the help given me by Mrs Aska Kalra, a computer technician at Leicester Polytechnic. She was unfailingly helpful when I asked for INGRES facilities to be put at my disposal at weekends or during holidays. She acted above the call of duty and with unfailing charm and courtesy.

Secondly, I would like to put on record my considerable debt to Graham Daniels, a systems analyst at Polytechnic SW. He kindly read my text, made coherent and sensible comments upon that text, and often suggested useful additions to the text (suggestions that I normally ignored because one can hardly take the ideas of someone who supports Wrexham Football Club at all seriously).

Mike Kretis, a colleague at Leicester Polytechnic, kindly read the opening chapters of this book and made a number of extremely pertinent comments. Mike's ideas I did take note of and incorporate into the completed text. I am only sorry that I could not have the benefit of his criticisms for the entire text.

While the above are the major debts that I incurred when writing this book, I would like to mention a number of others to whom I am grateful. The first is David Howe, the Head of the Department of Information Systems at Leicester Polytechnic. Dr Howe provided my first ever context in which I genuinely felt that I was being encouraged to learn about information technology, and it was he who very much set that tone. After I left Leicester Polytechnic, Dr Howe continued to respond to any pleas for assistance with both speed and charm. Apart from him and Mike Kretis, there were numerous other members of that department who I am sure contributed to this book in a number of tangential ways—Ray, Stuart, Mary, Brian, and John, for instance—if only in making the Polytechnic such an agreeable place in which to work and think.

Outside Leicester Polytechnic, I am grateful to Mr John P. G. Roper, Acting Director of the Computer Centre at the University of East Anglia, who kindly arranged for me to use the INGRES facilities at UEA during one holiday. Miss Pat Newby, the INGRES expert at UEA, was most helpful and obliging in lending me books and dealing with my queries when I was using UEA facilities. I also found Andrew Ware, publisher from McGraw-Hill, a most agreeable, patient, and understanding publishing professional.

My wife and children regarded the writing of this book as a harmless eccentricity and ignored it completely, but their very existence was a major factor in my ever completing it. I might, as a punishment, force them to read it.

Finally, of course, all the books that are mentioned in the text, and dozens that are not, were of immeasurable help in instructing and guiding me. Thank you to a lot of authors.

PART ONE

Plan, purpose, and procedures

1
Introduction: the object of the exercise

Since computer science, information technology, or whatever synonym you care to use is commonly regarded as a precise and exact study, I shall begin with a piece of imagination. I imagine that you are in a bookshop and have picked up this book with some form of curiosity. How idle that curiosity is, I will not attempt to wager. You have picked it up, however, and you may even be wondering whether or not to buy it. This short, introductory chapter is designed to explain exactly what sort of book it is. With that sort of information, you are then in the informed position necessary to make a reasoned judgement.

Since you are in a bookshop, you may not have time even to read the whole of this short chapter. Consequently, let me list in summary form the intentions and purpose of this book.

1. Total clarity. If you are so uninformed as to believe that INGRES was a Greek mythological monster (it was not), then you will none the less still be able to understand this book. No previous knowledge is assumed. It is, however, assumed that you are literate and of at least reasonable intelligence. (Since we do not know what the word 'intelligence' means, I shall simply assume that you combine the qualities of Socrates, Leonardo da Vinci, Mozart and Einstein.)

2. Interest. Far too many computer books make a railway timetable look gripping in comparison. (Actually, I do have a brother-in-law who does regard railway timetables as gripping.) This is a shame—not my brother-in-law's quaint tastes, but that computer books are often dull. Computer science is an interesting subject, and INGRES is an interesting and exciting product of computer science. I shall attempt to convey some of that interest and excitement.

3. A logical progression. Computer science is a cumulative subject. Most of the time you cannot understand section D unless you have already learnt about sections A, B, and C. Hence I shall try to develop the subject in such a way that you can see the manifold wonders of INGRES slowly reveal themselves as we build in an incremental fashion. Unfortunately, this does mean that you cannot begin this book on Chapter 9 and expect it to make any sense at all.

4. Practicality. This book is designed to enable you not only to understand what INGRES is and what INGRES can do, but also to make you competent in sitting at a computer keyboard and actually using INGRES.

This, then, is the object of the exercise. Hence it follows that if you really did pick up this book in the belief that INGRES was a mythological monster, then it is probably not quite the sort of volume you want. Furthermore, if you are already an experienced database manager just looking for a breakdown of the differing versions of INGRES, then this is not your book either. If, however, you work for a company that uses INGRES and you would like a relatively painless way of learning about it, then I suggest this might be your book. If you are studying computer science at university or polytechnic and have a course on INGRES, then again I think that this book will be helpful. Certainly that is its intention. Again, if you are that convenient lay person who is interested in information technology but is put off by the jargon-ridden tomes that confront you, I can promise that this will be a more approachable avenue into the vital world of relational databases than many other books (with honourable exceptions) seem concerned to offer. Indeed, although INGRES is the specific relational database with which this book is concerned, it is hoped that this book would also be of help even if the database with which you were concerned was Informix, Oracle, DB2, or any other.

So far as I know, there are only four other books on the market devoted entirely to INGRES. The first, C. J. Date's *A Guide to INGRES* (1987), published by Addison-Wesley, is an excellent book. Certainly Date fulfils the first three objectives that I laid down above. He is clear, interesting, and logical. The book, however, is not designed as a step-by-step guide to using INGRES. Nor, although it is very clear, is it designed for the total ignoramus. Date does assume at least some basic knowledge of computer science. He does not, for instance, bother to define the word 'database'. This is fine if you know what a database is, but not so fine if you are just a little uncertain. Hence Date's book, I would suggest, is the second book that you ought to read about INGRES. I found it absorbing and, with a little knowledge, so will you.

The second book of which I am aware is Carl Malamud's *INGRES: Tools for Building an Information Architecture*, published in 1989 by Van Nostrand Reinhold. This you can forget about immediately. Malamud's book, I am afraid, is not designed for anyone ignorant of databases, or, I regret to say, for anyone remotely sensitive to the use of the English language.

The third book is also the oldest, which in so rapidly changing a field as computer science can itself be a disadvantage. Not so, however, with this book. Called *The INGRES Papers: Anatomy of a Relational Database System*, it is a collection of 22 papers edited by Michael Stonebraker. Many of the essays are concerned with the design and development of INGRES itself, and some of them are fascinating. However, with titles like 'Locking Granularity Revisited' and 'Data Abstraction, Views and Updates in REGEL', you will appreciate that it is not aimed at the beginner or as a primer for using INGRES.

The fourth book, *INGRES User Guide: Visual Programming Tools*, by Peter Matthews was only published when this book had already been written. It has many of the same aims as this book, yet, not surprisingly, is none the less very different. Matthews only concerns himself with Version 6 of INGRES, while I am mostly concerned with Version 5 but do also include Version 6 in many instances. Matthews also pays no attention to Structured Query Language (SQL) which seems to me to be a mistake. Indeed, Matthews is only concerned to provide a user's guide. He provides no explanation of the intellectual rationale for any given procedure, or any background understanding. Normalization, for instance, which I regard as a crucial technique for preparing data for computer entry, is dealt by Matthews in so cursory a fashion as to be somewhat indigestible. Nor, although Mr Matthews does set exercises, is much guidance given for their successful completion, and no attempt is made to provide self-testing questions by which a reader can evaluate his or her own memory recall and intellectual understanding. His Glossary is also considerably sparser than my own, which seems to me to be a shame for an introductory book presumably read by students for whom relational databases are an entirely new world. Indeed, my book gives a much fuller understanding of the theoretical basis of INGRES. Hence it depends upon your own priorities. If you want a workmanlike, practical guide, then Matthews's book would probably be perfectly adequate. I have to confess that I have an aversion to such practical guides because they strike me as being a negation of the human desire to understand, but tastes differ. In addition, Matthews states on his second page that anyone reading his book should have some basic computer literacy. This is not a qualification necessary for reading this one.

Of course, you are not limited to commercially produced books. Relational Technology, who developed INGRES as a commercial product, do produce a whole series of user manuals, including one deliberately aimed at the beginner. I have not always found these manuals 100 per cent accurate, but, on the whole, they do a good job. But they, like Matthews, are completely user-orientated. The RT manuals will tell you what to do, but they will not discuss the operation in more theoretical terms; they will not explain what is

happening in terms of relational *raison d'être*. If, for whatever reason, you
want to learn how to use INGRES, then it is a *sine qua non* that you also
learn why such a procedure exists. Any fool can learn the words 'je suis', 'tu
es', and 'il est', but there is not much point in learning them unless you
understand that they are the French equivalent of 'I am', 'you are', and 'he
is'. Equally any fool can learn that INGRES is built round the concept of the
table, which is then translated into a form—that sort of object we are always
being asked to fill in for various unfathomable bureaucratic reasons. There is
no point, however, in learning that INGRES is so modelled without learning
why this is the case. This book will not transform you into an expert user of
all the facilities of INGRES, but at least you will *understand* the facilities that
you have learnt to use, and you will be in a good position to extend your user
awareness. Of course, if you do already know about relational databases and
just want a user's guide, then the RT manuals will be fine, though even then
they do present some problems in locating the information that you actually
want when you want it. The RT handbooks are a reference source. They are
not designed as a comfortable guide. Hence one can often find, when working
through Chapter 5, that you need to refer to material in Chapter 16, and so
on. This is not a criticism of those guides. It was through them that I learnt
most of what I now know about INGRES. None the less, both I and the
students I supervised did not always find the RT tomes as approachable or as
structured as a purpose-built guide needs to be. From that point of view, the
Matthews book might be a better option.

Let me then return to the objectives that I expressed earlier in summary
form.

The first was CLARITY. Do excuse the pretention of printing the word in
capitals, but it is an objective more honoured in the breach than in the
observance. Unless an exposition is clear, no one learns anything from it.
Such a truism is so self-evident that one is almost ashamed of writing it, but
we all know that clarity is a virtue far from commonly evident. Yet it is
placed first amongst my four objectives because it seems to me to be by far
the most crucial. Unfortunately, however, the quest for total clarity does
bear with it a danger. If I am determined never to use a remotely technical
word without first of all definining it, then the exposition is inevitably slowed
down (which is irritating for everyone) and those who knew what the term
meant anyway are bored rigid (which might be terminal for them). Two
remarks are relevant here. First of all, my definitions will attempt always to
be brief, so that we are slowed down as little as possible. Secondly, even if
you do know what a parameter is (or a database, or an interface, or
whatever), it is not without interest to see how writer X defines it. Words are
slippery things. For instance, the Oxford University Press *Dictionary of
Computing* (1983) defines a database as 'A collection of interrelated data
values of such a nature that they might be represented as a number of files
but not a single file.' But what is a data value? What is a file? Above all,

what are 'interrelated' values. The towns of Prague, Paris, Oxford, and London are interrelated because they are all the nicknames of symphonies. They are interrelated because they are all cities in Europe. They are interrelated because they are all university towns. And so one could go on. A word like 'interrelated' is a subjective word. Its meaning is only evident through its context, and in the Oxford *Dictionary of Computing* it is barely given sufficient context for it to have any meaning at all. Hence I ask for indulgence in my passion for defining my terms of reference. It is not an idle exercise. I fear, however, that there is another danger into which it is easy to run. If I am writing for the uninformed, and, at the same time, determined to be clear, there is a serious risk of oversimplification. The English Civil War was a religious conflict. That statement is true. But the English Civil War was also many other things. It was an economic struggle. It was an embryonic class war. It was a war of political ideologies. And so one could go on. Hence, to say that the English Civil War was a religious conflict, and to say only that, is to mislead. Yet, to some extent, this dilemma is like trying to square the circle. This book is not designed for someone doing his or her Ph.D. in database design. Consequently there is bound to be a certain amount of oversimplification. All that I can attempt is to ensure that the simplification never becomes either misleading or patronizing. I recall too well my own painful introduction to INGRES to become patronizing. I can only thank in retrospect the students I supervised; they taught me much. Obviously too I shall try hard never to mislead. Also, because one does forget the meanings of words even if they have been clearly defined, I have included a glossary at the end of the book that tries to gather together all the remotely technical words used in this book. If I have inadvertently missed any out, I would be grateful if you could direct my attention to such omissions.

My second objective was INTEREST. I find INGRES an artefact of considerable interest. Consequently I hope to convey this interest. None the less, I shall not attempt to do so by writing like this:

> Now comes the beginning of our adventure. We shall now, for the first time, enter the absorbing world of INGRES itself. I want you to type at your computer keyboard the word 'addingres'. This mystic slogan will transport you away from the barren and limited world you and I normally inhabit. It will, instead, convey you into that fairy-land of wonders, the INGRES database.

There will be, I hope, no melodrama in this book, no purple passages of tortured prose. Nor, I hope, will there be too much of that pedestrian prose which aims at accuracy, but certainly accomplishes tedium. Indeed, I hope and believe that the interest flows from the clarity. INGRES is interesting. Hence any book that clearly explains what INGRES is and how to use it is, by the nature of the subject, bound to be interesting. Indeed, since most subjects are interesting—the English Civil War, the poems of Gerard Manley

Hopkins, the geology of the Lake District, the fauna of Australia—it ought, by definition, to be impossible to write a dull book. To our cost we all know the falsity of that pious belief. All the same, interest is a spurious objective. If something that is of inherent interest is clearly explained, then the explanation will be interesting. Six years ago I had no interest in databases. I then read Peter Laurie's book on the subject. *Ergo*: I became interested. It is also worthwhile, in passing, to quote the first sentence of Laurie's first chapter: 'A database is a bunch of information held in a computer's memory' (*Databases*, Chapman & Hall/Methuen, 1985, p. 9). That is the sort of writing at which I aim. It is brief and requires no further explication. Of course it is a limited definition. It does require some expansion and refinement. Laurie provides this, but never loses clarity and never relapses into jargon. Indeed, he begins his second chapter with the sentence 'A database is simply a collection of lumps of information stored on a computer' (p. 39). Because Laurie is simple, straightforward and clear, he never loses your attention. I shall be pleased if I am able to do the same.

My third objective was LOGICAL PROGRESSION. Indeed, to be fair, it is the combination of clarity *with* logical progression that will produce the interest. This book is not a detective story. You are not going to find out who killed the countess by unravelling skilfully placed clues. But you are going to watch the construction of a marvellously designed object. You are going to see how a very simple concept—the table—can be used and built upon so as to create an intricate and masterly tool. You will also be able to talk knowledgeably to your database administrator (DBA) or write impressive university essays. But that is a by-product. You will not impress your DBA with fumbling stabs at half-understood concepts. Only if you can really see, and be interested by, the structure of INGRES (and relational databases in general) do you stand very much chance of impressing anybody within the IT world. I believe that presenting this subject with an emphasis on logical structure will provide you with that understanding.

Finally, computer science is, above all, a PRACTICAL SUBJECT. It might be fine to know all about parameter passing or embedded objects, but it is totally meaningless unless you can transfer that knowledge to doing something practical on a computer. INGRES has been designed to be used. I want this book to give you a theoretical background in relational databases in general and INGRES in particular, but most of all I want this book to get you feeling at home at the computer keyboard when using INGRES. Indeed, this was the very origin of this book. I was called upon to take some tutorials in INGRES. While I did not think that INGRES was a mythological Greek monster, I none the less knew nothing at all about it other than the fact that it was a relational database. I therefore looked for aids. I did not find them. The RT handbooks were very helpful, but they did not give me the understanding I sought. Date's book was exciting, but was marginal in increasing my confidence at the keyboard. Hence the book I wanted had to be written. This is the result. I hope that it saves you the traumas that I endured when I first grappled with INGRES. Indeed, if you are still in that bookshop and still reading this first chapter, here, at long last, is the real reason for buying this book: it will save you pain. INGRES is a complex tool. I, and the students I was supposedly supervising, sweated in sheer frustration. This book is designed to banish the frustration.

Worthy though such an aim may be, I must end with at least two warnings. Because I am trying to do two things—give a *practical* introduction to INGRES and provide a *theoretical* understanding of that practice—you will find that the chapters of this book will be almost exclusively slanted in one or other of those two directions. Hence, if you only want a practical knowledge of INGRES, you will doubtless skip some or all of the theoretical chapters. Clearly you are free to do so, but if you do, you will be missing out on the entire object of the exercise.

Secondly, although I do try to give some practical 'hands-on' guidance, this may not always be entirely accurate. There are again two reasons for this. First of all, implementations of the same version of INGRES can be slightly different, particularly since some organizations and/or academic institutions deliberately 'doctor' their version for their own particular purposes. In addition, of course, there are differing versions of INGRES. I began writing this book while using Version 5 at Leicester Polytechnic. I finished it while using Version 6 at the University of East Anglia. There are considerable differences between the two versions. I have tried to remain aware of both throughout the book. Even so, it is inevitable that my 'instructions' will, from time to time, fail to work for you. Although I regret this, I do believe that linking the theory and the practice, as is done in this book, will aid each user to overcome most practical problems that he or she encounters. Furthermore, most users are going to have some literature available at their place of work giving information about their particular implementation of INGRES. Since this book is designed, in part, as an interface between the user and the technical manuals that normally confront such users, it will, I hope, be found that the understanding provided by this book will make the technical manuals completely accessible.

In the ideal world, of course, this book should be totally unnecessary. INGRES would be uniform in every implementation; technical manuals would be limpid in their clarity. Such, alas, is not the case. As Dr Michael Giddings, a GCSE examiner in computer studies, once commented to me, 'The trouble with IT is not that x is not compatible with y, but that x is normally not even compatible with x.' Everyone that I have ever met excuses this by saying, 'Well, IT is still a very young subject.' One wishes that it would grow up more rapidly than it seems to be doing. INGRES, and relational databases generally, are marvellous tools; it is a shame that such tools are presented in such a forbidding form. This book is intended to demystify relational databases in general and the INGRES database in particular.

2
Relational databases: the backcloth to INGRES

Having stated in the previous chapter that this book was designed as a practical aid to using INGRES, it might come as a let-down to discover that this chapter barely mentions INGRES at all and certainly provides absolutely no hands-on advice. There is method in this apparent madness.

While I do not doubt that it is possible to learn to swim by jumping into the deep end of a swimming bath, such an approach does carry not insignificant risks. It is perhaps possible to learn to drive by leaping into a friend's Jaguar and proceeding to navigate from Birmingham to Coventry. I would not, however, wager much money on either you or the Jaguar emerging from this escapade in an entirely unblemished state.

Analogies are deceptive and misleading, but you will, I have no doubt, have taken my point. If you are hoping to learn to swim, a few words about the nature of water might well be in order before you actually immerse yourself in the substance. It is handy to know the respective positions of the brake, clutch, and accelerator before attempting to drive a car. So it is with INGRES. As you know, INGRES is a relational database. It is useful to know something about relational databases and the sort of data with which they cope before beginning a practical study of any one specific such database. It is to this end that this chapter is devoted, and, given this, should be helpful whatever relational database you are confronted with.

I have divided this chapter into two broad sections. The first is concerned with explaining what a relational database is, and, in passing, what other sorts of database exist and how they are different from relational ones. The second is concerned with showing how the data that you wish to be managed by INGRES needs to be given to INGRES in the first place. Obviously

INGRES cannot manage data that it does not understand—I speak metaphorically. Hence we have to learn how to give data to INGRES that it can understand. Both of these topics are covered by most general books on databases, but it would be absurd to omit them in a book on one specific database. They are, after all, essential, and you might not have any other texts to hand. Nor is it convenient to have to keep swapping from book to book. Indeed, you will find that this will be the case on other topics also. You cannot write about anything in information technology without trespassing upon a series of related topics. Hence, while our centre is firmly INGRES, it will be necessary to refer from time to time to related topics like networks or security. Equally obviously, if INGRES is a relational database, one needs to know what is meant by those words. So let us move immediately to the entity of which INGRES is an example, the relational database itself.

2.1 Relational databases

Before looking at relational databases in particular, we do need to glance briefly at databases in general.

The question as to what exactly constitutes a database was raised in the brief first chapter, and I do not want to repeat what was said there. One distinction, however, does need making: the distinction between data and information.

Imagine you are presented with a series of numbers like the following:

$$60 \quad 67 \quad 92 \quad 125$$

Such a series has no meaning. It cannot, therefore, be accounted as being information. It is data. If, however, you are told that the numbers are the opus numbers of Beethoven's 3rd, 5th, 7th, and 9th symphonies, then the series has acquired meaning. It has suddenly become information.

A computer processes data. A computer neither knows nor cares that you are presenting it with the birth dates of your children or the pints of milk delivered to the Manor Fields estate this week. To the computer it is all data. The computer will do things to that data according to the instructions that you have given it. In other words, the computer will process the data. But it will remain data. The computer could not care less if it was being instructed to cast your horoscope or select your marriage partner. Indeed, in neither case would the computer even know which, if either, it was doing. Hence data is simply material presented to a computer.

The stark statements presented in the preceding paragraph will rouse the ire of many engaged in an exciting field of computer studies, a field called artificial intelligence (AI). G. L. Simons, who wrote an excellent book on the subject, *Introducing Artificial Intelligence* (1984), would quite rightly berate me for massive oversimplification. None the less, for our purposes, my statements will stand. You may be giving information to your computer, and you will certainly want to gain information from the computer. But to the computer itself, it is simply data. As a consequence, that data needs to be presented to the computer in a particular form. The data needs to be 'normalized'. What 'normalization' means is the topic of our second section, but I did want to indicate from the start that we must not, in dealing with databases, ever think that the computer understands anything about the data with which it is dealing.

So then, a database is just a collection of data. It comes into existence because that data is needed and because it consequently needs to be accessed frequently and quickly. It has the further advantage of taking up very little space, and using no paper—and, therefore, no trees. None the less, although a database is little more than a glorified filing cabinet, the databases with which we are concerned do have certain further characteristics. A database is only an inert bulk of data. The entity that makes that data useful is a database management system. There is room for confusion here. When people talk about a database, they are almost always really talking about a database management system (which I shall refer to hereafter as a DBMS). Thus, when people refer to a relational database, strictly speaking they ought to be referring to a relational DBMS. It would be pointless and unnecessary to deplore this form of verbal shorthand. If someone says that he has been to see a football match, we all know that he means a soccer football match. So it is with databases. Hence, when, in this book, I refer to a database, I shall almost certainly be referring to a database management system.

A DBMS is an extremely complex set of software, the details of which need not concern us. What does concern us are the capabilities of this DBMS. If we are trying to run a business, administer a charity, or even just write a book, we need a database that can cater to our needs. What capabilities does a DBMS really need?

First of all, it needs to provide a quick and comprehensible way in which the data can be managed. The user is going to want to add, retrieve, select, modify, and delete data. A good DBMS will provide simple facilities for so doing.

Most databases have many people working on them simultaneously. The check-out in the store indicates that 20 more tins of Growler dog food had been sold. The purchase clerk in the same store places an order for 900 extra writing pads. The security officer indicates that a bill needs paying. The accountant implements a 6 per cent rise to all managerial staff. The manager himself sends a memo to all the cleaning staff. And all these things happen at exactly the same time. A DBMS needs to be able to provide accurate concurrent access to the database.

An effective DBMS also needs to act as a watchdog. It would not be greatly appreciated if all the staff in the shop could find out how much the manager earned simply by pressing a few buttons. It would lead to chaos if every shop assistant could, on his or her own account, order fresh goods for the store. So a DBMS has to have the ability to limit access to data, and, ideally, to check on the validity of the data with which it is presented.

Furthermore, computer systems can go wrong. More frequently, there can be electric cuts. A good DBMS has to have the ability to recover from acts of God, preferably without losing any data in the process.

A database may be an inert mass of data, but a DBMS is a dynamic and versatile provider. All modern database management systems provide the facilities that I have just listed. There does, however, remain one further facility that is particularly crucial. If you or I look at a disk, we cannot see the data stored upon it, and even if we could, it would make no sense to us. Most fundamentally of all, a DBMS has to provide the user with a comprehensible representation of that data. That representation should contain within it procedures for dealing with relationships between differing items of data, methods for reducing too much data redundancy, and, as I have already indicated (and most apparent to the user), it should allow the user to see the data in understandable terms. Clearly the ability of a DBMS to do this will depend upon the sort of internal indexing system and accessing system that the DBMS possesses. This 'data model', as it is usually called, is what distinguishes one type of DBMS from another.

Broadly speaking, and again this is an oversimplification, there are three types of database: hierarchical, network, and relational. As you will have gathered, INGRES is an example of a relational database. Everyone agrees that, out of the three broad types, the relational type is greatly superior to the other two. I shall not, therefore, spend any time in explaining what a hierarchical or network database is. If you really do want to know, then Peter Laurie briefly explains on pages 93–5 of his book, while Smith and Barnes in their *Files and Databases: An Introduction* (1987) give a much more complex analysis in their 11th chapter. If you really get excited about the topic of databases, Alfonso F. Cardenas examines in some depth four non-relational systems in his *Data Base Management Systems* (2nd edn 1985). It is worth mentioning, though, that Cardenas then goes on to devote three complete chapters to the relational database approach.

A relational database, as its name suggests, is concerned with relations. But then most things are. There is a relation between Jaques Snodgrass and the number 0372-820434, because the latter happens to be Jaques' phone-number. There is a relation between Amnesia Snooze and 'Dope Cottage' because 'Dope Cottage' happens to be where Amnesia lives. There is a relation between 'Treasury', 'Exchequer', and 'Funding' because they are all types of gilt-edged stocks. And that is the most important thing that we need to know about relational databases. Everything in a relational database is stored in such a way as to reveal, clearly and obviously, the relationship between them. There are two technical methods of describing relational operations known respectively as relational algebra and relational calculus. Anyone seriously concerned with databases in a professional sense needs to come to grips with these. There are scores of texts that explore them. Jeffrey Ullman's 1982 *Principles of Database Systems* or his 1988 replacement of that book, *Principles of Database and Knowledge-Base Systems* are excellent guides. None the less, I have little shame in ignoring them here. One can learn to use INGRES, or any other database system, without plunging into these mathematically based formalisms. Certainly, as far as relational database systems are concerned, one only really needs to understand that everything in the DBMS is stored as a table. Conceptually, all that this means is that every item of data is stored in a row, and every item in that row is also a member of a column. The columns represent types of value or characteristic, while the rows represent values or characteristics that are intimately linked to each other.

That well-known publishing house, Recondite Reading, keep a table of their publications. It looks like this.

Author	Title	Year
Broadbean, P. J.	*Images of Provence*	1990
Bristle, A. S.	*The End Game*	1990
Dunking, C. W.	*Descartes and Doubt*	1990
Earnest, O. G.	*Bach and the Diminished Seventh*	1990

As you can see, each column represents a particular value: author, title, year. Consequently, each row represents three values that are intimately linked. P. J. Broadbean is intimately linked to *Images of Provence* because he wrote it. *Images of Provence* is intimately linked to 1990, because that was the year in which the book was published. It is a very limited table, but it serves to illustrate the point.

The database that we will be constructing in this book is concerned with a chain of department stores. We are only going to construct a few tables for this chain of shops. If we tried to create a realistic database for the entire entity, you would have to spend months of your life typing data into the computer. None the less, one of the things that we will be doing is devising tables for our database. Tables are an essential feature of everybody's life, but far too often those tables are incomplete or inadequate. One has, for instance, considerable reservations about the utility of the table devised by Recondite Reading; no mention of price, ISBN number, pagination, and so on. One of the virtues of a relational database is that it allows us to make the most productive use of the data concerned. It cannot, of course, make up for human error or omission, but, as we shall see, it can help to minimize both.

This minimization of error or omission is perfectly humdrum and simple. If you draw, in a book, three columns and give those columns appropriate headings, it is more than a little irking to realize, six months later, that you really needed five columns. You are confronted with two alternatives: either start a new book with five columns and copy into that book all the data contained in the first book, or shrug your shoulders and just make do with three columns. We all know what the most common human response to such a dilemma is likely to be. However, with a computerized database, the problem does not exist. If, after six months, you decide to add an extra couple of columns, then it takes about 20 seconds worth of effort. Filling those columns with the missing data will obviously take longer, but it is infinitely easier than having to start all over again from scratch. If you make a mistake in your superbly indexed file of customers, it will, at the least, mean some unsightly crossings out. At the worst, it could mean rewriting considerable sections of your file. With a computerized database, it means either one simple correction or, at the outside, a brief operation. If your correction affects other data in the database, then your powerful piece of inbuilt software, the database manager, will automatically update all the relevant items.

From a practical point of view, the thing that makes a relational DBMS superior to other database managers is the ease with which, in a relational system, you can get hold of data other than the specific data upon which you are currently working. As Rob Healey comments in his *A Relational Data Base and 4GL in Action* (Savant, 1987), 'Such systems demonstrate more flexibility than other data storage media, but usually at a cost of extra indexing and more processor power required at run time for any specific application.' Let me illustrate.

Let us imagine that you have constructed a series of files devoted to parliamentary reform acts. One section, hardly surprisingly, is given over to the Great Reform Act of 1832. You have divided that mass of data into a number of separate files: one is devoted to boroughs; another is given over to counties; a third is concerned with specific elections held between 1832 and 1866; another examines government expenditure; a fifth covers journalistic coverage of parliamentary affairs during those years. And so we could go on. All database systems—hierarchical, network, or relational—will have means of jumping from file to file in order to make comparisons or highlight disparities. However, let us assume, which is hardly unreasonable, that you want to make a comparison between the constituency of Westminster in 1841 and that same constituency in 1918. In a network database, this will be a tiresome process. In a hierarchical database, it will be even more time-consuming and even more tiresome, perhaps prohibitively so. In a relational database, however, it will be as easy and as rapid as if you had wanted to compare Westminster fortunes in the 1841 election and the 1846 election. In other words, the relational system gives a far greater ease of access between disparate and distant data than either of the other two types of system can manage. With a relational system, you, the user, are not conscious of the data being arranged in a whole series of separate files at all. All the data seems to be immediately accessible. Consequently, it is no surprise that everyone in the database field would agree that relational databases are greatly superior to all other types. Of course, there is a cost to this. The greater stark computing power needed and the more sophisticated indexing required are the penalty to pay—a penalty largely measured in money terms. None the less, in terms of simplicity and cohesion, it is a penalty regarded as necessary by most organizations that need really effective data processing. There is a network system called the Integrated Database Management System (IDMS), but for real integration, relational systems win every time.

I have no intention of going into the structure and mode of operation of a DBMS, but it is important that we are very clear about the nature of such an object. The April 1971 report of the CODASYL Data Base Task Group defined a DBMS as 'the data processing system providing the means to access, organise and control all information stored in the database'. While this is only a very basic definition, it strikes me as being perfectly adequate. Obviously, as has already been indicated, a DBMS can organize its data in a variety of ways: hierarchic, network, or relational. The way in which a DBMS does so organize (and retrieve) its data is known as the architecture of the DBMS. This concept of an architecture is a purely conceptual one. It does not necessarily indicate anything about the way in which the items of data are actually stored; it simply indicates the way in which the human mind can visualize the retrieval of that data. Indeed, in a DBMS, one of the most significant elements within it is the interface or connection between the conceptual or logical database and the physical database. The physical database is simply the way in which the data is stored on the disk. The conceptual database is the way in which that actual data can be accessed, presented, and combined. Hence a DBMS, among other things, attempts to ensure that the data values remain correct, secure, and can be shared among a variety of users, all of whom may be attempting to access it simultaneously. Indeed, much of the *raison d'être* of a DBMS lies in its ability to enable concurrent users to extract information for a variety of applications with total reliability.

Again, while it is far from central to our purposes, it would be misleading if I did not mention another element in this data processing matrix. A good DBMS may be vital, but even something as complex (and expensive) as a DBMS is itself subservient to the operating system of the computers in question. It is, after all, the operating system that is fundamentally in control of the computer or computer system in question. The entire environment within which a DBMS operates is an environment created by the operating system. There are many different ways, all of them valid, of viewing an operating system. Peterson and Silberschatz, in their *Operating System Concepts* (2nd edn 1985), see it as a government, a resource allocator, and as a control program. There would be little point here in partaking in any semantic quibbles as to the nature of an operating system. What the user of INGRES or any DBMS has to remember is that is that it is the operating system that provides the context for his or her DBMS to perform. This book was written with MS-DOS and VMS as the operating systems (not simultaneously). In theory, at least, it should not matter which operating system you are using to run INGRES. It is, after all, one of the functions of the operating system to remain invisible. In an ideal computer context, you should never even be aware that the operating system exists. It should perform its central role with total unobtrusiveness. None the less, the operating system is crucial. INGRES, or any other DBMS, may have slightly different manifestations under UNIX than it does under MS-DOS or under VMS as opposed to PICK. These differences ought to be minimal, but it might be as well to be aware that, if your operating system is OS/2 or whatever, INGRES might be slightly different from the way in which it is presented in this book. Michael Stonebraker, in the eighth paper presented in *The INGRES Papers*, even states that operating system services in many existing systems are either too slow or inappropriate to provide an adequate backcloth to INGRES, but his essay was originally written in 1981, and most current operating systems can cope with reasonable ease. It would be misleading, though, to present INGRES or any sort of DBMS as if it were solely in control of your processing environment. It isn't.

Regardless of the operating system, however, in order for a database, relational or any other sort, to be really effective, the data with which it is presented has to be 'normalised' data, and it is to this that we must now turn.

2.2 Normalization

Normalization is a process for expressing relations in an unambiguous and computer-convenient form. In fact the word 'relation' has a mathematical origin and you will find many books define 'relation' in such a form. For instance, the Oxford *Dictionary of Computing* begins its definition like this:

(defined as sets $S_1, S_2, \ldots, S_n$) A subset of R of the Cartesian product

$$S_1 * S_2 * \ldots * S_n$$

of the n sets $S_1, \ldots, S_n$. This is called an n-ary relation.

If this is meaningful to you, then normalization will hold no problems. If, however, it is a form of pidgin English, then what follows will, I hope, make all things clear.

Let us just return briefly to the question of what a relation actually is. As I have already indicated, a relation in the computer sense has a mathematical origin. I shall ignore this fact. I am well aware that doing so offends certain rigorous members of the computing community, but I see no point in introducing complexities when those complexities play no part in securing a basic understanding of the concept in question. Normalization is a process of ensuring that redundant elements are removed from the database and that

the consequent database has complete consistency. This normalization process is based upon a concept known as functional dependency. Sometimes
referred to as *determinacy*, all this means is that in a row of data items,
everyone of those data items is determined by the first. Let us give some
examples.

Zodiac Splirt has a National Insurance Number. He is the only person in
the world to have this particular number. Hence there is a unique one-to-one
relation between Zodiac Splirt and his National Insurance Number. Hence
the National Insurance Number determines Zodiac Splirt. He is functionally
dependent upon that number.

Kretsin Blob teaches on the B.Sc. Spectrum course. Hence Kretsin Blob
has a relation with that particular course. Unfortunately, it is not a simple
one-to-one relationship. To start with, Kretsin is not the only person to teach
on the Spectrum degree course; many other people do so as well. Secondly,
Spectrum is not the only course Kretsin Blob teaches on. So we would be in
trouble if we expressed the relation between Kretsin Blob and Spectrum as a
unique one-to-one relation. There is no way in which Kretsin determines the
existence of Spectrum. But this is what a computer would like us to do.
Computers are very simple things, and they have the brain power of a senile
earthworm. So normalization is the process whereby we break down relations
into a form that a computer can understand and handle.

There is also another factor that is vital in this normalization game. It is
called redundancy. Let me explain.

In an ideal world, any object or entity in a database would appear only
once. There are very good reasons for this. Let us take the entity 'Mary
Taciturn'. Mary teaches on a number of different courses. Mary has a number
of differing administrative roles. Mary receives a salary. And so we could go
on, but the position is obvious. Mary's name will appear in the file for every
course upon which she teaches. Mary's name will appear in each file for each
committee upon which she serves. Mary will appear on the payroll file.
Hence the name of Mary Taciturn will be present in about a dozen different
files. There are two consequences of this. First of all, it costs time and money
to store Mary's name so many times. She takes space on the database.
Appearing, as she does, so many times, she is helping to make the database
bigger, and therefore slower, than if she only appeared once. Secondly, I
happen to know that Mary is going to be run over by a bus tonight.
Consequently she will teach on no courses, serve on no committees, and
receive no salary. As a result, her name is going to have to be deleted from a
dozen files or so. How much more convenient it would be if her name only
had to be deleted once.

Now the fact that some entity or other appears lots of time in a database
does not necessarily mean that such appearances are redundant. They may,
in fact, be necessary duplications. But one of the purposes of normalization
is to remove entities or attributes that are redundant. In the example that I

have just given, let us imagine that 'Mary Taciturn' is the key in a table entitled 'Staff Employment', and that this relation lists the courses upon which Mary teaches. This may be a little obscure, so let me explain. There exists a database that stores all the necessary data for the college at which Mary works. One of those segments of data—a file, a table, or whatever term is used—contains information about staff and the courses that those staff teach. Hence there is a row of data given over to each member of staff. Obviously, the name of the member of staff concerned is the key to each row, in that we know, once we have seen the name concerned, that every item of data following will refer to that name and only to that name. The name of the member of staff in question determines the subject names that follow. Hence the data contained in the Staff Employment table pertaining to Mary Taciturn contains, among other things, the titles of the courses that Mary teaches:

B.Sc. in Brewing
M.Sc. in Tatting
HND in Goldfish Breeding
'A'-level Sanskrit
BTECH plumbing

Let us also imagine that each course has a file or table that lists the members of staff teaching that course. But Mary Taciturn's name in the 'B.Sc. in Brewing' file is redundant, because we already know from the Staff Employment file that this is one of the courses she teaches. The careful construction of normalized tables will not eliminate duplication, but it will eliminate redundancy. I do not propose to discuss the issue of duplication and redundancy any further. The distinction between the two is fairly obvious, but if you want a more in-depth discussion of the two, D. S. Bowers provides one in his *From Data to Database* (1988), as does D. R. Howe in his *Data Analysis for Data Base Design* (2nd edn 1989).

We need now to look at what exactly we mean by normalization. To do so will mean the introduction of some computer science jargon, but at least it is fairly straightforward jargon, and should cause no problems. It will also be introduced in the happy and convivial atmosphere of the Nether Bilton Chess Club.

Nether Bilton is a large village in the county of Mercia. Through various accidents of fate (and a certain amount of incest), Nether Bilton has, over the years, developed a fierce pride in the fortunes of its Chess Club. The club meets every Wednesday in the village pub and, apart from these weekly meetings, also takes an active part in the Mercian Chess League. When the club was established in 1945 by Crowther Parkin, a membership book was immediately established, a book that has been righteously maintained ever since. If you walk into the village pub, The King's Gambit, you can still see the first volume of Nether Bilton's Chess Club membership book. It looks

Table 2.1

Membership Number	Name	Address	Date of Birth	Year of Joining	Year of Leaving
001	Crowther Parkin	'The Lodge'	12.06.20	1945	
002	William Daniels	6 Cow Lane	25.03.11	1945	1966
003	Perdita Dawn	'The Rectory'	16.09.24	1945	1975
004	Sebastian Flug	2 Midden Close	09.02.06	1945	1958
005	Grimble Short	11 Cow Lane	07.11.21	1945	
006	George Witch	School House	14.08.29	1945	
007	Miranda Toss	7 The Byre	03.01.27	1945	
008	Clayton Purdy	9 Midden Close	26.10.19	1945	1988

like Table 2.1. And we will, for the moment, leave it there, because these were the founding members of the Nether Bilton Chess Club. As you can see, four of them are still members. However, what concerns us is to examine the nature of the entries themselves.

Note, first of all, that at the intersection of every row and every column there is presented an *atomic* value. But that, I mean that the entry in each column is a simple single value, not a set of values. Furthermore, it is a good rule to ensure that a value cannot be broken down into anything simpler. 'Membership Number' is patently atomic. You could, I suppose, break name down into 'Christian Name' and 'Surname', but it is, after all, the combination of the two that provides a distinguishing label. To call someone 'Sebastian Flug' is to make a distinction between him and his brother Ernest Flug. Equally with address; there is only one '7 The Byre'. Again there is only one 7 November 1921. So, when Crowther Parkin founded the club in 1945, he was sensible enough to establish a membership book that was clear and unamibiguous. And the same rule holds for data fed into a database. Every item of data, every value, must be atomic.

The Nether Bilton Chess Club membership book also illustrates another important attribute for the handling of data. Just look at the Membership Number. That number uniquely identifies one member, and only one member. In other words, 'Name' is *functionally dependent* on 'Membership Number'. Crowther Parkin can only be member no. 001; he cannot also be member no. 064. Thus one value, Membership Number, *determines* another value, Name. Nor is that all: the attribute 'Name' determines the attribute 'Address'. Miranda Toss only lives at 7 The Byre. Hence address is functionally dependent upon name. And this too is vitally important in a database. There has to be a dependency between the various elements of a row of data. As a casual glance will show, however, the various rows in the table so far presented of the Nether Bilton Chess Club membership book are less than rigorous in the dependency they exhibit. As we have seen, 'Name' is dependent upon 'Membership Number'. But in what way is 'Address' dependent upon 'Membership Number'? Clearly 'Address' is dependent upon 'Name'. George Witch lives at School House; those two items, name and address, are dependent upon each other. But if George moved from School House and went to live at 14 Cow Lane, his membership number would still remain 006. The two items have no necessary linkage. So let us look again at the records in the Chess Club membership book, and work out which items are fully dependent upon each other.

With a simple table like the one we have at the moment, certain things are perfectly obvious. 'Address' is dependent upon 'Name'; William Daniels can only live in one place at a time. Hence, if we say 'William Daniels', we imply that we are talking about the man who lives at 6 Cow Lane. Equally obviously, 'Date of Birth' is functionally dependent upon 'Name'. Doubtless hundreds and hundreds of people were born on 25 March 1911, but that was the only date upon which William Daniels was born. Equally, 1945 was the only year in which William joined the Nether Bilton Chess Club, and 1966 was the year in which he left it. Hence we have four attributes, 'Address', 'Date of Birth', 'Year of Joining', and 'Year of Leaving', which are all functionally dependent upon the *key attribute* 'Name'. The remaining attribute, 'Membership Number', has no necessary connection with address or date of birth or even year of joining. None the less, it is 'Membership Number' that determines 'Name'. It was Clayton Purdy, and only Clayton Purdy, who was given the membership number 008. Hence, if we are to observe the rule of functional dependency, we need to take the Nether Bilton Chess Club membership book and transform it into two tables. The first we could call 'Membership Catalogue'. It would simply consist of two attributes, 'Membership Number' and 'Name'. The first attribute would be the key attribute because it determines the second attribute. We would also, of course, reorder the name column so that the surname came first, since it is the surname that is likely to be the more significant and identifying element.

Membership Catalogue   001   Parkin, Crowther
                        002   Daniels, William
                        003   Dawn, Perdita
                        004   Flug, Sebastian
                        005   Short, Grimble
                        006   Witch, George
                        007   Toss, Miranda
                        008   Purdy, Clayton

The second table could be called 'Membership Details'. 'Name' would be the key attribute because it determines all the other attributes.

Membership	Parkin, Crowther	'The Lodge'	12.06.20	1945	—
Details	Daniels, William	6 Cow Lane	25.03.11	1945	1966
	Dawn, Perdita	'The Rectory'	16.09.24	1945	1975
	Flug, Sebastian	2 Midden Close	09.02.06	1945	1958
	Short, Grimble	11 Cow Lane	07.11.21	1945	—
	Witch, George	School House	14.08.29	1945	—
	Toss, Miranda	7 The Byre	03.01.27	1945	—
	Purdy, Clayton	9 Midden Close	26.10.19	1945	1988

And when we had done all this, we would have achieved two normalized tables. There is, perhaps, a potential problem in that one attribute of this table, the date of leaving the Chess Club, can be a non-existent entity or a *null value* as computer scientists tend to call it. We will leave this problem for the moment, since it is not relevant in the present context, though in a database context, null values ought to be avoided. Furthermore, as you can see, the names of these founding members now appear in two tables. Yet there is no redundancy here. A relational database can and does lead to duplication, but that is because the construction of well-normalized tables has to be regarded as the prime objective. The waste of space engendered by some repetition is as nothing compared to the total chaos that can be produced by badly normalized tables. I am aware that I have not justified the concept of normalization. To do so would require a somewhat lengthy and technical discussion. I am afraid that I must just ask you to take it on trust that, in a database, rows of data must comprise a *primary key* upon which all the other attributes in that row are dependent. There will be more about this in the next chapter. I ought, though, to point out that the DBMS itself rarely cares whether or not your data is normalized; it will do its best with whatever disorganized mish-mash you give it. Only, however, if your data is normalized will *you* be able to do all the convenient things with that data that was, after all, your basic reason for setting up the database in the first place.

There is, of course, nothing wrong with the Nether Bilton Chess Club membership book. Crowther Parkin was not trying to construct normalized tables for a computer database. If he had been, however, he would have needed to perform the sort of procedure in which we have just been engaged.

This operation of normalization was first expounded by E. F. Codd in a 1970 article in *Communications of the ACM*. As a consequence, it has given rise to the following legalistic parody:

I swear that all attributes will be dependent upon the key,
the whole key, and nothing but the key.
So help me Codd.

But at least that mock oath has the merit of helping one to remember the primary requisite of normalization.

We can, I think, sum up. As you know, data within a relational database is stored in a table. In order for these tables to be efficient storage houses, the data within them needs to be normalized. As a result of this normalizing process, the resulting tables should manifest five important qualities:

1. Each item of data should be a single value and only a single value.
2. All items of data within the same column in a table should be items of data of the same kind.
3. Each column within a table should have a distinct name that separates and distinguishes it from any other column within that table.
4. Every row (or tuple) within a table should be unique.
5. It is irrelevant as to in what order the rows and columns are arranged.

If the tables of data that you construct for a database exemplify those five qualities, then your data is well normalized and you should have few difficulties in managing the resulting database.

Needless to say, the whole topic of normalization is more complex and complicated than I have presented it here. Most textbooks define First Normal Form, Second Normal Form, and Third Normal Form. Some then go on to distinguish Third Normal Form from the Boyce–Codd rule, and even define Fourth Normal Form and Fifth Normal Form. For our purposes, none of this is necessary. If you remember that all attributes have to be atomic, and that in any one table, all the attributes have to be fully dependent upon the key of that table, then you have mastered the most significant aspects of normalization.

Now that you have learnt how to do this, you can start building your database. This mammoth operation is the subject of our next chapter.

3
Building a database

Since INGRES is a database management system (DBMS), we cannot start using INGRES properly until we have some data for it to manage. Hence this penultimate chapter of Part 1 will be concerned to provide that data. In other words, we are going to build a database. Most databases, of course, comprise tens of thousands of items of data. Ours will not. You are perfectly free to experiment on your own, feeding in every fact culled from the *Encyclopedia Britannica* or entering the entire London Telephone Directory. You are likely, however, to die before completing the operation. Hence the database that we shall construct in this chapter will be miniscule in comparison with most real databases. None the less, it will serve to illustrate, in part at least, the most important functions of INGRES. Indeed, the very act of building our database will give both guidance and instruction in the facilities of INGRES.

Furthermore, this chapter will act upon the assumption that you have access to a computer already loaded with INGRES. If you do not have such access, I would advise you to stop reading now. In this chapter you are going to load a tiny database into INGRES. In all the chapters that follow, you will be engaged in persuading INGRES to manage that data in various ways. Hence access to INGRES is, from now on, imperative. You could, of course, dash out and buy INGRES at once, but, apart from the expense, INGRES does fill 16 5¼-in. disks. Consequently you need a machine with a capacious hard disk in order to store it at all. Hence, you may recall, I stated on the first page of this book that it was aimed primarily at people working within a company that uses INGRES or at students at a university or polytechnic that run an INGRES course. Almost all statements that follow in this book will therefore assume that you are sitting at a computer keyboard, and can put into practice the operations and procedures discussed.

Alas, there is at least one impediment to your putting anything into practice. As INGRES has developed, so differing versions have been produced and sold. The bulk of this book was written when I was using INGRES Version 5 (or 5.7 to be precise). I have, however, also been able to do some work with INGRES Version 6 (or 6.3 to be fully precise). There are considerable differences between the two versions. I shall try to give the alternative procedures wherever possible. Almost invariably, the earlier of my alternatives will be the Version 5 one, though there again, each INGRES version can be found in a number of slightly differing implementations. It is not my fault that the computer world is a Tower of Babel, but it does make learning about that world unnecessarily difficult. None the less, I shall presuppose that you have sufficient tenacity not to be overwhelmed by such barriers.

Acting upon that assumption (and assuming too that you have switched the computer on and that you have resident on your hard disk a Version 5 of INGRES), I want you to type the word 'addingres'—just the word, not the single inverted commas. Your screen should therefore show the operating system prompt—something like A\> or C\>—and the word you have typed:

C\> addingres

You will now press the Enter (or Return) Key. (From now on, I shall use Enter or Return as the whim takes me; in this context, the two words are synonymous.) The simple action of typing 'addingres', however, has moved you into the INGRES world, because the word 'addingres' is a system level command which has the effect of loading the INGRES data manager into memory.

However, 'addingres' will not work for every implementation of INGRES. When working within the VAX/VMS context, where the prompt is $, not C\>, one has, first of all, to enter either

$ ACCESS/SOFTWARE = SECURE_INGRES

or

$ ACCESS/SOFTWARE = INSECURE_INGRES

Assuming that someone has already registered you as an INGRES user, you will then be placed within the INGRES world, with a secure and protected context if we typed SECURE_INGRES, and a less secure and protected one if we typed INSECURE_INGRES.

We cannot, however, do anything in that world, because we have no data upon which to operate. We must, first of all, create a database. Hence we type at the prompt the word 'createdb'. This word, 'createdb', is another system level command, but it cannot do anything by itself. It cannot create a database without that database being given a name. Hence, after you have typed 'createdb', press the spacebar once and then type 'sos':

C\> createdb sos

or

$ createdb sos

Now you can press Return. When you do, your instruction disappears, to be replaced, in Version 5, at the top of the screen, with a menu:

   Tables Forms JoinDefs Reports Applications Languages Help Quit

A whitish, rectangular cursor should be nestling over the word 'Tables'. As I said in the second chapter, 'everything in a relational database is stored as a table.' Hence, if we want to create a database, we are going to create several tables. Those tables will constitute the database. Indeed, the fact that the cursor is placed over the word 'Tables' means, as INGRES kindly explains, just beneath the cursor, that your options are:

   Tables Forms JoinDefs Reports Applications Languages Help Quit
Create, update or lookup tables in the database
                                          Database: sos

Obviously you cannot update or lookup tables because, as yet, none exist. Yet, as you can also see, your database does exist. It is a completely empty database, but at least INGRES acknowledges its existence. In Version 6, however, you are likely to get a number of screen messages, all of them explaining what is happening:

Creating database 'sos' ...
   Creating DBMS Core System Catalogs ...
   Creating DBMS System Catalogs ...
   Modifying DBMS System Catalogs ...
   Creating Frontend System Catalogs ...
   Creating Standard Catalog Interface ...
   Modifying Frontend System Catalogs ...

You may not find this the most gripping of reading, but it does not last for very long. The screen will then announce 'Creation of database "sos" completed successfully'. Ideally you ought next to give another instruction at the operating system prompt:

$ sysmod sos

This instruction will ensure that your database tables (when you come to create them) are internally organized in the most efficient manner. It may also take a few minutes for the sysmod instruction to be carried out. When it is, then you need to type

$ ingmenu sos

Tables	Create/examine tables or query/report on table data.
Forms	Create/edit/use forms for customized data access.
Joindefs	Create/edit/use join definitions on multiple files.
Reports	Create/edit/run/reports.
Graphs	Create/edit/plot/graphs.
Applications	Create/edit/run 4GL applications.
Queries	Query data using Query-By_Forms or a query language.

Place the cursor on your choice and select "Go".
Go(Enter) Tables(2) Forms(3) JoinDefs(4) Reports(5) >

Figure 3.1

and you will see the INGRES/MENU screen for INGRES Version 6 as shown in Fig. 3.1. In a few moments we will create our first table, but I need beforehand to explain why our database has been called 'sos'. I did not assume that you would be crying for help, so the title 'sos' does not refer to the panic I imagined you to be feeling. Our database refers to a chain of department stores called 'SOS: Save On Shopping'. The origin of these stores is not without interest.

In 1950 an entrepreneur called Jason Willspend realized that Britain was recovering from the austerity of the Second World War. He also realized that Britain had close on full employment, and that those so employed were earning increasing sums of money. Now was the time, he argued, for a new chain of shops, a chain that offered a wide range of goods at low prices, a chain that could dethrone Woolworths. Himself a wealthy man, Jason knew that the only way to make even more money was to spend the money he already had. This he promptly did. The fashionable cosmetic store, Woadstick, in Regent Street, London came up for sale. Jason promptly bought it. To the horror of the West End, Jason transformed Woadstick into an up-market Woolworths. Jason, you see, recognized that even the cultured, toffee-nosed middle and upper classes would not object to buying goods they wanted if they could buy them more cheaply than they could acquire them elsewhere. The store itself, while not as grand as Harrods, was made to look appealing. A massive advertising campaign did the rest. For six months, Jason lost alarming sums of money. He even sold some items in the store at cost price. But he got his public. After 18 months, 'SOS: Save On Shopping' did twice the business of near-by Libertys. Thereafter, it was an almost

Create Destroy Examine Query-By-Forms Report Find [F1=Help] [F10=End]
_____

INGRES TABLE UTILITY   Database: sos

Table Name	Owner

Position the cursor over the name of the
table you wish to select, then use the
menu to perform the appropriate
operation on that table.

Figure 3.2

unbroken catalogue of success, and Jason now runs SOS stores in almost
every major British city.

Despite his business acumen, Jason Willspend was not and is not computer-
literate. It is only now that he has realized that data processing is essential if
he is to maintain his department store supremacy. Hence we have been
called in to design a computer system for him. Colleagues of ours have set up
a wide area Novell network of Tandon computers. What we have to do is
create his database.

As we have already seen, a database (sometimes called a data bank), is
quite simply a collection of related items. The most obvious items in SOS are
the stores themselves, and so our first table in the database will simply list
those stores. With the cursor still resting over the word 'Tables', we can now
press Return (or Enter). The menu at the top of the screen disappears, to be
replaced with another menu (in Version 5) as shown in Fig. 3.2. Obviously
we cannot obey the instruction given alongside the empty columns because
there are, as yet, no tables for us to select. The cursor, as you will notice, is
resting over the word 'Create'. Since this is what we want to do, we simply
press Return. A new menu will now appear:

Insert Delete Blank Move GetTableDef Save Find[F1=Help] [F10=End]

Below the menu will appear the words 'Enter the name of the new table'.
Since we are going to list the stores owned by SOS, we might as well call our
first table 'Store'. Having typed in 'Store' immediately after the words 'Enter
the name of the new table', we press Return and the cursor moves to the
two-column table also depicted on the screen. As you can see, the columns
of this table are entitled 'Column Name' and 'Data Type' and an instruction
alongside the blank table tells us to 'Enter the column specifications of the
new table'. Before we can do this, we need to think. We also need some
further information.

The thinking is necessary to decide what data we need to store in our table. We already know that the data stored in each column will have to be atomic. We also know that one column will have to act as a primary key which determines the contents of all the other columns. Hence we have to decide first of all what our primary key is going to be. Obviously each SOS store resides in a town. Could 'Town' be the primary key? Perhaps you would care to stop for a moment and work out why 'Town' would be a disastrous choice. I'll give you the gap between paragraphs to think about it.

'Town' would be a perfectly acceptable primary key for the table 'Store' if there was only one SOS store in each town. Unfortunately, at the moment there are three towns that have two SOS stores within them. The attribute 'Town' could not, therefore, serve as a primary key. As you will doubtless have realized, the simplest choice is also the most convenient: give each store a number. The number will, of course, be unique to each store. The attribute value 'Store Number' will thus determine each store. That store will be functionally dependent upon the store number value. We could also build in a further benefit. If we call the first store established—the one in Regent Street—number 1, the second store founded number 2, and so on, we would be able at a glance to see that Manchester was the third place to be blessed with an SOS store, that Leicester was the 15th, and so on.

One further embellishment might also be helpful. If we prefixed each number with the letter 'S', we would then be able to tell immediately, when looking at a table, that it was a table of stores. After all, we are likely to use numbers as a primary key in other tables too. It is surely an advantage to have some distinguishing element prefixed to those numbers.

We have now, then, made our first decision in creating our table. One column within that table will be entitled 'Store Number', and that number will be prefixed by the letter 'S'. Unfortunately, the matter is not quite ended. There are two reasons why we cannot enter 'Store Number' as our first entry in the column headed 'Column Name'. To start with, INGRES will not accept spaces within its column names, and we have understandably left such a space between the two words 'Store' and 'Number'. Secondly, although INGRES will accept a maximum of 12 characters for any column heading, only the first eight of those characters are counted as being a unique identifier. Hence we can save ourselves potential trouble if we ensure that each of our column headings does only consist of eight characters.

It is easy enough to resolve these minor problems. We can shorten 'Number' to the common enough abbreviation 'No', and we can eliminate the space, either by entering our column heading as 'StoreNo' or by linking 'Store' and 'No' with an underscore: 'Store_No'. Perhaps the underscore is slightly preferable because it gives our heading exactly eight characters, and Store_No is marginally clearer than StoreNo. Incidentally, if you are not overfamiliar with a computer keyboard, the underscore character is found by pressing Shift and the key normally found on the top row of the keyboard just to the right of the row of numbers. Note also that INGRES will not accept a full stop after the characters 'No'. INGRES cares nothing for your grammatical purity of placing a full stop after every abbreviation. Indeed, the only non-alphanumeric character that INGRES will accept in such a context is the underscore. Furthermore, although INGRES will accept numbers in a column heading, each heading *must* begin with a letter. Hence 'STORE99' is an acceptable heading, while '99STORE' is not.

We can, at long last, make our first entry into an INGRES column. With the cursor immediately under 'Column Name', we can now enter 'Store_No'—do not, of course, include the single inverted commas within your entry.

Now we are confronted with the heading 'Data Format', and some explanation is needed here. All that the Data Format column wants to know is what type of data is going to be entered into the column that we have just named. INGRES will accept eight types of data, and we may as well explain what these types are:

- *integer1* is a one-byte integer ranging from -128 to $+127$;
- *integer2* is a two-byte integer ranging from $-32\ 768$ to $+32\ 767$;
- *integer4* is a four-byte integer ranging from $-2\ 147\ 483\ 648$ to $+2\ 147\ 483\ 647$;
- *float4* is a four-byte number which may not be an integer and which ranges from 8.43×10^{-37} to $3.37 \times 10^{+38}$;
- *float8* is an eight-byte number, also floating, which ranges from 4.19×10^{-307} to 1.67×10^{308};
- *vchar(n)* is a character string where (n) is the maximum number of characters stores in that string;
- *date* can contain any valid date, date and time, or time interval;
- *money* allows you to store data of up to 14 digits, including commas, £ or \$ signs, plus or minus signs, and decimal points.

We will encounter many of these data types later, but our primary concern at the moment is to choose a suitable data type for our column name 'Store_No'. Obviously, if we had contented ourselves with just a number, our data type could have been integer1. Even Jason Willspend does not anticipate SOS stores ever numbering more than 127. However, we have prefixed the number with the letter 'S', so our data format has to be vchar(n). What number do we replace 'n' with? At the moment, there are only 18 SOS stores. The highest entry that we can so far make in the Store_No column is, therefore, S18. Nor is it foreseeable that SOS stores will ever exceed S99. Consequently, we only need to allow for three characters in the 'Store_No' column. We therefore state the data format of 'Store_No' as being 'vchar(3)'. As a result, our first data definition in our database will look like Fig. 3.3.

I ought, as a parathesis, just to pause and clarify a possible confusion. In the list of data types given above you will have noticed the appearance of the word 'byte'. You may not understand what that word means. As you know,

Column Name	Data Format
Store_No	vchar(3)

Figure 3.3

a computer only handles two numbers, 0 and 1. Each number is called a bit, which is a shortened version of the phrase '*bi*nary digi*t*'. Obviously, one bit does not convey a great deal. If, however, you lump bits together in sequences of eight, then you can store quite a lot of information. Eight bits can be arranged in 256 different ways. Thus you could have a unique arrangement of bits to represent each letter, number and punctuation mark. One such arrangement is called the American Standard Code for Information Interchance (ASCII), which uses seven bits to represent the letters, numbers, and so on, and then uses the remaining eighth bit as a sort of check digit. Anyway, the widespread use of bits clumped together into groups of eight has led to such groups being called bytes. Hence a byte is just a sequence of eight bits.

Before we move on to our next column, I have to delay us further by admitting to an oversimplification. The data types that I listed above are the data types accepted by a data definition language called SQL. The whole question of data definition languages/data manipulation languages is dealt with in Chapter 9 entitled 'Talking with INGRES', and I do not want to anticipate that chapter too much. However, INGRES supports two such languages, SQL and QUEL. (Actually, the latest version of INGRES supports three such languages, but I know nothing about the third, VQL, so I am hoping you will not notice the omission.) These two languages, SQL and QUEL, have slightly differing names for the data types that I have listed. Since SQL is the more common of the two languages, I simply listed the SQL labels. It is possible, however, that you work in a QUEL environment. Hence I list in Table 3.1 the QUEL equivalents to the data types already given. As you can see, two of them are identical to each other and it should not take too much effort to memorize the differences between the others should you need to do so.

However, so far we have only succeeded in creating the database itself, SOS, one table within that database, Store, and one data value or attribute within that table, Store_No. The next attribute, however, should provide no problems. We have chosen Store_No as our key attribute. In other words, Store_No will determine the attribute or attributes that follow it. Consequently the most obvious second attribute for our table should be 'Town' because, self-evidently, every SOS store resides within a town. If you pressed Return after entering 'vchar(3)', the cursor should now be placed immediately below 'Store_No'. Hence all we have to do is to type the word 'Town' and press Return. The cursor will now move to the Data format column, immediately beneath 'vchar(3)'. The data type for 'Town' will obviously be

Table 3.1

	SQL	*QUEL*
	integer1	i1
	integer2	i2
	integer4	i4
	float4	f4
	float8	f8
	vhcar(n)	text(n)
	date	date
	money	money

vchar, so all we have to worry about is what number to put in the brackets immediately following vchar. The longest town in which SOS currently have a store is Newcastle upon Tyne. That takes 19 characters. It is difficult to think of any major British towns that are going to be longer than that. Even if there are such towns, it should not be beyond our wits to provide a meaningful abbreviation so that it fits within our stated confines. Consequently, it does seem perfectly reasonable to limit our vchar data type for Town to 20 characters. Certainly that will manage to cope with Ashby de la Zouch, Burton upon Trent and similar lengthy place names should SOS ever establish stores in those towns. As a result, our table will now look like Fig. 3.4. And we can say that we have at last created a meaningful table. It is, perhaps, worth celebrating this, so let us store this table within our database.

To save our table is simple enough. Upon your computer keyboard are a group of keys all prefixed with the letter 'F' (for function). Find 'F2' and press it. You will then be given a menu. Move the cursor by pressing the appropriate arrow key until the cursor rests over the menu word 'Save'. Now press Return. The table that we have just created has now been made a permanent member of our database. Actually you do not have to move the cursor over the menu word 'Save'; you could just press F3, which is the Save key.

If you are operating with INGRES Version 6, the principles remain identical, but the manifestation upon the screen is very different. If you remember, you invoke the INGRES/MENU screen by typing INGMENU

Column Name	Data Type
Store_No	vchar(3)
Town	vchar(20)

Figure 3.4

TABLES—Create a Table

Enter the name of the new table:

Enter the column specifications for the new table:

Column Name	Data Type	Key #	Nulls	Defaults

Insert(1)　Delete(2)　Blank(3)　Move(4)　GetTableDef(5)　>

Figure 3.5

SOS. You then opt for Tables by placing the cursor over the row labelled Tables and then pressing Enter (which, on the VAX keyboard, is not the same as Return). You will then be presented with a list of Table Utilities:

Create　Destroy　Examine　Find　Top　Bottom　Help　End

Obviously you choose Create, and, upon so doing, will be presented with the screen shown in Fig. 3.5. Most of this is fairly straightforward. You move the cursor to the end of the line reading 'Enter the name of the new table:' and type in the word 'Store' or 'store'. The first column name will be Store_No and the data type, vchar(3), as before. The Key # column we can ignore. It is concerned with the question of indexing, and, important though this issue undoubtedly is, we shall have to pass it over at the moment. The next column, Nulls, wants to know whether or not you will accept a non-entry in the Store_No column. Since Store_No is the primary key of the table row, it would clearly be absurd to leave it blank, so one types 'No' in that column. As a result, the Defaults column also automatically changes to 'No'. You then repeat the operation for the Town column. Then, when you wish to save your completed table, you are likely to have to press the 0 key on the right-side numeric keypad. You have, then, created your first table within Version 6 of INGRES.

As you know, although we have now got a table consisting of two attributes, the table itself contains no data. Since the objective of this entire book is to teach you how to handle data within INGRES, we had better start filling our table with such data.

You are still located in the Table Create Screen. We have, however, created and saved our table, so we need to move into a context where we can start loading our empty table with data. The first thing to do is to press the key F10 or, in Version 6, FP3. This always has the effect of moving you back to the screen inhabited previously. The result of pressing F10 (FP3) returns us now to the Table Utility Screen. This, fortunately, is the screen we need. When we last used it, we pressed Return when the cursor was placed over the key word Tables. This time, however, we need to move that cursor until it overlays the key word Query-By-Forms. The Query-By-Forms function, always abbreviated to QBF, is a very powerful INGRES facility, and we shall encounter it often in this book. We do not need now to explore those facilities, but if you now press Return, you will be presented with a choice. The menu as the top of the screen now offers you Simple Fields or Table Fields. If you choose Simple Fields, the screen will just show you one record or entry at a time. If you choose Table Fields, the screen will display a number of successive records or entries. Since we now want to make a number of entries into our table Store, we might as well choose Table Fields, and then press Return.

A table outline with the headings 'Store_No' and 'Town' will now appear. All we have to do is to place entries into this framework. Placing the cursor in the column headed 'Store_No', we simply type S1 and press Return. The cursor will now shoot into the Town column, and we simply type 'London' and again press Return. The cursor will now shoot back into the first column, only this time on the second line. Now we type S2, press Return, then type Birmingham, and press Return again. And so the process continues. Once you have reached S10, the cursor will automatically jump into the next column, because S10 is three characters long, the maximum we allowed for this entry. Obviously you are free to make your own entries into our table. For what it is worth, I give my own entries in Fig. 3.6, but if you have some sentimental attachment to Nottingham or Bangor, there is nothing to stop you making them part of your database. A student in a tutorial group on database design that I was once taking had a passion for Basingstoke. This Hampshire town appeared in every table he created. You are free to do the same. Equally you are free to copy the table that I created. There are also advantages of convenience if we are both using exactly the same data.

As you can see, London, Swansea, and Liverpool all have two SOS stores within their boundaries, while, as yet, many important British cities have yet to be so graced. If the injustice done to Nottingham, Coventry, Belfast, and so on concerns you, the remedy lies with yourself. You can add as many as you wish.

If you look at the table in Fig. 3.6 you will see that it certainly fulfils the requirements of normalization: each attribute is atomic, and the attribute Town is functionally dependent upon the key attribute, Store_No. None the less, the Store table does give remarkably little information. Surely it would be more useful if it also contained the precise address of each store, and

Store_No	Town
S1	London
S2	Birmingham
S3	Manchester
S4	Swansea
S5	Newcastle-upon-Tyne
S6	Liverpool
S7	Glasgow
S8	Reading
S9	Edinburgh
S10	Swansea
S11	Exeter
S12	Leeds
S13	Bradford
S14	London
S15	Leicester
S16	Cardiff
S17	Sheffield
S18	Liverpool

Figure 3.6

possibly the store's telephone number as well. Both of those attributes could be added to the table without infringing the rules of normalization.

If you were thinking such thoughts, you were entirely reasonable in so doing. I made our first table so limited for this very reason. When you construct a database, you *always* discover that you have missed out some useful attribute or attributes from a table or so. Consequently, you have go back and amend the table or tables in question. Certainly the table Store would be more useful if it had the address and telephone number of each store included within it. I want, therefore, to show you how to add extra columns to a table that has already been created.

While I trust that it is clear that I like INGRES and regard it as a most creditable relational database, it cannot be pretended that altering a table that you have already created and saved is the most straightforward operation in the world. Ideally it would be pleasant if one could just re-enter the table and add one or more attributes to that table. Alas, this is not possible. Of course, there is some sense in not making it so easy. If a table has been created, it could lead to mayhem if all and sundry could alter the format, structure, and composition of that table with consummate ease. As a result, what you have to do is to create another table, which will, of course, be empty of data, and then copy into that new table all the data from the old one. Let me just spell this operation out in terms of our SOS database.

Column Name	Data Format
Store_No	vchar(3)
Town	vchar(20)
Address	vchar(30)
Tel_No	vchar(14)

Figure 3.7

First of all, you must decide upon the composition of your expanded table. I would suggest that we need the attributes shown in Fig. 3.7.

The attributes themselves we had already decided upon, though you might be a little surprised by the data format for Tel_No. Since a telephone number consists entirely of numbers, why not make the data format integer4? There are two very good reasons. Many phone numbers in Britain will begin with the digit 0. If your data format is integer4 and you enter the number 017948273, then INGRES will automatically delete the initial 0. Secondly, it is easier to comprehend a telephone number if one splits it into 071-794-8273 rather than presenting it as one nine-digit number. Integer formats (or floats) will not accept the dash separating the groups of numbers. Hence we have to have recourse again to vchar.

Having now decided what we want our expanded table to include, we need to begin a somewhat tortuous process. Return to the INGRES/MENU screen and move the cursor to the Languages option. Press Enter. You will then be offered the language range that your system supports. Both SQL and QUEL should be shown. Move the cursor to SQL (the cursor is probably already resting over it) and press Return. You will then be presented with a blank area into which you can type SQL command. All you need to do is to write:

```
copy table store ( ) into 'storebkp';
```

You then press F2 and the command should be obeyed. What has happened is that you have copied the entire Store table into a backup file. The empty brackets () indicate that you wanted all the attributes of Store transferring. Since our temporary file 'storebkp' now contains all the data of our table Store, we can destroy the table itself. Return to the Table Utility screen, place the cursor on the S of Store, press F2, select Destroy from the options offered, and press Return. The Store table will now disappear. Ironically, we shall now have to construct a new Store table in its place. We know what the attributes are and what data format those attributes should take. Hence we create our second Store table in exactly the same way as we created our first. Having done so, we need to transfer the data contained in our temporary file 'storebkp' into our table. This is done by returning to the SQL screen and typing the command:

Store_No	Town	Address	Tel_No
S1	London	6–9 Regent St., W1	01-356-9634
S2	Birmingham	The Cowring, B1 9HZ	021-92817
S3	Manchester	11 Deansdoor, M1 3PE	061-761933

Figure 3.8

copy store ( ) from 'storebkp';

Obviously your new table will not contain any addresses or telephone numbers. It will be your job to provide them. It will clearly not be necessary in the Address column to specify the town, since that is given in the preceding · column. Consequently I contented myself with a postcode, as you can see from the first three entries that I made (see Fig. 3.8). I trust that any inhabitants of Birmingham or Manchester who are reading this will not be offended by the spurious addresses that I gave to the SOS stores in those cities. There are 15 more invented locations that you will encounter shortly, should that be any consolation. Do not, therefore, phone me up to complain that you have been unable to find any SOS stores.

While the instructions for creating new columns that I have given ought to work, there is, unfortunately, a lack of compatability between differing INGRES systems. The RT Reference Manual that I am working with now states that, in order to add or remove columns from a Table, one needs to use the GetTableDef operation. Let me just quote from the RT Manual:

> To copy or change a copy of the specifications for an existing table's structure, use the GetTableDef operation. INGRES prompts for the name of an existing table and then copies the column specifications for that table into the list on the screen. You can then proceed to edit or delete any name or data type, using the Tab and arrow keys to move through the list.

Alas, these instructions were quite invalid on the INGRES systems that I used while writing this book, one system on an Olivetti M24 terminal and the other system on a Tandon. If the method that I have outlined does not work, then you should try the one quoted above. If that does not work either, I suggest that you return to my method and make some slight alterations. For instance, my copy command reads:

copy table store ( ) from 'storebkp';

Maybe your system does not like the brackets being left blank. Hence you could try the laborious instruction given below:

copy table store (store_no=vchar(3), town=vchar(20),
address=vchar(30), tel_no=vchar(14)) from 'storebkp';

Some systems may want system commands to be printed in capitals. Hence you would type:

```
COPY TABLE store ( ) FROM 'storebkp';
```

Always check your entry carefully; have you included the single inverted commas around store? have you included the semicolon? However, should none of my suggestions work, I am afraid that your only recourse is to approach someone with much more experience on your system or, if no such person exists, get in touch with Relational Technology, or whoever it is that has now replaced them.

Despite my forebodings in the preceding paragraph, it is highly likely that you have been successful in copying the data from 'storebkp' into 'Store'. It is a wearisome process, and I hope that Relational Technology, in a future version of INGRES, do something to facilitate what is, after all, a frequent enough demand. In fact, there is another method that you could employ. This technique involves using the menu option 'Insert', but to do so entails meeting another INGRES utility called the Visual-Forms-Editor (better known as VIFRED). We shall, in fact, have to encounter VIFRED in a moment, so I shall delay my further explanation until then.

You might, at this point, think that we had finished with our first table. I am sorry to detain you for so long a time over one simple table, but it is surely more sensible to explore our first table fully so that we are then superbly equipped to create other tables. There is only one more aspect concerning Stores that I wish to look at.

Our table 'Store' exists, and once we have filled it with data—not very much data, but at least enough to handle meaningfully—we will be able to relax. We consequently wonder what on earth can be left to do.

The table that we have created is fine. Were you to have filled in all the addresses and phone numbers, the table would contain a bulk of useful data. (If you have not done so, you may prefer to copy my version given towards the end of this chapter.) However, it is still a small table. We can only assume that SOS will continue to open new stores in different towns as they have been doing for the last 40 years. Consequently, from time to time, new data will need to be added to our Stores table. Just a little experience in the data processing world is needed to convince us that if there is an incorrect method of adding data, someone will find it and use it. Someone in your company never talks about SOS stores, they always refer to SOS branches. Consequently, when they come to make a new entry, they unconsciously enter the Store_No as B19, because they have Branch on their mind rather than Store. INGRES will not object. After all, it does not know that Store Numbers have to begin with the letter S, because no one has told it. Someone else is told to enter a new store in King's Lynn. They do so, but completely forget to enter a new Store Number at all. Again INGRES will not object. Hence what we need for our new table are some validation checks just to guard against human error (or even human spite). Fortunately INGRES can provide such checks.

Since Store_No is our primary key, it seems sensible to make it a mandatory key. In other words, one cannot make an entry into the Stores table without including a Store_No. You might also want to make it impossible for anyone to delete a Store_No. Who knows, you might also want to emphasize the significance of Store_No by having it displayed as dark characters on a bright background, or even have it attract attention by blinking on and off. All these, and others, can be done by INGRES.

Some of the changes can be made by means of the Attributes screen, which lists for you the following options:

- Box Field   Highlights the field by placing a box round it.
- Reverse Video   Changes the screen from light on dark to dark on light.
- Blinking   Makes the attribute value blink on and off.
- Underline   Underlines the word or words in the specified field.
- Brightness Change   Self-evident. This changes the brightness for a field.
- Force Lower Case   Changes any capital letters into lower-case ones instead.
- Force Upper Case   The reverse of the above, printing everything in capital letters.
- No Auto Tab   Prevents you overshooting one field and typing by mistake in another one.
- No Echo   Prevents data from actually being displayed on the screen.
- Display Only   Displays the data in a field but prevents any changes to it being made.
- Colour   If you have a colour monitor, this will allow you to change the colour.

Nor is this all. Various validation checks are also possible within INGRES. I do not think that there is much point in listing them all at the moment, but at least two of them would be useful to us. The first has already been mentioned: the mandatory field. If you decided to make Store_No mandatory—and it would, I think, be wise so to do—then INGRES prevents the cursor leaving the Store_No field until such a Store_No has been entered. You can also persuade INGRES to give you an error message if you do try to input invalid data. In addition, INGRES can ensure that the right type of Store_No is input. We already know that INGRES will not allow a Store_No to exceed three characters, but we can also ensure that INGRES refuses to accept any store number that does not begin with the letter S.

Clearly such facilities are an advantage. Together they will help to keep your data more secure and to display that data in a more striking fashion.

In order to implement such facilities, we need to meet another of INGRES's user-interface tools. We have already encountered Query-By-Forms

Create   Destroy   Edit   Rename   Utilities   Find   [F1=Help]   Quit
_____

VIFRED - Forms Catalogue

Name	Owner
Store	pc

Position cursor on the name of the
form you wish to select, then use
the menu to perform the appropriate
operation on that table.

Figure 3.9

(always referred to hereafter as QBF). The one we need now is called the
Visual Forms Editor (hereafter referred to, as I suggested a moment ago, as
VIFRED).

For the purpose of explaining how to enter VIFRED, I shall assume that
you are back at the INGRES/MENU screen. When we have been present in
this screen before, we have selected Tables as the facility that we wished to
use. This time, however, just move the cursor one space to the right so that
it is resting over Forms. Now press Enter. The cursor will now be resting
over the menu item 'Edit-Forms'. Press Return and the so-called Forms
Catalogue screen is now presented (see Fig. 3.9). Place the cursor on the S
of Stores and press F2. The cursor will now return to the menu line. Move
the cursor to Edit and press Return. You will now be presented with the
outline of the table required as shown in Fig. 3.10.

Since we wish to create some validation checks, you should place the
cursor over the c in the Store_No column, press F2 so as to return to the
menu, move the cursor to Edit, and then press Return. You will now be
offered more options (see Fig. 3.11).

What you next have to do is fairly obvious from the default screen with

Create   Delete   Edit   Move   Undo   Order   Save   [fl=Help]   [F10—End]   Quit
_____

    Query Target Name is store
TABLE(S): Stores

Store_No	town	address	Tel_No
c ..	c...............	c	c ....

Figure 3.10

Insert Delete EditAttr Move GetTableDef Forget Find [F1=Help]

VIFRED - Table Field

Name of Table Field: Number of Rows to Display:
Display Line?(y/n): y

Title of a Column	Data Format	Internal Name of a Column

Figure 3.11

which you have been presented. Move the cursor to the space immediately
following 'Name of Table Field'. Since we only have one field, Stores, our
entry here is inevitable. Indeed, INGRES may have already placed 'Stores'
there ready for you. If not, type the word Stores yourself and then move the
cursor to just after the colon that concludes the heading 'Number of Rows to
Display', and type in the number of rows that you want to see. Since we have
only created four attributes in this field, Store_No, Town, Address and
Tel_No, we are obviously limited to a maximum of four. Now move the
cursor to the Display Line question, and type the letter 'y'. In the 'Title of
Column' column you should now type in Store_No. Now press F2, which, as
always, moves your cursor back to the top-line menu. Now move the cursor
along until it rests over EditAttr. Press Return. You will be presented with
the Attributes for Field screen shown in Fig. 3.12.

From now on the procedure is very straightforward. For Store_No, for
instance, we wish to make such an attribute mandatory. Hence you just
position the cursor over the 'n' next to 'Mandatory Value' and type a 'y'. If
that is the only change you wish to make among the options provided, you
next press the Tab key; that is the one with two arrows pointing in opposite
directions. That will move your cursor to the colon following the 'Internal
Name for Field' heading. Here you type in the entry 'Store_No'. You do,
however, wish to make a genuine validation check on Store_No. Hence you
move the cursor to the space beside 'Validation Check to Perform on Field'
and type:

store_no = S* OR store_no = M*

That ensure that INGRES will not accept a Store_No that begins with
anything other than a capital S or a capital M. (The reason for the M is given
in five paragraphs' time; just take it on trust for the moment.) The * sign
stands for any character or characters that may follow the S or M. Consequently your validation check does not prevent someone typing Sabc or

---

VIFRED - Attributes for Field

Default Value for Field:

Attribute	Set
Box Field	n
Keep Previous Value	n
Mandatory Field	n
Reverse Video	n
Blinking	n
Underline	n
Brightness Change	n
Query Only	n
Force Lower Case	n
Force Upper Case	n
No Auto Tab	n
Display Only	n
END OF ATTRIBUTES	

Internal Name for Field (12 characters only):

Validation Check to Perform on Field:

Validation Error Message:

Color: 0

Figure 3.12

M98361, though the fact that Store_No has a maximum storage capacity of three characters would outlaw both of those anyway. Still, somebody could type Sab or Mgz if they wished. Both entries would be accepted by INGRES, but the likelihood of anyone being so uninformed as to make such entries does seem too slim to safeguard against.

Having set your validation check, you may wish to give a message to anyone who does try to enter a Store_No incorrectly. Place the cursor after the words Validation Error Message and type in an appropriate remark. It is unlikely to do much for departmental loyalties if you type a message like 'Learn the correct format, peabrain!' I would suggest a neutral comment like 'Store numbers must begin with the letter S or M'.

Frankly, once you have made Store_No mandatory, I do not really think that any further validation checks or visual embellishments are necessary. Remember that, for each attribute addition you make, you are consuming more of the computer's resources. In other words, you are taking up memory space. Obviously, for a database as small as ours currently is, this hardly matters. The computer, and INGRES, will cope quite happily if you decide to capitalize every town, force every phone number to blink on and off, and underline every post code. In a large database, however, the more attribute embellishments you include, the more memory you will tie down and the more slowly you will force the operating system to run. It is probably a good idea at the moment to experiment with creating a large number of attribute qualifications, but it would be sensible at the end to nullify them all except for the very few that you regard as really essential. A mandatory Store_No is the only one that strikes me as imperative. Play around by all means. The best way of coming to grips with INGRES is to experiment as much as possible. I shall, however, assume that you have, at the end, been content to make the first field of our first table mandatory, and that all the other fields—Town, Address, and Tel_No—have remained untouched.

It is, however, possible that you have not been able to carry out the foregoing instructions. This will not be because you have misunderstood them, or because I have misinformed you. Some student-orientated versions of INGRES will not implement the validation checks. For reasons beyond my understanding, it is argued that students, because they are not designing a real database, do not need all the security functions that such a real database would require. Hence, although you will have been able to carry out most of the procedures that I have indicated, no valid achievement has been possible. This is tiresome. I can only apologize for the small-mindedness of your university or polytechnic. They, in turn, will point to budget constraints. Hence you are left with little recourse. The assassination of the Minister of Education is unlikely to change very much and could terminate your education completely if you get caught. There are some who feel that sticking hot needles into a puppet manifestation of the Prime Minister is effective, but I have never found it so. Your only sane response is to reflect that at least you have managed to do most of the necessary operations in the creation of a database.

Now that we have met VIFRED, however, let us see how we can use it to create extra columns.

Once again, I shall assume that we are placed in the INGRES/MENU screen. We move the cursor to Forms again, press Enter, position the cursor over Edit-Forms and again press Enter. Once more we are in the VIFRED Forms Catalogue, although, of course, we only have one form, and that form has just as many columns as it needs. However, for the sake of practice, we are going to give it a fifth column.

Place the cursor on the S of Store and press F2. This will move the cursor to rest over the option Create. Press Return and then move the cursor to rest upon the option TableDefault. Again press Return. You will now be presented with an unspoken query:

Table:

You just type the name Store, press F2, move the cursor to TableField, and press Return again. This brings you to the Query Target screen shown in Fig. 3.13. You now place the cursor on Create and press Return. Next place the cursor on TableField and press Return. You will then be presented with the VIFRED Table Field, which contains the option Insert that I mentioned earlier. This time we shall be able to use it, and in so doing learn another

Create Delete Edit Move Undo Order Save [F1=Help] [F10–End] Quit

_____

Query Target Name is store

TABLE(S): Stores

Store_No	Town	Address	Tel_No
c	c...............	c	c ....

Figure 3.13

technique for adding columns to our already existing tables. Figure 3.14 shows the VIFRED Table Field. If you want it full of attributes as I show it, you must move the cursor to GetTableDef and press Return.

To add another column to our table, you must position the cursor on the row above which you wish to add the extra column. Let us, therefore, place the cursor on the 't' of town. Now press F2. That will move the cursor to rest upon Insert. Press Return. Immediately VIFRED places a new row between store–no and town. The new row will be called something inappropriate like NEW1, so we move the cursor to the N of NEW and type in our new attribute, Manager. We will give it a data type of c15 and an internal column name of Manager. Now, if we press F10, we should find ourselves in the Form Layout screen, on which our amended form will appear. Neither method of adding new domains to our table are quick and easy, but, to repeat myself, just think of the chaos that would ensue if all and sundry

Insert   Delete   EditAttr   Move   GetTableDef   Forget   Find   [F1=Help]

_____

VIFRED — Table Field
Name of Table Field: Number of rows to display: 4
Display Lines? (y/n): y

Table of a Column	Data Format	Internal Name of a Column
store_no	vch(3)	store_no
town	vchar(20)	town
address	vchar(30)	address
tel_no	vchar(14)	tel_no

Figure 3.14

NIN	vchar(14)
store_no	vchar(3)
name	vchar(20)
role	vchar(15)
salary	money
hire_date	date

Figure 3.15

could, almost by accident, alter the very structure of the database that all used. Clearly INGRES has to safeguard against such relational disasters.

None the less, important though this topic is, we have been indulging in something of an extended paranthesis. Let us rapidly return to our main thread.

Obviously SOS employs people—as shop assistants, managers, buyers, accountants, advertising men, cleaners, security guards, drivers, and so on. Equally obviously, even though we have limited SOS to a mere 18 stores, the total number of people that it employs runs into thousands. Hence, for our Employec table, I shall limit myself largely to the employees linked to a single store. Our concern now must be to choose the attributes for our Employee table.

The primary key is not difficult to choose. We could, of course, have E1, E2, E3, . . . just as we had S1, S2, S3, . . . in our first table. Certainly there would be nothing wrong in so doing. None the less, since a National Insurance Number (or Social Security Number, if you are based in the United States) is going to be needed for every employee, we could use that as the primary key. We would have to store it somewhere in the table anyway, it is unique for each person, and hence can act as a perfect primary key.

Virtually all employees will, however, be based in a single store. Hence it would be sensible to link the Insurance Number to the relevant store number. We would then have a dual key: National Insurance Number (NIN) and Store Number. Employees who were not attached to a specific store—people like regional managers or the occasional accountant—could be given a store number prefixed, not by S, but by M, standing for management. We could arrange our validation checks so that this presented no problem. Then would follow employee name, position in the company, salary, and date of appointment. The resulting Table Create Screen would contain the entries shown in Fig. 3.15. We would, I think, want to make NIN and store–no mandatory. If you want visual effects as well, you are welcome to implement them in exactly the same cumbersome way as we did for the Stores table.

Nobody can be expected to fill out our newly created Emp–Store table and form with hundreds and hundreds of data items. Since this chapter was written in Leicester (as, indeed, were most of the others), I confined myself largely to employees of the Leicester SOS store, though I did take care to give every store, all 18 of them, a manager. The table is, of course, too large to fit into a single screen (or page), but my early entries looked like this:

NW_90_66_23_A	S15	Pecksnort, Daniel	Manager	£18,750.00	01_06_71
ZS_45_61_88_D	S15	Fussup, Beryl	Sales Dir	£15,250.00	30_09_68
BS_37_82_49_K	S15	Bleary, Felix	Janitor	£9,700.00	16_03_65
VR_34_16_95_B	S15	Nittle, Sarah	Assistant	£7,300.00	25_11_89

Unfortunately, if we are going to really use our database in a fashion that gives a reasonable indication of its range, we cannot confine ourselves to employees at only the Leicester branch. I give my full table entries in a few pages time, and, as you will then be able to see, I did content myself with the minimum data input that was possible.

SOS is a successful chain store because it sells, at reasonable prices, a large range of goods. Clearly, therefore, it needs to keep tags on its range of suppliers, and the orders it makes to those suppliers. Two more obvious tables (and forms) are called for here.

The Supplier table is fairly straightforward. Each supplier is given a unique supplier number, preceded by the letters Sp. Then follows the supplier's name, address, and phone number.

Sp1	Filcham, Cyril	7 The Toerow, LEEDS L1 6YR	0367–239841
Sp2	Wallop, S.T. & Co	Etruria Rd, STOKE-o-TRENT ST6 9GV	0581–688439

Once again, as you can see, the table is simple and unambiguous. Every attribute within the row is dependent upon the primary key. Obviously we will want to know what goods each supplier can provide, but that is dealt with in the Prod-Sup table, where the joint key of Product Number and Supplier Number is followed in each case by one product and its price. While the relational approach does lead to some duplication (as in Supplier Number appearing in two different tables), the resulting simplicity and ease of management more than compensates for this. Never try to be clever when constructing tables. One's cleverness has the irritating habit of rebounding upon oneself.

The Purchases Table is composed of the following attributes:

- Order Number.
- Supplier Number.
- Date.
- Contents.

Yet, upon reflection, we could simplify this a little. We could construct our Order Number in such a way that it contained a plenitude of information. Let us stay with the Leicester branch of SOS. The first order from that store could have been numbered as follows:

0000001/S15/Sp7/150689

The first seven-digit number is the order number; the second item is clearly the store number; then follows the supplier number, and the entire entry concludes with the date: 15 June 1989. While I would agree that this made the Order Number entry unwieldy, the compensating advantages atone for this. You have saved yourself storage space for Store_No, Suppl_No, and Date, as well as making the so-called Order Number verifiable on a number of elements. For instance, you could force the order number itself to comprise seven digits, you could ensure that the second element always began with a capital S, that the third element always began with the letters Sp, and that the final element always contained six digits. And, of course, you could be more rigorous than that. You could ensure that no one entered a date like 331423. You could ensure that no one entered a Store Number S92 when there were only 18 stores in existence. (Indeed, you could force S15 for all orders made from the Leicester store.) You could even ensure, when the last order number had been 0001063, that the next one was 0001064. Above all, of course, such an entry is unmistakably unique. Hence, if anyone did make a mistake, the error could be tracked down. If, furthermore, it was made company policy that no order form was allowed to contain more than one type of product, each order would be fully normalized and atomic. You might want to order six different items from the same supplier. It is hardly a great deal of effort to make out six separate forms, particularly since the bulk of the Purchases Form would be preprinted anyway.

I hope that you can explain why such a primary key would be quite unacceptable? All writers place a considerable emphasis upon the primary key. I was recently re-reading one of C. J. Date's books and it was pleasing to be reminded of the importance of the primary key (see C. J. Date, *Relational Database: Selected Writings*, Addison-Wesley, 1986). But rarely do writers provide any dicta on elongated primary keys. What then is wrong with the elongated primary key that I have suggested?

There was one aspect that I mentioned earlier. Attributes within a table must be atomic attributes. The elongated key that I suggested is far from atomic. It is blatantly composed of four elements. Hence we have to disallow it. This digression, however, does illustrate that, even at a relatively elementary level, it is very easy to confront quite complex issues. Normalization is a relatively simple topic. Designing a relational database is a relatively simple topic. Why, then, do both topics engender argument, discussion, doubt and disagreement? In a sense, it is because they are simple topics like riding a bicycle. Almost anyone can ride a bicycle. Yet confront a group of cyclists on topics like gears, or mudguards, or tyre pressures, and you will be confronted by controversy. So it is with database designers. And it is important. None the less, Date himself warns against our making it too important: 'I certainly believe that anyone doing database design should be familiar with normalisation. But it should not be viewed as a panacea. There is a lot more to database design than just normalising' (ibid., p. 488). Let us then return to our Purchases table.

With a Purchases table, the temptation is to overload: there is so much that can be included. We have seen how my suggested primary key contains far too much information, but there are many attributes that we could now add:

- Description of goods ordered.
- Quantity of goods ordered.
- Cost of goods ordered.
- Discount rate.
- Date for delivery.
- Address to which order should be delivered.

To construct a table containing such attributes is asking for trouble, just as an elongated Purchase Order number would be. Clearly one is justified in having a description of the product that one is ordering. One will also want to know how many items of that product have been ordered. The rest, however, we can ignore. The supplier will inform us of the cost and our discount rate on his invoice. The address for delivery will be shown on the Purchase Form anyway. The date for delivery is both mythical and superfluous: mythical in that there are too many variables for a delivery date ever to be much more than a guess, and superflous because it is as much in the interest of the supplier to get the goods to you as quickly as possible as it is in your own interest.

How, then, can we finally construct our Purchase Order table? I think that it is clear that the Purchase Order number has to be the primary key. How, then, can we construct such a key? Let us retain the seven-digit number intact, but preface that number with two letters. The letters will represent the store that placed the order. Thus one could have RE standing for Reading, BR standing for Bradford, and so on. Thus one could have 18 Purchase Order numbers that are all 0000001, but they would be rendered unique by the two letters that preceded them.

Of course, there is the problem of towns that have more than one SOS store, but this is not a serious problem. One Swansea store is signified by the letters SW, the other by the letters SA. Equally London could be LN for one store and LO for the other, while Sheffield could be SH and SD. By this stratagem one has, I think, resolved the problem. We can still, if we wish, retain Store_No, Supplier_No, and Date within our table, but this time as separate attributes, not as one non-atomic concatenated key.

You might, quite rightly, point out that the primary key that we have now settled upon is still something of a hybrid, incorporating, as it does, Town and Order Number. Such a hybrid will not, however, give rise to problems. The basic reason for forbidding hybrid attributes is concerned with the question of joining different tables together, and we can suspend

Table 3.2   Store Table

S1	London	6−9 Regent Street, W.1	01-356-9634
S2	Birmingham	The Cowring, B1 9HZ	021-92817
S3	Manchester	11 Deansdoor, M1 3PE	061-761933
S4	Swansea	28 Viola St, SW2 7OT	0792-78130
S5	N'castle-o-T	56 Ferdinand Close, NE4 7WF	0632-100245
S6	Liverpool	1−5 Sebastian Rd, L12 8PO	051-99321
S7	Glasgow	103 Belch Row, GL3 6RS	041-37825
S8	Reading	12−14 Iago St, RE4 8OL	0734-12994
S9	Edinburgh	Agucheek House, E83 1LG	031-814425
S10	Swansea	16 Fenton St, SW5 9PX	0792-23657
S11	Exeter	Page Mansion, EX2 7GF	0392-79251
S12	Leeds	Malvolio Cres., L13 8HV	0532-71335
S13	Bradford	Katherine Close, BR6 30J	0274-92274
S14	London	Ophelia Rd., NW3 6TK	01-793-3487
S15	Leicester	11−13 Richard St, LE2 5RG	0533-551552
S16	Cardiff	14 Feste St, CR3 8YF	0222-16953
S17	Sheffield	Gaunt Close, SH4 5PV	0742-94472
S18	Liverpool	Banquo Mansion, L15 7YB	051-66182

discussion of this topic until we reach Chapter 7. One might also point out in passing that the Liverpool store will have on its database only the orders placed by the Liverpool store itself. Only on the central database at Headquarters will all the orders of all the stores be kept. The fact that each store has a database confined to data appertaining to that store alone and that a central SOS database contains all the data from all the stores merits considerable explanation and discussion. INGRES can cope quite happily with distributed databases of this kind, but to discuss it here would take us away from our primary concern, using INGRES, and the topic is, anyway, an exceedingly complex one to which many books are already devoted. None the less, it is always well to be reminded that one topic within the information technology field always inevitably leads on to other related topics.

These, then, are the four tables with which we will be dealing in the chapters to come. I am well aware that filling in data is a tedious operation, but it is important that you do so before moving onto Part Two of this book. If it is any help, Tables 3.2–3.5 show the tables that I constructed. You may prefer to listen to the radio while mechanically copying my tables rather than devising your own.

Table 3.2 shows the stores currently owned and managed by SOS. Now let us look at Table 3.3, the Emp–Store one. As indicated, we shall confine ourselves mostly to the Leicester branch, but, for the sake of handling our data realistically, some staff from other stores will have to be included.

Table 3.3   Employee-Store table

NW_90_66_23_A	S15	Pecksnort, Daniel	Manager	£18,750	01_06_71
BC_14_83_92_L	S17	Wain, Rocco	Assistant	£7,300	18_07_89
ZS_45_61_88_D	S15	Fussup, Beryl	Sales Dir	£15,250	30_09_78
GN_37_94_61_M	S8	Cobol, Vaunt	Manager	£18,750	16_10_88
DC_83_26_10_F	S1	Machin, Turd	Driver	£9,400	25_03_81
NX_61_73_49_A	S2	Essendal, Modula	Manager	£18,750	31_12_76
MT_82_55_68_V	S7	Cleary, Maud	Cleaner	£6,000	23_05_84
BS_37_82_49_K	S15	Bleary, Felix	Janitor	£9,700	16_03_75
BN_79_86_79_P	S5	Wayne, Crispin	Manager	£18,750	01_04_79
WR_34_16_95_B	S15	Nittle, Sarah	Assistant	£7,300	25_11_89
TQ_66_71_38_A	S6	Prune, Alex	Manager	£18,750	01_03_81
UY_27_41_63_N	S15	Popsill, Nerd	Assistant	£7,300	01_04_75
HD_74_26_19_Y	S10	Yap, Rover	Manager	£18,750	14_03_78
JS_44_17_91_P	S18	Esendall, Gwyn	Assistant	£7,300	30_07_90
VN_55_71_94_A	S15	Yarduit, Sask	Accountant	£16,500	12_10_85
TV_91_45_83_Y	S3	Cringe, Norman	Manager	£18,750	22_12_78
RT_36_95_17_F	S15	Everton, Flange	Assistant	£7,300	01_09_88
ME_34_71_94_J	S4	Whisker, Job	Manager	£18,750	01_01_83
NW_62_53_39_N	S15	Locoway, Reginald	Purchase D	£15,250	01_06_71
RS_51_93_83_W	S1	Bushkell, Fay	Manager	£18,750	15_07_86
EU_84_71_44_P	S15	Maroon, Grace	Assistant	£7,300	25_05_83
TQ_71_75_96_L	S2	Kai, Mordecai	Sales Dir	£15,250	01_11_85
HW_44_82_97_B	S7	Keel, Howard	Manager	£18,750	01_05_79
OJ_86_39_40_T	S15	Blenkins, Brindle	Assistant	£7,300	01_01_89
YW_54_37_18_R	S11	Broadhurst, Jim	Manager	£18,750	18_07_84
VN_83_19_52_O	S5	Bushed, Lee	Assistant	£7,300	23_12_85
CR_63_71_92_S	S9	Prinz, Luke	Manager	£18,750	01_03_74
PR_45_23_67_M	S15	Wattle, Verge	Assistant	£7,300	18_04_90
VJ_82_17_55_X	S18	Murdstone, Joe	Manager	£18,750	22_06_78
GD_77_26_91_P	S16	Yallop, Gurd	Manager	£18,750	01_01_79
MC_63_17_83_Y	S9	Whinge, Karl	Manager	£18,750	19_10_87
NH_73_29_11_K	S17	Blench, Tugrel	Manager	£18,750	01_11_79
LU_93_22_18_O	S14	Claude, William	Manager	£18,750	28_03_81
TQ_77_35_29_P	S12	Minge, Leonore	Manager	£18,750	01_04_90
DS_99_14_58_B	S13	Fleck, Nigel	Manager	£18,750	21_02_80

I am well aware that remarkably few staff are shown in Table 3.3, but I find filling in tables just as boring as you do, and all I want to do is to provide enough data to make INGRES exercises meaningful. Table 3.4 is the Suppliers table.

And now, thank goodness, all that we have left is our Purchases table (Table 3.5). Clearly this will present a vast amount of data, and I have no intention of presenting more than a tiny fraction of such data. Since the Order table was not constructed until June 1989, I shall content myself with a few of the purchases made in the second half of that year.

Table 3.4   Suppliers table

Sp1	Filcham, Cyril	7 The Toerow, LEEDS L1 6YR	0367-239841
Sp2	Wallop, S.T. & Co	Etruria Rd, STOKE-on-TRENT ST6 9GV	0581-688439
Sp3	Sludge, B.Y. & Co	Satis House, MANCHESTER M13 7UV	061-952576
Sp4	Fake, Percy	15 Blenheim Gate, LEICESTER LE1 4SD	0503-832167
Sp5	Dodger, O.R.	1–6 Bayswater Rd, W11 8GH	01-674-3481
Sp6	Con, Wendy	Bleak St, BRADFORD BR4 6DC	0328-74492
Sp7	Hurtis & Co	Slaughter St, BIRMINGHAM B3 7CS	021-672-6693
Sp8	Brandish Ltd	Vertigo St, SHEFFIELD SH2 5YB	0743-99152
Sp9	Torque, H.S.	Gripe Road, PORTSMOUTH PO5 3DK	0391-88427
Sp10	Slime & Co	14 Trauma St, MANCHESTER M12 4ZL	061-337521
Sp11	Carker, G.L.	Marshalsea Depot, EC4 8FE	01-634-2763
Sp12	Carton Ltd	Lowood, BIRMINGHAM B11 9OP	021-385-2271

Table 3.5   Purchases table

LR0000001	S15	Sp7	150689	Wheelbarrows	10
L00000001	S1	Sp2	030789	Rulers	700
LR0000002	S15	Sp4	070789	Writing Pads	1200
MA0000001	S3	Sp6	180689	Table Lamps	50
EX0000001	S11	Sp2	210689	Typewriters	35
L00000002	S1	Sp1	080789	Saucepans	125
L00000001	S14	Sp7	180789	Electric drills	40
SH0000001	S17	Sp12	200689	Portable radios	65
BI0000001	S2	Sp4	300689	Typing paper	300
LE0000001	S12	Sp12	240689	Televisions	45
BI0000002	S2	Sp5	140689	Pillows	50
ED0000001	S9	Sp3	060689	Chess sets	25

I cannot pretend that filling out tables full of data is anything other than monstrously tedious. It has the stultifying impact of a Conservative Party Conference, without the saving grace of the latter's elements of farce. However, it was a necessary operation, and we have reduced our own tables to the barest minimum. Indeed, in the case of the final table, we will have to make many more additions to it before it can be a really useful set of data. We have, though, created a database. In Part Two, we will be able to manage that database.

To conclude. We have, in fact, covered an alarming amount of material in this chapter. I am well aware that it is not easy to remember all the details of constructing a table, adding new columns to a table, and placing validation checks upon that table, let alone coping with the problems of normalization. Consequently I have included, in an appendix, step-by-step notes on how to perform the operations with which this table has been concerned. Hence, should you want to create some tables of your own, add new domains to existing tables, or change the appearance of your tables, those notes should be adequate in reminding you of the necessary steps.

4
Taking stock

At the end of each section of this book, there will be a chapter like this one, a chapter that attempts to sum up what we have so far learned and to place that knowledge within a more conceptual framework. Let us, then, begin.

One of the besetting sins of information technology is its use of the English language. One might be forgiven if one felt that the prime aim of computer scientists was to induce linguistic paranoia. There are a number of plausible reasons as to why writers on data processing tend to write confusingly.

1. Computer science is a new subject. Like all subjects, it genuinely does need a vocabulary of its own. As zoologists refer to primates or marsupials, so computer scientists refer to B-trees or hashing. This is inevitable. One of the troubles, though, is the tendency for six different computer scientists independently to coin a new word for the same thing. Hence it is possible for the words attribute, data item, element, field, and value to be used as complete synonyms. For someone new to computer science, this can cause alarm and confusion.
2. It has to be sadly admitted that some computer scientists might be superb at programming in FORTRAN or wizard at designing a database, but that their command of correct and clear English is minimal. There are lots of honourable exceptions to this aspersion, and I am also aware of that merry proverb that states that people who live in glass houses shouldn't throw stones. My sincere apologies if you have ever found me obscure or ambiguous.
3. Computer science is really an amalgam of disciplines. This book is about a relational database, but it will have to occasionally refer to systems analysis, hardware considerations, programming techniques, and mathematical aspects. Each of those is a separate discipline (or even collection

of disciplines). It is no wonder that vocabulary distinctions and differences come to play their part.

Hence the first subsection of this chapter is concerned with vocabulary. In that section I try to define all the technical terms that we have so far encountered, and to provide some guidance as to the synonyms that you might encounter in your further reading. One or two other relevant terms that you might encounter are also introduced.

In the second section, I look at the concept of a database more closely. We have just created a small database, but what are the real advantages of so doing? Are there, for that matter, any disadvantages to having a database?

Next I look at the role of the database administrator. Unless you understand his or her work, you will not get to grips with managing your own database.

Finally, I glance at the differing ways in which a DBMS can be seen. In a sense, this concluding section is just an attempt to understand the nature of INGRES more fully, and, through INGRES, the nature of all databases.

Let us, then, begin with that most slippery of subjects: words. The Glossary at the end of this book does try to give some short definitions of the technical terms used in this book, but such short cuts have severe limitations. It is never possible in a dictionary format to give the penumbra of meaning that most words possess. Yet, even in a 'science' like information technology, it is such penumbra that create the problems.

4.1   Vocabulary

As you are well aware, this opening section of the book has been concerned with building a small database that we can, in subsequent sections, move on to use in the variety of ways that INGRES allows. As you are also aware, we have spent considerable time in constructing tables for our database. It is with those tables that I shall be primarily concerned in this subsection.

A *table* is sometimes referred to as a *relation*. This term comes from the mathematical origin of database design, and points, properly enough, to the fact that everything within a table is related to all the other elements within that table. Date, on page 81 of his *Relational Database* points out that 'a relation should be regarded not as "just a table", but rather as a *disciplined* table'. Even more commonly, a table is referred to as a *file*. Thus we have a file on Suppliers and another file on Purchases. The term 'file' is nowadays regarded as belonging more to pre-relational database days.

A table is made up of *rows*. Each individual row is often called a *tuple*. Why anyone uses the word 'tuple' instead of the word 'row' I am unable to explain, but it is a word that you will often hear. Hence you need to know its meaning. A silly rhyme might help, particularly since it indicates the correct pronounciation of the word 'tuple':

> Store number and town make a splendid couple,
> Since they are items within a tuple.

Of course, we do use the word 'tuple' as an element in words like 'quintuple', and so, strictly speaking, you ought to refer to a row as a 4-tuple or a 6-tuple, depending on how many attributes there are in that row. The number of rows in a table (or relation) is known as the *cardinality* of the table. Thus our table 'Stores' has a current cardinality of 18, though I ought to add that I have so far managed to go through life without ever using the word cardinality. I have not found this denial in any way constricting. However, to return to our subject, each row or tuple can be referred to as a *record*, though I would advise against the use of this word: it has so many meanings that ambiguity is almost inevitable if you use it in this context as well.

Each row within a table is made up of a number of individual items of data, items like Store Number, Town, Address, and Telephone Number. I have tended to call such individual items *attributes*, but the word *field* is also commonly used. I indicated in the third paragraph of this chapter that other synonyms can also be encountered: data item, value, element, and, doubtless, others.

While each attribute rests within a row, it is also part of a column of functionally identical attributes. Thus Sarah Nittle is an attribute within the row that begins with her National Insurance Number, but she shares the same column as Verge Wattle, Daniel Pecksnort, and others. The column that they all share is often called a *domain*. Thus, in the third table that we designed, there are four domains: Supplier Number, Supplier Name, Address, and Telephone Number. The number of columns or domains in a table (or relation) is called the *degree* of the relation.

Each row of attributes will have a *primary key*, which can be seen as the unique identifier of the entire row. One may need to tie two attributes together for them to form a composite or compound primary key, as is the case in the Employee-Store table, though such a practice is not, perhaps, the wisest.

Each row within a table should consist of *fully normalized* data, in that each attribute in that row should be wholly dependent upon the primary key of that row.

Of course, your fully normalized data consists of *characters*. A character can be a letter (either upper or lower case), a one-digit number, or a range of special characters, like punctuation marks, that are regarded as valid by the operating system your computer is controlled by.

A *character string* is simply a sequence of characters, like 'dog' or '2 + 2 = 4'.

If you understand and are at home with the italicized words in this subsection, you are well on the way to becoming computer literate. S. M. Deen, in the sixth chapter of his *Fundamentals of Data Base Systems*,

(Macmillan, 1977), has a useful breakdown of such concerns if you would like to sample someone else's prose.

4.2   The database

Human beings often have a remarkable tendency to accept the status quo.

Databases exist, so databases must be a useful entity.

Once one expresses the unspoken concept in such a fashion, its complete illogicality becomes obvious. It is exactly like saying "The Conservative Party exists, so the Conservative Party must be a useful entity', and the blatant foolishness of that remark beggars belief. (I always believe that authors should keep their personal prejudices to themselves.)

Anyway, before I allow myself to be distracted by irrelevancies, let us look at why a database, (or, strictly speaking, a database management system), is so useful. Some of the issues have already been mentioned, but it will be useful to tie them together here.

The most obvious advantage of a database rests on the economy of effort and resources that it can bring. The principle here is exactly the same as the one that impels my wife during her shopping expeditions. I am always coerced into accompanying her, and my function is obvious. My wife wishes to buy some washing powder. She has worked out that the bigger packet of powder she buys, the cheaper in real terms each washing day becomes. Unfortunately, the really massive packets of washing powder require a team of trained navvies to move. This is where I come in. Disregarding my fears of a hernia, my wife forces me to crouch while she levers a packet of Persil unto my back. Then, with a quick flick of her whip, I am driven towards the check-out and ultimately the car. It is the same with a DBMS. They are expensive to build and install, but, once constructed, they offer you all the facilities that you will ever need. You and your staff will be able to service all applications that require the data you have stored. The economy of effort and scale is considerable. Not only do you have all the data instantly accessible, you have it stored with remarkable compactness, retrieved with almost no effort and at considerable speed, updated with ease, and are consequently always up to date. On top of all these advantages is another, which is regarded by C. J. Date in his *An Introduction to Database Systems* (Vol. 1) as being overriding:

The database system provides the enterprise with centralized control of its operational data.

For Date, this aspect is crucial. In an organization without a database, files or records tend to be allied to the department that most uses such a file. Thus the payroll file will be kept in the Accounts Department, the suppliers file in the Marketing Department, and so on. But other departments often need data that is based in a department other than their own. Either they then borrow the file concerned, or they construct their own. The inevitable result is the repetition of data (i.e. redundancy) and/or inconsistency between files. With a database, however, the same data can be shared, and procedures can be implemented to ensure the integrity or consistency of that data is maintained. In other words, standards can be enforced, security checks can be applied, and conflicting requirements can be balanced. Of course, all this can be done in a non-database environment; but it rarely is. Standards, security, and consistency are extremely difficult to enforce when files are the preserve of an entire galaxy of differing departments. A database, however, makes such housekeeping extremely easy. It is a consequence of what Elmasri and Navathe in their *Fundamentals of Database Systems* (Benjamin/Cummings, 1989) refer to as the self-contained nature of a database system.

Linked with this is the very important question of *data independence*. It is not appropriate to indulge here in a lengthy discussion of this vital concept. Date deals with it in p. 15–19 of his *Introduction to Database Systems*, while Smith and Barnes distinguish between physical, logical, and geographical data independence in their *Files and Databases* (Addison-Wesley, 1987). Very broadly, data independence means that the same data can be accessed by many different applications without those applications needing to worry about where the data is stored or even in what format it is stored.

There is, of course, a price to be paid for this. A DBMS is extremely expensive. Your company will not purchase INGRES for 30 pieces of silver. Furthermore, having purchased INGRES, they will need the staff to manage it, and such staff tend to be expensive also (which is why, perhaps, you are reading this book). In addition, once you have purchased a DBMS, you can find yourself tied to particular processes, particularly modes of operation, and even particular types of hardware. A DBMS may liberate you in countless ways, but it can also circumscribe you as well. It is likely to cost more to run as well; filing cabinets do not need electricity. And a DBMS commits you. You are, after all, putting all your eggs into one basket. I have not, however, heard anyone argue that, instead of relying solely on nuclear weapons, the armed forces should also keep a ready supply of bows and arrows. My analogy is not as far-fetched as it may appear.

If, then, a DBMS is more wonderful than sliced bread (and most things are), it does need someone of experience and intelligence to be in charge of it. This is the task of the Database Administrator (DBA). Since you are engaged in constructing your own database, and will then be concerned and responsible for managing it, the conclusion is obvious: you are, pro tem, a database administrator. Since this is the role that you will be playing for the succeeding chapters of this book, it is important to offer some guidance as to the nature of such a role.

4.3   The database administrator

In a large company, the database administrator—hereafter known as the DBA—is rarely a single individual. There may be a database planner, a database technician, a database analyst, and so on. However, we are only constructing a tiny database, and, perforce, you are the only administrator. Hence, before we move in the next section to managing our data, you need to know the nature of your task.

Joseph A. Vasta, in his *Understanding Data Base Management Systems*, (Wadsworth, 1985), defines the role of the DBA in a very succinct fashion:

> The major functions of the data base administrator are to perform planning as it relates to the data base management system; to establish, publish, update, and enforce standards; to perform data base design; to implement data integrity procedures; to coordinate users to the data base; to implement quality-control procedures; and to perform data base tuning and monitor performance.   (p. 296)

Most of what Vasta has to say is fairly straightforward and expected. Indeed, we have already been engaged in performing some of the DBA's functions. We have established some standards, we have performed a small database design, and we have implemented some quality-control procedures. Equally, some of the functions Vasta cites will not be relevant to us. It is likely that you will be the only user of the SOS database, so you are not going to have to coordinate other users. Nor, although you will need to enforce standards, does it seem necessary to publish them. None the less this mention of publishing does suggest a function of the DBA that Vasta fails to highlight. Richard C. Perkinson, in his *Data Analysis: The Key to Data Base Design*, (QED Information Sciences, 1984), devotes a complete paragraph to this function:

> *Documentation.* In a data base environment documentation is essential. One of the major responsibilities of the job of data base administrator is the creation and maintenance of data documentation. This documentation includes cataloging the physical data base description, creating and maintaining the organizational standards, procedures, and passwords, plus defining the usage measurement procedures and standards.   (p. 151)

Clearly, while you are only concerned with SOS, there will be little need for extensive documentation. But there will be the need for some. Particularly if you extend and develop the database as you proceed through this book, you will need to keep a record of your own procedures. I am peculiarly fortunate here. I seem capable of forgetting almost anything at a minute's notice. Hence, unless I make a written or computer record of things that I need to recall, the data is lost for ever in the murky caverns of my mind. Hence, most of the time, I force myself to make such a record. It is the only way that I can recall my wife's name. I strongly advise you to do the same.

This, then, in outline, is the job of the DBA. Concerned with standards, planning, integrity, security, design, coordination, control, and documentation, he or she needs to have a good, overall understanding, not just of INGRES, but of the database environment as a whole. David Howe, in his quite difficult but richly rewarding book, *Data Analysis for Data Base Design* (Arnold, 2nd edn 1989), uses the term 'data administrator' to cover three aspects of the database world, namely the conceptual schema; the internal schema; and the external schema. Needless to say, other books refer to this threefold demarcation with different terminology: the conceptual or logical schema; the internal, storage, or physical schema; and the external schema.

We shall conclude this entire section by looking briefly at what this threefold demarcation means.

4.4 Views of a database

Ever since Caesar divided Gaul into three parts, there seems to have been a passion for demarcating things in a threefold fashion. Virtually all books on databases do so with respect to the so-called architecture of a database system. I shall consequently be very brief. Fuller discussions can be found in the books by Date and Howe already cited in this chapter.

The conceptual schema of a database is the one that you have in your own mind. Assuming your mind to be powerful and well-disciplined (as, of course, it is, or you would not have read so far in this book), then the conceptual level is a paradigm of accuracy, consistency, and completeness.

The internal schema is concerned with how the DBMA actually stores your perfect conceptual database. When you type a row of your Suppliers Table, how does the DBMS store this row, where does it put it, and with what sort of retrieval machanism is it stored?

The external schema is what you actually encounter when you sit down at the keyboard and try to extract information out of your database. How do you find out how many suppliers of SOS are based in Manchester? Did the Shcfficld branch makc any purchascs of coffcc tablcs last Junc?

In learning to use INGRES, it is the external level with which we shall be mostly concerned. But, as a DBA, you will certainly need to have a conceptual schema as well, and at least sufficient understanding of the internal level so as not to try and load further data into a disk that is already full.

One useful facility of a database we have already encountered in part: the use of function keys. We have seen that pressing F2 returns one's cursor to the menu at the top of the screen, that F3 saves the data that you have recently input, and that F10 takes you back to the screen you inhabited immediately before your current one. Indeed, we could have saved ourselves just a little effort by a more extensive use of the function keys, so it seems a good idea to provide a breakdown of them all here. Quite apart from the function that these keys perform, pressing them will often obviate the necessity for pressing F2 and then moving the cursor to the command you need. We have seen that pressing F3 avoids our having to press F2 and then move the cursor to the word Save. As you will see in the complete list below, other vital operations can also be implemented in like fashion.

F1   This is the Help key. Press F1 whenever you are confused and require help concerning the operation you are currently attempting to accomplish. The help you will then be given on the screen is not always the precise help you need, but it often is, and F1 should always be your port of call when in difficulties.

F2   As you already know, pressing this key moves the cursor back to the menu at the top of the screen. If you then press F2 again, the cursor will return to the position on the screen that it left when you first pressed F2.

F3   This saves the work on the screen and then returns the cursor back to that same screen.

F4   This is the Edit function key. We could have used this a number of times in some of the operations we have already done, though I decided that it was not useful to bombard you with too many function keys all at once.

F5   This is the Find key, which searches for a specified number of characters on the screen.

F6   This is the Quit key. If you are in QBF or VIFRED, it will return you to the INGRES/MENU screen. If you are already on the MENU screen, it will return you to the operating system.

F7   If you make a mistake in performing an operation, the F7 key will undo the operation for you.

F8   This key will take you temporarily back to the operating system. If you want to return to the screen that you left, you just have to type 'exit' at the operating system prompt.

F9   Pressing this key will ensure that the command or operation that you have just entered will immediately be executed.

F10   Returns you to the previous screen.

As you will probably have noticed, F1 and F10 normally appear among the options given in the menu at the top of the screen.

In the VAX/VMS version, of course, it is PF3 and PF2 in particular and the numeric section generally (e.g. 0 for Save) that takes over from the function keys.

In the next section we shall learn about some primary operations that you can perform on the data of a database. In other words, we shall actually be managing the data of SOS. Before, however, you dash off to do so, try to answer the questions which conclude Part One. After all, you cannot start managing data until you understand the fundamentals, and the test that follows will demonstrate whether or not you do. And anyway, suffering, they tell me, is good for the soul.

Questions on Part One

1. What is the difference between redundant data and duplicated data?
2. In the table below, give an example of an attribute, a domain, and a primary key.

SPOONLEY ORCHESTRA	Id_No	Name	Instrument
	001	Tremulo, S.D.	violin
	002	Quaver, P.J.	violin
	003	Clef, Y.N.A.	sackbut
	004	Legato, M.E.	cello

3. Fill in the missing words in the following paragraph:

   The primary purpose of a database is to store ——. The thing, however, which distinguishes a DBMS from a file management system is that the data in a DBMS is —— data. This sharing helps to reduce —— and the problem of maintaining —— between duplicate values.

4. What do the abbreviations QBF, VIFRED, ASCII, DBMS, and RT stand for?
5. Milton Parva has a bridge club. Construct a normalized table for their register of members.
6. Give five advantages of a DBMS.
7. Define data security and explain why it is a significant factor.
8. A table of the recording of Mozart's works has been constructed with the following attributes. One entry in the table is also shown.

MOZART RECORDS	Work	Date	Performers	Record_Co
	Cosi Fan Tutti	1790	Karl Böhm, E. Schwarzkopf C. Ludwig	EMI

What is wrong with such a table?

9. What is the role of a database administrator?
10. What are the disadvantages of using a database system?

Answers

1. Redundant data is data that is not necessary; duplicated data will appear more than once in a database, but is necessary to each of its appearances.
2. Tremulo, S.D. is an attribute to the domain 'Name', 003 is an attribute of the domain 'Id-No', and cello is an attribute to the domain 'Instrument'. 001 is the primary key of the first row of the table, 002 is the primary key of the second row, and so on.
3. Data, shared, duplication, consistency.
4. Query-By-Forms, Visual Forms Editor, American Standard Code for Information Interchange, Data Base Management System, Relational Technology.
5. The simplest would be:

MEMBERSHIP TABLE	Number	Name

   You could have date of joining the club, sex, status, and date of leaving as well. You could not have address.
6. (a) Data independence; (b) non-redundant data; (c) data security; (d) data integrity; (e) economy of scale.
7. Data security is concerned with ensuring that each individual working at a database can retrieve and alter only the data necessary to perform his or her function within the organization or enterprise concerned. Consequently users are prevented from changing the data that is needed by other members of the organization, either accidentally or deliberately.
8. The attribute Performers is not atomic, there is no clear primary key, and there is consequently no total dependence of the attributes upon each other. For instance, the date of the work in question has no relationship to the performers of that work or the record company that recorded it.
9. A DBA safeguards standards, does long-range planning, provides quality control, and may also provide assistance in database design.

10. A database system is very expensive, often very complex, may give rise to security and integrity problems, and almost always leads to more hardware being needed, higher operating costs, and extra personnel.

PART TWO

Primary operations

5
Select

Obviously, one of the most fundamental functions that a DBMS can perform is to select data from a table. You have, after all, built up the database because you know that the data it contains is going to be necessary to you. Consequently you are frequently going to want to retrieve this data. INGRES offers two ways of so doing. The first method, by means of QBF, is very limited, but still useful. The second method, by using SQL, is more versatile. None the less, both techniques have their uses, and I shall examine each in turn. The specific instructions given will relate to INGRES Version 5. In Chapter 7 I do give some attention to Version 6, but, for these primary operations, though the format of the two versions is different, the procedures are identical in principle, so I saw little point in giving constant copies of the varying screens.

5.1 Selection through QBF

Although I stated that QBF was a limited instrument for the selection of data, many users of INGRES none the less cope quite happily by only using QBF. Let us see what can be accomplished by means of our QBF facility.

  We shall, for the moment, concern ourselves with the Store table. We will also begin at the beginning, even though we have already encountered QBF. Imagine then that you are on the INGRES/MENU screen. The cursor is resting over the menu option Tables, so you press Return. Then, by using the arrow keys, you move the cursor until it rests over the table name Store. You should next press F2 and then move the cursor along until it rests over the option Query-By-Forms. Pressing Enter again, we have next to choose between SimpleField or Tablefield. Opting for the latter, we press Return and are presented with the QBF Execution Phase screen. From the options offered, we select Retrieve, and, upon pressing Enter, are presented with an empty form. It is from this point onwards that we can begin to test the retrieval capabilities of QBF.

(Imagine that this is a footnote, but I felt that it was worth pointing out that you can access QBF from the operating system prompt by simply typing QBF.)

5.1.1 TO RETRIEVE A WHOLE TABLE

You doubtless recall that, in order to view an entire table, all that you have to do is to press F2, whereby the cursor will be moved up to the menu line, and will be nestling over the command Go. If one then presses Return, the screen is then filled with the data from the selected table. (Alternatively, you can just press F9.) Clearly, of course, if the table is too large to fit into a single screen, pressing the downward-pointing arrow key will scroll the table before you. Hence, having retrieved the table, you can browse merrily through it. By pressing the Tab key—the one with two arrows upon it—you can jump from column to column. Given the size of our Store table, there is not a great deal of point in this, but it might give you a feeling of power and consequently assuage your desire to smash the china.

5.1.2 ORDERING DATA UNDER QBF

You may have noticed that when you were on the Retrieve screen, the options offered included not only Go but Blank and Order also. Blank is not very useful for selecting data; instead, it merely clears any current entries from the screen. Order, however, is worth a brief mention.

If you select Order, you then have the ability to arrange your data in a prearranged sequence. Let us imagine that you would like the towns listed in the Store table to be presented in alphabetical order. You place the cursor on the relevant column heading—in this case, town—and type the number 1. When you execute the query, the table will be shown to you as follows:

S2	Birmingham	The Cowring, B1 9HZ	021-92817
S13	Bradford	Katherine Close, BR6 3OJ	0332-92274
S16	Cardiff	14 Feste St, CR3 8YF	0377-16953
S9	Edinburgh	Agucheek House, E83 1LG	0346-814425

And so on. Should you want these towns presented to you in reverse order, you would type 1d, the d standing for descending. In such an instance, Swansea would be the town given at the head of the table. Of course, since there are two SOS stores in Swansea, you might want to legislate as to the order in which such duplicates are presented. Let us assume that you wanted duplicate towns presented in the order of their Store Number. In that case, after having typed 1d in the field town, you would type 2 in the field Store_No.

This Order facility can be particularly useful when one has joined tables together. This will have to wait until we have learnt how to so join such tables.

5.1.3 QUALIFYING SELECTION IN QBF

It is clearly useful to be able to retrieve an entire table. It may also be useful to sort or present or arrange that table in a variety of ways. None the less, there can surely be little argument that the most useful mode of QBF selection is the number of ways in which you can select the data with which you are presented. If you retrieve an entire table, you are not doing very much selection. Nor, if you use Order, are you selecting; you are merely sorting the entirety. If, however, you specify that you want particular types of data falling under certain specified constraints, then you are genuinely selecting. Let us see what methods QBF can offer us for so doing.

The first procedure that we can opt for is to ask QBF to give us data according to some prearranged mode of comparison. For instance, we might want to know what stores were run by SOS in towns beginning with the letter B. You know that, when presented with the Query Target screen, if you left the default form blank and opted for the menu instruction Go, the form was filled with the entire table, or as much of it as was possible. You can, however, move the cursor to the field town and specify that you wanted only towns beginning with B, as shown in Fig. 5.1.

As a consequence of such an insertion, the table will display the Birmingham and Bradford branches (or whatever stores beginning with B that you have placed in your own database). Alternatively, let us assume that you wish to know which SOS employees earn more than £15 000 per annum. You will consequently call up the Query Target screen for the Employee-Store table and make the entry shown in Fig. 5.2. As a result, you will be shown that Daniel Pecksnort, Beryl Fussup, Sask Yarduit, and others are in this relatively happy position. Indeed, INGRES will allow the following comparative symbols to be used within the Query Target Screen:

$=$	equal to
$!=$	not equal to
$<$	less than
$>$	greater than
$<=$	less than or equal to
$>=$	greater than or equal to

Thus quite a wide range of comparative evaluations can be effected within QBF.

It is also possible within QBF to perform some limited logical operations.

Store_No	Town	Address	Tel_No
	B*		

Figure 5.1

NIN	Store_No	Name	Role	Salary	Hire_date
				>15000	

Figure 5.2

One can link two different attributes by an implied logical AND operation. Imagine, for instance, that the entry shown in Fig. 5.3 was made on the Query Target screen. This would be asking for all employees whose surnames began with the letter M AND who earned over £15 000 per annum.

One can also perform a logical OR operation. This is identical to the AND procedure except that one places the data requests upon consecutive rows instead of upon the same row (Fig. 5.4). Clearly this is asking for employees whose names begin with the letter B or whose salaries are greater than £15 000 per annum. Clearly too, one can express an AND query within a SimpleField context, while one needs the TableField screen for an OR query.

Thus I think enough has been done to demonstrate that the selection procedure of QBF are in no way negligible. Users who never stray beyond the use of QBF can still accomplish a considerable amount.

NIN	Store_No	Name	Role	Salary	Hire_date
		M*		>15000	

Figure 5.3

NIN	Store_No	Name	Role	Salary	Hire_date
		B*			
				>15000	

Figure 5.4

5.2   Selection through SQL

Obviously, all the things that you can do through QBF can also be accomplished by using SQL. INGRES will do this for you by means of the keyword SELECT, though you do not have to capitalize the word unless you wish to. It will also follow that some of the elements in this section will be nearly identical to the previous section on QBF. This you will immediately perceive stems from my desire to make this book of such a respectable length as to be seen as academically viable. Operating upon the principle that nothing is true unless it is said three times—I seem to recall some dictum to this effect in *Alice in Wonderland*—move on to the next paragraph, which will be a paraphrase of the section that you have just read.

Let us begin with the most all-embracing of commands; imagine again that you wish to see the entire contents of the table Store. From the INGRES/ MENU screen you move the cursor to Languages and press Return. You then select SQL and again press Return. On the blank screen that now follows you type

SELECT *
FROM store;

You will then be presented with the entire Store table. The * character, as you also know, is known as a wildcard character and can be handily used to represent either the entire contents of the table or some sequence of characters that you have forgotten. Let us imagine, for instance, that you know that SOS employed someone called Nittle, but you could not remember anything else. All that you would need to do would be to enter this command:

SELECT Nittle, *
FROM emp_store

and you would be presented with the row

WR_34_16_95_B   S15   Nittle, Sarah   Assistant   £7,300   25_11_89.

Imagine again that you knew that there was an SOS store in Glasgow, but you could remember neither its address nor its phone number. You would enter the command

SELECT Glasgow
FROM store

and then be presented with the exciting data

S7   Glasgow   103 Belch Row, GL3 6RD   0561-37825

None the less, you might well be feeling that the keyword SELECT does not do anything more than a good card index system could not do equally well. To a considerable extent, you would be right. After all, a database is nothing more than a big card index system. It takes up less room and you tend to find the data more quickly, but a database is only a convenient way of storing data. It does, however, cost a great deal more than half a dozen filing cabinets. Can its existence be justified?

It is worth pointing out that the SELECT function is only *one* of the functions of a DBMS. It would be wise to suspend judgement until you have encountered rather more database facilities. None the less, even with SELECT, I would suggest that a database provides a speed, a convenience, *and* a skill that the best-trained office staff would find it hard to match. Hence, what I propose to do now, having just introduced the SELECT command at its simplest, is to itemize the various ways in which this fundamental command can be used.

5.2.1 TO RECALL AN ENTIRE TABLE

This one we have already encountered, but I repeat it now so as to facilitate a reader's ease in looking up facilities. As you recall, all you need to do is to type SELECT * FROM [table name]. Specific instances would be

```
SELECT *
FROM emp_store
```

and

```
SELECT *
FROM purchase;
```

5.2.2 TO RECALL A ROW FROM A TABLE

We have already encountered this one also. The basic format is SELECT [attribute name] FROM [table name]. Hence we could have the following:

```
SELECT Manchester
FROM store;
```

and

```
SELECT Fake, Percy
FROM suppliers;
```

5.2.3 TO RECALL ALL DATA FROM ONE COLUMN

You might, for instance, want to know in which towns SOS had a store. The general format is SELECT [column title] FROM [table name]. Hence, for this specific example, you would type

```
SELECT town
FROM store;
```

However, as you know, SOS had two stores in London, Swansea, and Liverpool. If you only wanted the names of the towns, and had no interest in how many stores SOS had in each of those towns, you would type

```
SELECT DISTINCT town
FROM store;
```

And you could, of course, put the command all on one line—I have only written them in this way for the sake of clarity—and you could write the entire command in either upper or lower case. Whatever mode you adopted, you would get 15 entries for the second command as opposed to the 18 entries given for the first, because, in the second one, London, Swansea, and Liverpool would only be shown once.

Not only can you exclude duplicate values, but you can also insist that the values with which you are presented are given you in a predetermined order. Let us imagine again that you wanted a list of towns in which SOS had a store, but that you wanted those towns presented to you in alphabetical order. In such an instance you would type

```
SELECT DISTINCT town
FROM store
ORDER BY town asc;
```

Should you, for bizarre alphabetical reasons of your own, want those towns to be presented in reverse alphabetical order, then your command would be

```
SELECT DISTINCT town
FROM store
ORDER BY town desc;
```

From those two instances, you can deduce the function of the operator's 'asc' and 'desc', though I also need to point out that if you are going to use ORDER BY within a command, you must also use the keyword DISTINCT. (There is an exception to that rule which we will shall encounter shortly.)

Fairly obviously, 'asc' and 'desc' can be applied to numerical data as well as alphabetic data. Hence, if you wanted to know the salary range offered by SOS, you would type

```
SELECT DISTINCT salary
FROM emp_store
ORDER BY salary asc;
```

Already, I would argue, our SELECT command is beginning to look more versatile than any card index system.

5.2.4 SELECTING DATA FROM MULTIPLE COLUMNS

Naturally, you are not limited to selecting only one attribute at a time. Imagine that you wanted to select both the name and the telephone number of SOS suppliers. All that you would need to do is to list the column names that you required:

```
SELECT name, tel_no
FROM suppliers;
```

As a consequence, the screen would show you data like the few instances cited below:

```
Filcham, Cyril      0367-239841
Wallop, S. T. & Co  0581-688439
Sludge, B. Y. & Co  061-952576
```

Were the same supplier to appear more than once in the Suppliers table—something that does not happen, and would be highly undesirable if it did—you could eliminate duplicate appearances by using DISTINCT.

5.2.5 SQL AND WHERE

I am sorry if this heading appears somewhat cryptic. Let me explain.

In the real world we often want to know what instances are true where another instance is also true. For instance, we might want to know how many tropical fish-breeders in the United Kingdom are also fluent in Serbo-Croat. If such an enquiry strikes you as being somewhat improbable, fear not. I am only anxious to introduce a principle. Under SQL you would express such a query in the following form:

```
SELECT tropical fish breeders
FROM occupations
WHERE skill = Serbo-Croat;
```

The example given is an absurd one, but the WHERE condition is an alarmingly useful one. Just look at the more realistic query expressed below:

```
SELECT name
FROM emp_store
WHERE salary > 15000
```

This is asking INGRES to select employees whose salary is greater than £15 000 per annum. The database will immediately give you people like Sask Yarduit, Reginald Locoway, and Mordecai Kai as falling into that category. Indeed, according to the Employee-Store table that I have constructed, you ought to be given eight names. If you have adopted my own tables, you ought to try the command to see if this is so. If you have not adopted my own tables, you should still do so, but this time you will have to work out manually whether or not the answer is correct.

5.2.6 COMPARISON OPERATORS WITH SQL

You will recall that under QBF we could use the logical comparative words AND and OR. Hardly surprisingly, you can do the same in the SQL context. You can, for instance, extend the WHERE command by linking one condition with another. Let us imagine that you wanted to know, as you did in the last subsection, which people earned more than £15 000 per annum and also had been joined SOS later than 1985. You would consequently express your SQL request as follows:

```
SELECT name
FROM emp_store
WHERE salary > 15000 and hire-date > *85;
```

Naturally, you can also use the OR construct in a fashion like the following example:

```
SELECT town
FROM store
WHERE   town = 'Reading'
OR      town = 'Exeter';
```

Furthermore, SQL will also permit the use of a NOT command:

```
SELECT name, role
FROM emp_store
WHERE role <> 'Assistant';
```

As is, I think, fairly obvious, the above is asking for all the names and roles of employees listed in the Emp-Store table except for those employees who happen to be assistants.

5.2.7 ARITHMETIC COMPARISON AND SELECTION

SQL also allows a number of operations with numbers and arithmetic comparisons. Obviously, some of the procedures at which we have already looked have involved numbers, e.g.

```
WHERE salary > 15000 and hire-date > *85.
```

Indeed, all the operations at which we have so far glanced can be performed as easily with numeric data as they can with alphanumeric. However, there are certain facilities within SQL that are best suited to numbers or can only be employed with numeric data.

The most obvious of such facilities is the COUNT function. Again it is quicker and easier to give an example rather than attempt to explain this function in words.

```
SELECT COUNT
FROM suppliers
```

What this is asking for is for SQL to count up the total number of suppliers used by SOS and to provide the answer. Consequently the number 12 will instantly (or fairly quickly, at any rate) appear upon the screen.

Again we could have the following query:

```
SELECT COUNT
FROM emp_store
WHERE salary = '9700'.
```

This is asking how many employees earn £9700 per annum.

In addition to COUNT, one can also use the following built-in functions:

- SUM   Adds up to the values of a column.
- AVG   Gives the average of the values of a column.
- MAX   Gives the largest value of a column.
- MIN   Gives the smallest value of a column.

Hence, when using the SELECT command with SQL one can also gain some of the facilities of a spreadsheet.

This is a long way from being a complete breakdown of the range of SELECT operations that one can perform in INGRES by using SQL. As I have mentioned before, there is an entire section, albeit a brief one, devoted to communication with INGRES. Consequently, a fuller and more logically orientated discussion will have to wait until one has reached Part Three. I do, however, believe that even this cursory survey of just one primary operation—SELECT—has given some indication of just how useful INGRES can be. It may only be an electronic filing cabinet, but it makes the traditional filing cabinet look prehistoric in comparison.

6

Update

We will assume that we have all our data stored conveniently in our database. We already know many ways in which to select that data. None the less, it is often going to happen that we need to change our data within a table or form. Personnel will leave and have to be deleted. That militant trade union, the Amalgamated Shop Staff Association, will pressure for a pay rise. Hence salaries will have to be updated. Jason Willspend will decide to add new suppliers to the SOS range. Consequently, with remarkable frequency, we shall need to change the data within our database. If SELECT is the most fundamental of all database operations, UPDATE must push it fairly close.

As with SELECT, the changing of a database can be performed either through QBF or by using SQL. I shall consequently, as in the previous chapter, consider each procedure in turn.

6.1 Update through QBF

Once again we need to enter QBF, either by typing 'qbf' at the operating system prompt or by selecting Forms from the INGRES/MENU screen and then choosing Query-By-Forms. This will bring you again to the QBF Start-Up screen. Choose Tables from that screen, and you will be presented with a catalogue of your tables. Let us consider separately the two operations of changing the data and deleting the data.

6.1.1 CHANGING DATA

Let us imagine that the Amalgamated Shop Staff Association have recently been pressing for an overall 35 per cent rise in salaries. Their General Secretary, Wilfred Putchz, has been arguing that shops are the life-blood of this country. Without manifold stores selling the goods that the people need, the entire country would grind to a miserable halt, the economy would collapse, and the next thing that we would know is that we had been invaded by Argentina, anxious to suck the blood from the British corpse. Aided by massive rallies and extensive television coverage, the Amalgamated Shop Staff Association (hereafter known as the ASSA), attracted much support. Jason Willspend, despite his very advanced age, also came in for a great deal of unfavourable comment. As a consequence, Jason was obliged to compromise. After acrimonious discussions, the ASSA agreed to accept an overall salary rise of 10 per cent provided that it was linked to better holiday terms and provided that every shop employing over 100 people established a crèche for the use of its married staff. These terms Jason and all the other retailing magnates of the UK were forced to accept. Hence we now need to update our Emp_Store table.

We are, at the moment, placed in the Catalog screen. We need to put the cursor in the E of Emp_Store, press F2, and then choose Go. Since it is a table that we need to amend, we now opt for TableField, and press Enter. On the QBF Execution Phase screen that we now see, we place the cursor on Retrieve and press Enter. We are now presented with an empty form. We specify that we wish to select the rows containing salary and then press F9 (or F2 followed by Enter). All the salaries will then be displayed. You now have to overtype the existing entries with the new salary. Since there would be, in the real world, thousands of them, updating by means of QBF is not a viable idea. Certainly it is worth while using QBF if you only have one or two changes to make. If, however, you need to change every entry in a domain, then SQL is infinitely to be preferred. However, since we will want to use QBF for updating purposes from time to time, we ought to complete our account.

Having made our alterations, we merely have to select Save by pressing F3, and those alterations are effected.

6.1.2 DELETING DATA

There are in fact various ways in which you can delete data within INGRES, many of them not requiring either QBF or SQL.

On the top row of your keyboard there should be two keys labelled 'DEL'. The one with an arrow pointing to the right will delete a character to the right. The other one, with an arrow pointing to the left, will delete a character to the left. Of course, if you place a finger on either of them and keep it there, they will continue to delete character after character until, eventually, you raise your finger from the key or the entire collection of data in that table has been removed.

You will also have noticed that many of the menus with which you have been confronted have contained the word 'Destroy' or the word 'Delete'.

Hence, were you, for instance, on the Table Utility screen, placed your cursor on the initial letter of 'Store', pressed F2, moved the cursor to rest over Destroy, and then pressed Enter, then the entire table would be extinguished.

Furthermore, if you had just instructed INGRES to do something and then changed your mind, you could always press F7. This would 'undo' the operation that you had just completed, and so would be a form of deletion. Equally, of course, if you did delete something and then changed your mind, you could always press F7 in order to restore that which you had just destroyed. Note, however, that you can only restore data immediately after you have removed it. It will be no use returning a week later and trying to undo something that you performed seven days earlier. Only politicians are allowed that luxury.

Despite these techniques, however, there will be occasions when you will want to delete data from within the QBF context. You need, therefore, to be on the QBF Execution Phase screen. Choose Retrieve again, and then, from the next menu, the command Update. The ensuing menu includes the word Delete. If you have previously specified that you wish to be presented with SimpleFields, you will only be able to delete one row at a time. If you specified TableFields, you will be presented with a number of options, not all of which will be meaningful to you at the moment:

```
Master
AllDetailRows
DetailRow
Detail
AllRows
Row
```

I do not intend to examine each of these at the moment (or, probably, ever), but even this terse list does indicate that QBF gives you the opportunity of deleting a single row or the entire table.

6.2 Update through SQL

6.2.1 CHANGING DATA

The operation here is simplicity itself, though it introduces us to a new SQL word, SET. I am sure that if you just look at the example below, the mode of changing data by means of the UPDATE command will be apparent.

```
UPDATE emp_store
SET salary = salary * 1.1
```

As you have doubtless worked out, this two-line command has the effect of raising everyone's salary by 10 per cent. Of course, we could be more discriminating:

```
UPDATE emp_store
SET salary = salary * 1.1
WHERE salary = 7300;
```

In that instance, only the salaries of the shop assistants have been raised by 10 per cent.

The structure and purpose of the UPDATE command is fairly clear. The UPDATE command itself always refers to a table:

```
UPDATE suppliers
```

The SET statement indicates the change or changes that are necessary:

```
SET address = 'Danton Road, BIRMINGHAM B9 6TR'
```

and the WHERE statement shows which row or rows have to have that change implemented:

```
WHERE address = 'Lowood, BIRMINGHAM B11 9OP'
```

Of course, it is not always that easy. There can be slight problems if you want to update every attribute in a column, and that column is an integral part of an index system. Fortunately, that need not detain us at the moment.

6.2.2 DELETING DATA

The delete operation in SQL is equally easy. Here is an example:

```
DELETE
FROM suppliers
WHERE suppliers_no = 'Sp9';
```

And, of course, you can link attibutes together with the word AND:

```
DELETE
FROM suppliers
WHERE supplier_no. = 'Sp9'
AND tel_no. = '0391-88427';
```

There are other updating circumstances, both in changing data and in deleting it, that we have not considered. They can wait until we move to Chapter 9, 'Talking with INGRES'. For most normal circumstances, however, you should now be able to cope with selecting data from the database and with deleting data too. Both operations are very frequent, and both operations, as we have seen, are very simple. The next process, however, that of joining together elements from different tables, is less simple, but it is one of the most powerful and useful operations that a DBMS can offer.

7
Joining tables

The storing of data in tables (or relations) is a convenient practice, and most of us do it. As you know, a relational database does it all the time. Unsurprisingly, though, one frequently wants information that is not to be found in any one table. It can, however, be found by combining two or more tables together. More commonly, all one needs to do is to combine specific domains from two or more tables. Hence, if a database is to be really useful, it must have some method of merging tables. Needless to say, INGRES does have such techniques. So, of course, do all databases, but it is the Join facility that most clearly distinguishes a relational database from its hierarchical or network brethren. Date in his *Guide to INGRES* states that 'it is the availability of the join operation, almost more than anything else, that distinguishes relational from nonrelational systems' (p. 62), a dictum that is emphasized also by Mark Gillenson in his step-by-step guide to database. You can join tables in hierarchical and network databases, but you do so implicitly rather than explicitly. Indeed, it is in the actual design process of the other database types that provision is made for potential joins, and, should you wish to create a join that has not been previously considered likely, the operation may well prove to be either impossible or extremely time consuming. It is true that if one wishes to perform a join within a hierarchical or network database where the pointers to accomplish such a join have already been established, then the join will be created more rapidly than it will be within a relational database, but it is only within a relational database that one can accomplish data integration virtually as the whim takes one.

Given the complexity of the task that we are asking INGRES to do, it is remarkably simple to join one or more tables together. None the less, it is more complicated than simple selection or updating, so I advise against reading this chapter while you are watching television or suffering from a hangover.

7.1   A simple join

A student of mine had been set an exercise on the JoinDef facility. ('JoinDefs' is just the code word used within INGRES to signify the facility of joining two or more tables.) His written report upon that assignment did not entirely follow traditional patterns:

> As the tired sun ached its way painfully across the western sky, its rays, old and haggard, endlessly seeking somewhere to warm, I found myself once again staring with bleary eyes at a monochrome monitor.
> 'O God, not another assignment,' I said to myself, 'Is there no end to them?'

You will be delighted to know that my student's sour mood did not continue. He went on in his melodramatic style to reveal the nature of the exercise, and as he approached the moment of specifying the JoinDef command itself, he wrote:

> Now I know that as you read the next exciting installment, demonstrating the ease by which all the above is achieved, you will be filled with wonderment at its simplicity.

Yet I quote my student's words, not just because his Hollywood style amused me, but because I agree with him. Imagine that you need to do some planning. Your son is going off to Greece for a fortnight in July ('Where is his itinerary?') Your bank manager suggests a second mortgage. ('Where are his figures?') You and your wife are thinking of visiting aunt Mabel in Exeter. ('Where is the AA route?') The architect's plans for the new study need to be looked at. ('Where did I put them?') And by the time that you have found everything, there will not be enough room on the table for you to examine them. I do not, of course, mean to suggest that having a relational database will put an end to such traumas, but it could help very considerably. There can be no database facility more saving of time and energy (and bad language) than the JoinDefs function. So let us see whether or not my student was right. Is it all really very simple?

For two tables to be merged, they *must* have at least one attribute in common. You are aware, for instance, that our Store table and our Employee-Store table both share 'Store_No' as a common attribute. Hence you will be able to join those two tables together. This facility in INGRES is known as a JoinDef, and can be implemented via the usage of QBF. Let us imagine, therefore, that you wanted to know the addresses and phone numbers of the various SOS stores, but also wanted to know the names and roles of the employees of each of those stores. You cannot find out this

Create Destroy Edit Rename Go Find [F1=Help] [F10=End] Quit

QBF - JoinDefs Catalog

JoinDef Name	Owner

Position cursor over the name
of the JoinDef you wish to select.
Use the appropriate menu item to
perform the desired operation
on that JoinDef.

Figure 7.1

information by using the SELECT facility that we looked at in Chapter 5, because SELECT will only operate within a single table. Hence we will have to join together two tables in order to gain the information that we seek. Of course, we do not need to join together two complete tables. We are, after all, not interested in the National Insurance Number of our employees, or their salaries or date of appointment. All we need, therefore, is the entire Store table linked to the employee names and roles.

To achieve this, we need to place the cursor on the JoinDef menu entry. This can be done from either the INGRES/MENU screen or the QBF Start-Up screen. Having done so, and pressed Enter, we will be presented with the JoinDefs Catalog screen. Obviously there will be nothing in the catalogue because we have not, as yet, created any JoinDefs. Figure 7.1 shows the screen with which one is presented in INGRES Version 5. In INGRES Version 6 in the VAX/VMS context, the appearance is different, but the procedure identical (see Fig. 7.2).

The differences between the two screens need not concern us at all. Both

QBF - JoinDefs Catalog

Name	Owner	Short Remark

Place cursor on row and select desired operation from menu.

Create(1) Destroy(2) Edit(3) Rename(4) MoreInfo(5) >

Figure 7.2

of them are blank. Since, however, we are now proposing to create a Join, we obviously leave the cursor on Create (or, in Version 6, press 1) and again press Return. This action will give us the JoinDef Definition screen. At first sight, this screen will appear somewhat problematic, since it is certainly asking for certain details that we have not so far encountered. There is, however, no serious difficulty to be faced, so let us just have a look at this JoinDef Definition screen, and learn how to cope with it. I shall give the Version 5 screen first. In fact, the Version 6 screen, as you will see, is more helpful than the earlier version. In any case, as those who have glanced at Date's *Guide to INGRES* or Malamud's *INGRES: Tools for Building an Information Architecture* will already have noticed, their reproductions of screens are both different from the ones that I have been giving in this book. As I keep on insisting, what matters when dealing with INGRES or any relational database is that one understands the principles behind the operations concerned. The screen formats are, after all, relatively easy to adjust to. Indeed, as Date states in the Preface to his INGRES book, 'there may be a few detail-level discrepancies between the discussions in the text and the product as it actually exists', but he goes on to affirm that 'such discrepancies are (I hope) minor'. I can only echo both his fears and his hopes. Figure 7.3 shows one screen presentation of the JoinDef Definition screen. The alternative screen is shown in Fig. 7.4.

The first thing that we have to do is to give our proposed table a name. I suggest that StoreEmp will do as well as anything else. So, in the highlighted section that follows the words 'JoinDef Name' we simply write the selected name, StoreEmp.

Next we have to deal with the strange columns with which we are presented. INGRES will allow three kinds of join:

1. Joining a master to master table.
2. Joining a detail to detail table.
3. Joining a master to detail table.

In order to do any of these, we do need to know what INGRES means by referring to some tables as master tables and others as detail tables. If you join a master table to another master table (or a detail table to another detail table), you are envisaging a one-to-one join. Thus, for instance, if you wanted to know which SOS store hosted the 1987 Annual General Meeting, you would join the Store table to the AGM table, both tables having Store Number as a common attribute. (Ignore the fact that we have created no such AGM table; I have just invented it for the sake of illustration.) If, however, you wanted to create a one-to-many join, you would be likely to use a master/detail construct. Thus, if you wanted to know, as we do now, which employees were employed by which stores, you would use a master/detail layout. This procedure, however, is not a prescriptive one. You can

Go   Blank   ChangeDisplay   Joins   Rules   Save   [F1=Help]   [F10=End]   Quit
_____

QBF - JoinDef Definition - Table Entry Form

JoinDef Name:

Enter table names and corresponding optional range variables in
the tables below.

Master Tables: Detail Tables:

Table Name	Range Variable		Table Name	Range Variable

Figure 7.3

QBF -   JoinDefs Definition Form
        JoinDef Name:
        For each table in the JoinDef, enter table name (with optional
        abbreviation for table name) below. For Master/Detail JoinDefs
        enter Master or Detail under Role. (Default is Master of blank.)

Role	Table Name	Abbreviation

                Table Field Format (y/n):
            Select the "Go" menu item to run the Join Definition
Go(Enter)   Blank(2)   Change Display(3)   Joins(4)   Rules(5) >

Figure 7.4

use whichever construct you please. INGRES will not object. Let us return
to our join procedure, and see how it works.

   Having filled in our table name—StoreEmp—we move the cursor to the
first column of the Master Tables grid, and type 'Store'. You do not have to
specify a range variable. In fact, a range variable is just a shortened name for
the table or tables that you are accessing. INGRES will not mind in any way
if you make no entry at all. Now you just need to press either the Tab key or
the Return key. Normally both will produce the effect of moving the cursor

Append   Retrieve   Update   [Fl=Help]   [FlO=End]   Quit
_____

Append data

                    INGRES QUERY-BY-FORMS
                    QBF Execution Frame

Figure 7.5

to the Table Name column of the Detail Tables diagram. However, let us
begin by seeing what happens if you join two master tables. Move the cursor
back to the Master Table grid and, immediately below Store type in
Emp–Store. Press F2, which will move the cursor so that it rests over the
word Go. Now press Return, and the screen will change so that you see a
very bare screen indeed, just like the one shown in Fig. 7.5.
   We, of course, are trying to Retrieve data, so we just press F2, move the
cursor so that it rests over Retrieve, and then press Enter. We will then be
presented with the screen shown in Fig. 7.6. And as you can see, the screen
display disappears off the screen. If you press Tab or the correct arrow key a
number of times, the remaining attributes will appear. In fact, because I have
abridged the space given to the various attributes, there is only Hire_date
remaining. None the less, it is irritating to have to keep on moving the cursor
to the right in order to see all the data, and anyway, the resulting join has
given us more data than we want. There are ways of obviating this situation.
   First of all, instead of making Store and Emp-Store a master/master join,
we could turn it into a master/detail join, which is what we ought to have
done to start with. If we did this, we would then be presented with the screen
shown in Fig. 7.7. As you can see, this enables all the data from both the
tables to be conveniently seen, though you will have to fill in the Store_No
and then access Go for the information to be delivered. But, of course, we
do not want all the data; we only want the name and role columns for each
store. It is not difficult to arrange this.
   You may not recall, but when we were formulating our Join on the JoinDef
Definition screen, the list of options presented at the top of that screen was
as follows:

Go Blank ChangeDisplay Joins Rules Save [Fl=Help] [FlO=End] Quit
_____

                    Query Target Name is emp_store

Store_No	Town	Address	Tel_No	NIN	Name	Role	Salary

Figure 7.6

Go Blank [F1=Help] [F10=End]

Query Target Name is store_emp

TABLE IS store

Store_No: town:

Address: Tel_No:

TABLE(S): emp_store

NIN	Name	Role	Salary	Hire_date

Figure 7.7

All that you now have to do is to move the cursor to the ChangeDisplay option and press Enter. You will then be presented with a complete list of all the attributes contained in both tables. All that you have to do is to place the cursor on the first letter of an attribute that you do not want, press F2 to move the cursor to the top of the screen, and then move that cursor to the word Destroy, which will be one of the new options given. You then press Return, and the attribute in question disappears. Thus, in the case that we are considering at the moment, you would destroy all the attributes of the Emp_Store table except the ones named Name and Role. As a result, when you enter S15 (or any other Store Number), you will be presented with a list of all the names and the respective roles of employees of Leicester or whatever is the appropriate store that you have entered.

There is just one small item still worthy of mentioning. You will note that towards the bottom of the screen, a question appears:

Table Field Format? (y/n):

If you only want one row at a time to appear, you will type 'n' to this query. If, however, as is the case now, you want a number of rows to appear, you will type 'y'. As a consequence of typing 'y', the screen will display all the employees of the store in question (or, at least, as many as it can squeeze onto the screen).

We have now completed our simple join. Indeed, we have made it a little less simple than it could have been by deciding to exclude some of the data that we could have retrieved. Even so, the operation is not a fiendishly complicated one. And having learnt how to do a simple join, it will be relatively simple to perform slightly more complex ones. It is to this that we next turn.

7.2   More complex joins

In this subsection, I want to look at two other types of join: joining more than two tables together, and joining one table to itself.

One can join a maximum of 10 tables together, though I find it difficult to believe that one would ever want to. The procedure is virtually identical to the one that we have just been examining. The matter is irrelevant in our case because we have only created four tables. We could, however, join all four together because they all have at least one column in common with at least one other table. We know that Store table and Employee-Store table both have Store Number in common. The Suppliers table and the Purchases table both have Supplier Number in common. Fortunately, the Purchases table also has Store Number as one of its columns. Consquently, there is enough linkage between the tables for all four to be merged. All one has to do is to enter the table names in the master and/or detail columns that we have just been using, and the job is done. Of course, in the real world, one would not join the totalities of all the tables. If one did, one would have a massive amount of information to play with, even in the circumscribed circumstances in which we are operating. One is likely, therefore, to call for the deletion of a number of columns. But we have already learnt how to do that by accessing the ChangeDisplay option, so to join together four tables is really no more complex than joining together two.

Although it does not affect our situation, one further point about joining tables together is worth mentioning, particularly if you go on yourself to create other SOS tables. Although, as I stated, you can theoretically join as many as 10 tables together, you can only make one master/detail join. Consequently, you could join four master-to-master tables, join one of the master tables to a detail table, and then join together five detail-to-detail tables. Obviously this operation could be performed with any allowable ratio:

1 master-to-detail
1 master-to-detail
8 detail-to-detail

or

7 master-to-master
1 master-to-detail
2 detail-to-detail

and so on. Whatever the combination, however, there can only be one master/detail join. This impediment is hardly likely to cause any great hardship, and it certainly does not increase the difficulty of the operation.

Nor is there anything difficult about joining one table to itself. It is necessary, however, to explain why such an apparently bizarre operation can be very useful. We will take the Emp_Store table as our example. We know how to call up the table and examine its contents. It is quite possible, however, that we might want to know which employees were responsible to which manager. We could, of course, find out by combing through the Emp_Store table itself, but it would take us a considerable time. If, though, we joined Emp_Store to itself, INGRES would do the operation for us. Let us see how this is effected.

Imagine that we are back on the JoinDefs Catalog screen. All that we need to do is to type a name for our projected JoinDef. The cursor will then move into the Master Tables section, whereupon we simply type the name of the single table that we wish to join to itself. Having then chosen Go, the table will be displayed upon the screen. This, of course, is no more use than a simple selection of the table in the first place. However, it does become of considerable use if one builds into one's JoinDef certain criteria that one specifically needs and which require, for their display, a JoinDef. Thus certain columns can be deleted, so that irrelevant data is not displayed or so that certain personnel do not see data to which they have no right. Equally, certain (or all) rows can be disabled from deletion. Or, as in the example mentioned in the preceding paragraph, data can be matched with other data from the same table; in this case, employees with their respective managers. You are likely to find in creating such JoinDefs that use of the Range Variable column on the JoinDef Join Specification screen becomes very useful.

8
The primacy of data

In Part One, among other things, we built ourselves a tiny database. In Part Two we have been examining three INGRES techniques for managing that database. We have been concerned with the most fundamental operations:

1. Selecting data from the database when needed.
2. Updating data from the database when needed.
3. Merging data from the database when needed.

With these three techniques, we have mastered the primary needs of any administration or business venture. Anyone who knows how to select, update, and join data in the INGRES relational database can honestly say that he or she is a competent database operator.

While this is a worthy-enough skill to gain, one must never forget that the most extensive techniques, the most enlightened approach, and the most stunning mind are all of them irrelevant if the data upon which to exercise those talents is incomplete, corrupted, or false. A good relational database is the best way of handling data, but the data itself has to come first.

As a consequence of this truth, when one is constructing a database, one first of all constructs a *data model*. This is nothing more than a description of the data that the database is going to need. Clearly that data needs structuring in a particular way. The result is a data model. As we have seen, in a relational database, the data is organized in sundry tables. When that structure has been decided upon, the tables themselves can be constructed, and the DBMS can then be called upon to select from the data, update the data, or join the data. This, after all, is what we have so far been doing.

It may, however, already have become apparent to you that there is an extremely large element of make-believe in what we have been doing. If SOS were a real chain of department stores, it would need a massive number of tables. There would have to be a table for products containing, at least, product number, product description, and product price. There would have to be a method of recording orders that customers placed. There would have to be a system of distinguishing between full-time and part-time employees. There would need to be an invoice system. Indeed, there would need to be at least two; one system of invoices for customers who bought items on account, and another for the invoices received from suppliers who delivered goods to the various stores. There would have to be a whole series of security checks to ensure that the data was only accessed by those with the professional right to do so. There would equally have to be a large number of validation checks, so that a data entry into one table did not contradict or clash with the data entry into another table. There would need to be communication channels between each store and the administrative head office. It would be absurd for the Bradford store to have access to the data appertaining to the Glasgow store or the Manchester shop, but vital that the central database had access to them all.

One of the major responsibilities of the database administrator is to devise a data model. Indeed, referring back to Chapter 4, one is concerned with three data models—the conceptual, the internal, and the external. It is clear, then, that the *ad hoc* and miniscule database so far constructed for SOS has been so constructed with little regard for the tenets of data modelling. Yet, if data is paramount, surely this is a cardinal sin.

The response has to be a shamed affirmative. It is, though, the proverbial question of swings and roundabouts. The primary concern of this book is INGRES and how to operate with INGRES. As has been indicated already, information technology is a genuine discipline of its own. Like most other disciplines, it is demarcated into several subdivisions. The skills of a programmer are different from the skills of a system designer. The approach of a systems analyst is different from the approach of a hardware technician. But because information technology is a genuine discipline of its own, all its subdivisions are intimately related to each other. I have indicated from the outset that it seems pointless to learn how to operate mechanically within the INGRES environment without at the same time understanding the entities with which one is dealing and the concepts that underpin those entities or operations. None the less, one has to draw the line somewhere. There can be no doubt about the primacy of data. After all, without data there would be no database. With no database, there would be no need for a database management system—relational or otherwise. Hence, perforcely having to concentrate on INGRES itself, one cannot pay a great deal of attention to designing the system that INGRES will manage. Of course, in the real world, one would need to spend a great deal of time in designing that system, but the people who design the system are unlikely to be the people who will then operate the system. We are concerned here with learning how to operate the system, not with how to design it. I have already referred to the occasional book on systems design. Should your particular concerns or needs lie in that direction, there is nothing to prevent you following it up.

Although some demarcation of coverage is inevitable, however, it does seem important to pay some attention to the relationships between data that one can encounter. Fundamentally, when one selects, updates, or merges within a database, one is concerned with such relationships. This was patently obvious in the chapters devoted to the Select and the Join functions. Hence it seemed useful to devote a little space to codifying such relationships.

There are three types of possible relationship:

- *One-to-one* There is a one-to-one relationship between National Insurance Number and employee name; each number refers to only one person, and each person has only one number.
- *One-to-many* There is a one-to-many relationship between store and employees. There is only one store, but it employs many people. Of course, in fact there are many stores, but since no employee works simultaneously in more than one store, the one-to-many relationship is preserved.
- *Many-to-many* There is a many-to-many relationship between store and supplier. Each store will receive goods from many suppliers, but each supplier is likely to service many stores.

The examples given above are examples of relationships between differing entities, but there can also be relationships between attributes. If, for instance, each employee was given an Employee Number, but the table also stored his or her National Insurance Number, then there would be a one-to-one relationship between Employee Number and National Insurance Number. There is a one-to-many relationship between the attribute Store Number and the attribute Role, because each store has a variety of employees fulfilling different roles. There is a many-to-many relationship between supplier and store. There are many suppliers and many stores. Each supplier may well supply several stores and each store will order from many suppliers.

These, then, are the types of relationship possible within a database. Clearly, the type of DBMS that one is using has a profound effect upon the efficacy of the operations that one wishes to perform upon the database concerned. In an hierarchical database, the relationship established between what one may call a dominant entity and a subordinate entity type is a one-to-many relationship. Each dominant entity (the parent) may have a number of subordinate entities (children), but each child has only one parent. In a network database, the situation is more complex (and more flexible) in that each entity can be both a parent and a child. In a relational database like INGRES, however, there is no such parent/child concept. Indeed, one can use such a database without being in any way concerned about the phyiscal representation of the data. Data requests, therefore, can be entirely non-procedural, not having to worry about positional dependencies between attributes or tables. The result is a considerable gain in user ease. The user need only be concerned about the information he or she wishes to extract, and not about the paths such data retrieval has to undergo. To Select, Update, or Join data in INGRES may well need some concentration because even tiny databases like ours require thought, but the primary operations at which we have been looking are none the less much simpler within the relational context than they are elsewhere.

Not uncommonly, textbooks at this point would be talking about four relational concepts: projection, restriction, Cartesian product, and join. I mention them now, less for their intrinsic importance than simply to indicate that there is no need to be alarmed if you encounter them. Projection is simply the label given to describe a vertical section of an existing table, in other words, a subset of the columns of a table. Thus the following instruction is an example of projection:

```
SELECT store_no, town
FROM store
```

Restriction, in the same way, constructs a horizontal section of a table by presenting rows that satisfy a specified condition. Clearly this will entail a use of the WHERE clause:

```
SELECT store_no, town, address
FROM store
WHERE store_no >10
```

A Cartesian product is the sum total of two separate tables. Hence would achieve a Cartesian product by an instruction like the following:

```
SELECT *
FROM store, emp_store
```

A join, so far as these relational concepts are concerned, is a combination of a Cartesian product followed by a restriction.

In fact, the examples given above are the SQL implementations of relational concepts. Many textbooks—those by D. S. Bowers and Elmasri and Navathe, for example—plunge into relational algebra at this point and use the terms union, difference, intersection, Cartesian product, and division. To do so would be entirely pointless for our own purposes and, as I suggest elsewhere, is these days fairly pointless for anybody's purposes. I only mention the matter here for the sake of clarity.

With or without relational algebra, one's life within the relational context (or any other), is made even more productive once one has learned how to communicate most effectively with that relational database. It is with this that our next section is concerned. Do not, however, move into Part Three without consolidating your understanding by answering the questions that conclude this section of the book.

Questions on Part Two

1. If you wanted to see the Purchases table presented with all the purchases made from Supplier 1 presented together, all the purchases made from Supplier 2 presented together, and so on, how would you express your request?
2. How, using SQL, would you delete a employee from the Employee-Store table if that employee had the National Insurance Number BN_79_86_79_P?
3. Using QBF, how would you retrieve the entire Purchases table?
4. Why might one wish to join one table to itself?
5. What do the following comparative symbols mean? (a) != (b) > (c) <=.
6. How, using SQL, would you increase the salary of all shop assistants by 5 per cent?
7. How would you find out how many SOS employees earned £18 750?
8. What is a data model?
9. Which function in SQL would you use to add up the values of a column?
10. What does it mean when we say that a relational database responds to non-procedural queries?

Answers

1. SELECT DISTINCT supplier_no
   FROM purchases
   ORDER BY supplier_no asc;
2. DELETE
   FROM emp_store
   WHERE NIN = 'BN_79_86_79_P'
3. From the INGRES/MENU screen, access Tables. Then place the cursor

over the P of Purchases, and press F2 followed by Return. Alternatively, you could place the cursor on the P of Purchases and then just press F9.

4. There may be a number of reasons. The two most important are that one can then delete unnecessary columns or protect columns from updates.

5. (a) Not equal to; (b) greater than; (c) less than or equal to.

6. UPDATE emp_store
   SET salary = salary * 1.01
   WHERE salary = '7300';

7. SELECT COUNT
   FROM emp_store
   WHERE salary = '18750';

8. A description of the data needed for a database, with, preferably, that data having been structured into some useful and convenient format.

9. SUM

10. It means that in a relational database one only needs to ask for the information needed without having to specify the route by which that information can be accessed.

PART THREE

INGRES and communication

9
Talking with INGRES

When we built our database and when we learnt the three primary operations of a relational database, we were constantly talking to INGRES. We were also often aware that we were talking to INGRES through the medium of a query language. Indeed, if you have worked through Part Two, you have noticed that one query language, SQL, has been specifically mentioned as being of aid in performing even primary operations. There are a number of books about SQL, and there can be little doubt that anyone seriously interested in coming to grips with INGRES will have to learn either SQL or QUEL. Yet such a statement is far from self-evident. We have, after all, built a small database, selected necessary items from it, and joined together various tables or elements from tables. Very rarely during these operations have we felt in any need of SQL. And yet, ironically, we have only been able to accomplish the things that we have accomplished because we have been using SQL (or, more probably, QUEL). Let me explain.

When we were creating our database, we performed the majority of operations by means of placing the cursor over a menu word. What was really happening was that INGRES was giving us a painless guide to QUEL. You will recall that when we created a table, we placed the cursor over the menu word CREATE, and then pressed Enter. From then on, with INGRES holding our hand all the way, we created a table and all the attributes within that table. In fact, however, we could have ignored the aid proffered by INGRES, have moved straight into QUEL (or SQL), and created the table ourselves. 'Why on earth bother?' is a natural question. If INGRES does the whole thing for us anyway, there seems no point in using yet another tool. One of the purposes of Part Three is to show that there is a considerable point. Indeed, INGRES and a query language are like bread and butter; there is not much point in having the one unless you also have the other.

This symbiotic relationship is looked at in the next brief chapter, 'Query Languages'. For the moment, let us sidestep the issue of whether or not one really does need to learn SQL. By the end of Part Three it should certainly have become obvious that one does. Let us, instead, forget that one can use QBF in order to create tables, and let us instead create a table by using SQL.

Just imagine for the moment that we did not have a table called STORE. We do, however, wish to create one. We switch the computer on, type 'addingres' or ACCESS/SOFTWARE = INGRES_SECURE, and wait for the C> or $ prompt to appear. When it does, we have two alternatives:

1. We could type 'isql sos', and we would immediately be presented with a blank screen into which we could type our SQL commands.
2. We could type 'ingres sos', be presented with the menu—Tables Forms JoinDefs Reports Applications Languages Help Quit—move the cursor to Languages, and press Return. We would then be offered two or three options—SQL, QUEL, etc.—and would select SQL. If, of course, you are within a VAX/VMS context, you would type 'ingmenu sos'.

Clearly the first method is quicker if you are just starting work, but selecting the Languages option may be quicker if you have already been working on existing data.

Whatever method you have adopted, I shall assume that you are now facing a blank SQL screen. You wish to create the table STORE. Hence you type at the keyboard the following:

```
CREATE TABLE store
  (store_no vchar(3),
   town vchar(20),
   address vchar(30),
   tel_no vchar(14))
```

You do not have to create your table exactly as I have set it out. You could create it in one long line:

```
CREATE TABLE store (store_no vchar(3), town vchar(20), address vchar(30),
tel_no vchar(14)
```

Personally I find the long line example less clear then the previous mode of setting each attribute upon a separate line, but *chacun à son goût*.

What you have been doing, of course, is creating consciously via SQL the table that we created in Chapter 3 via the INGRES menu. In fact, the INGRES menu was QUEL directed, but the principle is identical. Every time that you use an in-built menu facility of INGRES, you are actually using a query language. We have already seen that, simply by using menu structures, you can accomplish a great deal. However, as we shall see, if you go on consciously to use a query language like SQL, you can accomplish much more than the in-built menu system will easily permit. Since it is so relatively easy to learn enough SQL to do so, it would be foolish to throw away the opportunity.

If using SQL (or QUEL) is a way of talking to INGRES, there is also a way of getting INGRES to talk to us. I refer to what is called the Data Dictionary.

Our database is composed of tables. Each table is constructed of a number of attributes, one of which is the primary key for that particular table. Our own database is currently so small that we can carry the details of each table quite comfortably in our memory. The real database of SOS, however, is enormous. There are hundreds of attributes and thousands of examples of each attribute. In the Pension table, for instance, there are details of which employees are members of the SOS pension scheme, which employees have joined a different independent pension scheme, which people have withdrawn from SERPS, and so on. In the Social Club table, there are details of venues, officers, events, and finances. No one could remember which store organized the SOS Pennine Walk, or in which tables an employee's National Insurance Number is stored, or how many bytes of memory is taken up by the Role field in the Store_Emp table. But the INGRES Data Dictionary can. Since you are currently the database administrator, you will find that the Data Dictionary is an invaluable tool.

There is also, of course, another aspect to communication: that of transferring data from one point to another. You may well be coming to grips with relational databases in general and INGRES in particular in solitary isolation, but in the world of business and commerce, one of the major functions of a database is to transmit its data to another office on the same site or even to another office thousands of miles away. It would obviously be absurd to have a section on communications that omitted this facet.

As you will have gathered, this section is concerned with communicating with INGRES and getting INGRES to communicate with us. No attempt is made to teach the whole of SQL, just as no attempt is made to describe all the facilities of a Data Dictionary or all the intricacies of data communication. You cannot, however, learn anything very meaningful about a relational database without learning the fundamentals of talking with it. You may at the end of this section (Chapters 10–15) still prefer talking with your wife/husband or children, but I think that you will find talking with INGRES more productive and less wearing.

The snide remark with which the last paragraph ended was not intended as an insult to your own, doubtless delightful, family, nor, for that matter, an indication that I cannot stand my own. Nobody can pretend that learning the basics of how to handle INGRES is an entirely entrancing task. It is often tedious. It is not, however, difficult (assuming that I have explained it clearly enough), and once you have learnt it, you are equipped for the next few decades. That is not true for our families. They change, often in disconcerting ways. INGRES does not (though the differing versions can be an irritant). If you can learn to communicate with INGRES, you have gained an invaluable, productive skill that may well serve you for your entire working life. Communicating with people is much more difficult, much more tenuous, and much more demanding. Talking with INGRES may not be as rewarding, but, once the graft is over, it is incomparably easier. But to talk effectively with INGRES, you have to use a query lanaguage, and it is to these that we next turn.

10
Query languages

A database is an inert mass. (Isn't it strange how the Conservative Party keeps popping into this book?) Let us begin this section by trying to summarize our current understanding of databases.

We begin with a mass of data:

Brown, B.N. 16 >PI 13 Rodean Grove £76
12.5% Manager Sp6 <>10 COVENTRY CV3
coffee $430000 !=7 Frost, G.R. a+b/2.6
13–6 Australia ½ 'S18' #68 Wilson, P

Such data, of course, is entirely useless. It needs to be ordered into some comprehensible framework. Consequently, we devise tables into which we can place our data.

Turner, S. T.	12_08_78	12450	DR10001
Fletcher, G. R.	07_02_73	13560	BN78119
Barnes, P. W.	23_11_79	11200	VW93725

Even then, the data is not very helpful. It will just sit in the database, doing nothing. Consequently we need some mechanism whereby we can perform a number of operations upon our data. We will want to select items of data, delete items, update items, join items together, and so on. In other words, we will want to perform all the functions to which Part Two of this book was devoted.

The nature and scope of the functions that one can perform on data is conditioned by two factors:

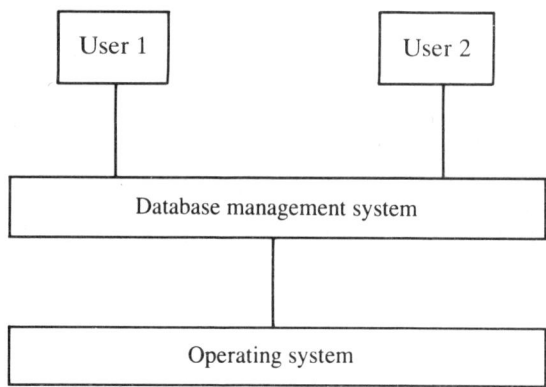

Figure 10.1

1. The nature of the database itself.
2. The nature of the query language used.

In effect, these two factors normally are interrelated, since all databases come with at least one query language built into their fabric. INGRES can use two or three query languages, though it was originally developed with QUEL as its data manipulation language, which is why the INGRES menu uses QUEL key words like RETRIEVE rather than SQL words like SELECT.

The nature of the database itself—whether it is hierarchical, network, or relational—clearly imposes certain constrictions, and, within any type, certain other questions like validation or modes of resolving conflicting requirements will also play their part. In addition, the very operating system upon which the database is placed will also be significant. The user thinks that he or she is working with a database, but at a fundamental level, that database itself is constrained by the operating system which acts as the conductor of the entire orchestra (see Fig. 10.1). Even Fig. 10.1 is a considerable simplification of the milieu. If you want to see a more realistic diagrammatic schema, have a look at the more complex diagram provided by Gio Wiederhold in his essay on databases included in the tutorial book, *Database Management*, published by the Computer Society of the IEEE.

We are not concerned here primarily with the problems of database design, though we have had to pay some attention to the question in designing our SOS tables. D. R. Howe, in the introductory chapter of his *Data Analysis for Data Base Design* (2nd edn 1989), gives a most illuminating survey of the traumas endured by Torg Ltd, a mythical manufacturing company, in constructing their own database. I would recommend that chapter as an excellent seven-page introduction to the quagmire of databases.

Fortunately we can sidestep most of these issues. This book is starting out with the assumption that you have INGRES installed upon a hard disk in a computer terminal that has MS-DOS or UNIX or some other acceptable operating system. Furthermore, as both Part One and Part Two indicated, I am assuming that you have access to the SQL query language. All that I want to do in this chapter is to have a glance at the very nature and role of query languages in general. Hence these opening paragraphs have only been trying to place query languages within the entire context of database management.

10.1. An interface

A query language is an interface between the user and the DBMS. Its purpose is to make life easier for the user. Frequently, as with INGRES, this is done by making the query language itself virtually invisible to the user. The varied menus that INGRES offers are just ways of making the query language effortless. Every time that you select a command like Retrieve, Order, or Help, you are in effect making a query language request. The function keys are also an implementation of query requests. Instead of entering the SQL screen and typing the word 'Save', one just presses F3 instead. The forms that INGRES presents are also an implementation of query language requests. Hence many people can survive in an INGRES environment without even knowing anything at all about query languages. As you are now aware, one is limited to fairly basic operations if one is tethered to the INGRES on-screen guidance, but they certainly perform a most useful function as a pain-free interface.

The idea behind the query language is also that it should offer a pain-free interface between the user and the database. To this end, a query language is a non-procedural language. In other words, it does not require the user to specify how the wanted data is to be retrieved. All that the user has to do is to state *what* he or she wants, not *how* the command should be obeyed. Jerome S. Burstein in his *Computers and Information Systems* (1986) goes so far as to exclaim that

> The beauty of databases really comes into play here, because the user need not have the slightest idea of the storage medium being used for the data item, how the data item's fields are defined, the hashing technique used, the relation of the data item to other data items, and so on.

It is not difficult to state

```
SELECT town
FROM store
WHERE town = 'Edinburgh';
```

but it would clearly be much more complex if one had to tell the computer which sections of memory it needed to access in order to fulfil this command.

Computer science may be less complicated and convoluted than many seem to think it is, but it is easy to confuse a query language with the DBMS itself. After all, a query language enables you retrieve, amend, merge, or destroy the database itself. Consquently it looks as if the query language itself is managing the database. Certainly this is the impression that the unsuspecting user gains. It is not, however, the case. The query language tells the database management system what it wants; it is the DBMS itself that then executes the request. After all, it is only the DBMS that knows where the data is. The query language has no idea where the various records and fields of the database are located. For this reason, a query language is often referred to as a data manipulation language (DML) because it is the use of the query language that persuades the DBMS to divulge its secrets.

Nor is a query language a programming language in the way that BASIC, COBOL or FORTRAN are. Those languages, known as third-generation languages, are procedural languages in that the user of them has to spell out how data is to be obtained. As we have already seen, query languages are non-procedural. They simply have to specify what they want. However, as you doubtless know, there are now a number of so-called fourth generation languages. They too are non-procedural, but even so, a query language is still not allied to a programming language, even a fourth-generation one. With a fourth-generation programming language, you can have a series of screen and report designing facilities and menu-creation utilities that are well beyond the scope of a query language. As a matter of fact, you can use a query language in combination with a third- or fourth-generation language, but the query language and the programming language none the less remain different and separable entities.

The last two paragraphs have been somewhat parenthetical. Returning to the itemization of those elements that make a query language an excellent interface between the DBMS and the user, a further facet of modern query languages that is worthy of note is that they should be capable of allowing one to make one's queries in something close to everyday English. I have seen claims that SQL is so close to normal usage as to pose no problems at all in its usage. This depends, I suppose, on your normal usage. The RT Reference Guide to INGRES claims that 'SQL is a language with a flow like ordinary English.' I must confess that I rarely speak or write like this:

```
UPDATE employee
SET salary = salary * 1.1
WHERE dnoIN (SELECT dnumber
             FROM department
             WHERE dname = 'Research');
```

I doubt if you do either. Still, despite the hyperbole, good query languages do bear a strong enough resemblance to everyday language as to make them relatively easy to learn.

Finally, and this may strike you as too obvious as to need mentioning, a query language needs to act interactively. In other words, when you enter a query language request, you need to be able to see that request obeyed. It is not a lot of use typing

```
SELECT name
FROM emp_store
WHERE name = 'Quilter';
```

and then having to come back an hour or so later to see if the request has been performed. As you have already seen, INGRES will deal with such a request in a matter of seconds.

There are other aspects to the interface role of query language that could well be mentioned. For instance, it is possible to 'embed' SQL within one's normal programming language and, as a consequence, run two different languages in harness. It is possible also to use a query language in the specifications for a report. However, this book is only intended as an introduction to INGRES and its associated aspects, and we need not concern ourselves with such issues.

10.2   The dual nature of a query language

Most commentators point out that a query language performs two distinct types of task. First of all, they are a data definition language. All that this means is that a query language can help to construct the very data structures needed for our relational system. We have, of course, already witnessed this. In the tables that have so far been created in our tiny database, we have accessed the query language command CREATE. Such a command is playing a part in defining the structure that we wish to establish. Equally, if we use a word like DESTROY (or DROP) or a word like ALTER (or AMEND), we are again helping to define the data within our database. Indeed, the first command that we used—CREATEDB—is clearly a fundamental data defi-nition term. Hence SQL or any other query language plays a vital role in the creation of the database itself, the tables within that database, and the index or indexes attached to that database or table.

Secondly, a query language enables us to manipulate data. We are manipulating data when we SELECT a particular data item. We are manipulating data when we RETRIEVE, UPDATE, INSERT, or DELETE a data item. Equally we are manipulating data when we use a query language to sort data into alphabetical order, or arrange some data into columns, or perform some mathematical operation upon the data.

Jonathan Sayles, in his entertaining book *SQL Spoken Here* (QED, 1989), makes a further category of task when he says that a query language also performs a data control function. Thus when you force an order number to comprise eight digits or when you prevent an employee of a store in Bristol from accessing data belonging to a branch in Sheffield, you are accessing the data control functions of the query language in question. Most writers would include such control operations as being part of data manipulation, but the matter is not worth a semantic quibble.

10.3   The level of query languages

Query languages are known as high-level languages. All that this means is that you express, by means of a query language, what it is that you want to do. You do not, however, have to specify how the operation is to be done. Hence, by means of the language, you may decide to SELECT some data from a table. All you have to do is to indicate what it is that you wish to select. You do not have go into a complicated procedural instruction as to how the items need to be selected. Just imagine what it would be like if you had, for instance, to specify whereabouts on the disk the items you wanted were placed.

In addition to this simple and pleasing non-procedural aspect, most query languages have a very accessible vocabulary. The most common commands in SQL are CREATE, DELETE, INSERT, UPDATE, JOIN, and SELECT. They can be modified or linked by words like BETWEEN, FROM, OR, and WHERE. Consequently, query languages are referred to as declarative languages because all that you need to do is to declare what you want.

Obviously a great deal more could be (and has been) written about the nature of query languages. One can, for instance, distinguish between algebraic languages and the even more declarative relational-calculus based languages. To do so, however, would be to venture into rarified fields, the utility of which I tend to doubt (to the despair and contempt of my computer-committed acquaintances). Let us, however, take a closer look at SQL.

10.4   SQL

Although we have not looked directly at SQL until this chapter, it has been mentioned (and, indeed, used) on a number of occasions. It is a structured query language (hence its acronym), and the nature of that structure is something that will be looked at in this section. However, I must first begin with a warning. If you ever hear anyone talking about 'Sequel', they are in fact talking about SQL. Personally I always refer to it as SQL (ess-queue-ell), but it is as well to be aware that there are two available pronunciations. Quite why anyone refers to SQL as Sequel these days has always baffled me, since the name Sequel is part of the history of database development. In 1974 (medieval times as far as relational databases were concerned), D. D. Chamberlin and R. F. Boyce published an article entitled 'SEQUEL: a structured English query language' in *Proc. ACM–SIGMOD Workshop on Data Description, Access, and Control* (Ann Arbor, MI) in which they suggested the structure of a proposed query language. As the title of the article indicates, the name of this proposed structured query language was SEQUEL. A year later, Chamberlin and Boyce teamed up with W. F. King and M. M. Hammer to propose an improved query language. Their article, published in *Comm. ACM* for November 1975, was concerned with expressing queries as relational expressions, and this time they named their data sublanguage SQUARE. A year later yet another article appeared, this time in *IBM Research and Development* and this time with eight authors. The name selected for the data sublanguage was now SEQUEL2, and it was this language that was incorporated into the so-called 'System R' research database developments undertaken by IBM. None the less, by 1980, when Chamberlin wrote yet another article, this time summarizing user experience with the language, the name of the language had been changed to SQL. Despite this, many people continue to refer to it as Sequel. Thus Date, in Chapter 4 of his *An Introduction to Database Systems*, Vol. I (1986), states that SQL was 'originally spelled SEQUEL, and usually pronounced as if it still were', and Emerson, Darnovsky, and Bowman in their 1989 *The Practical SQL Handbook* (Addision-Wesley) state, for reasons quite beyond my understanding, that 'In this book, we use the term SQL as if it were pronounced "sequel".' Calling SQL 'Sequel' seems to me to be about as sensible as calling a row a 'tuple', but fortunately the issue is hardly one of earth-shattering significance.

Whenever SQL has been mentioned previously, the implication has been given that SQL is an unambiguous entity. Would that it were. Like everything else in the computer universe, SQL exists in sundry modifications, none of which are compatible with each other. However, since SQL has become the *de facto* 'standard' query language, attempts have been made to rectify this confusion. The major date is 1986, for it was then that the ANSI SQL standard was proclaimed. Unfortunately, two elements have prevented this laudable urge towards standardization being as useful as it might have been. First of all, the very fact that there were already differing versions of SQL has meant that these differing versions have continued to exist. The mere announcement of a so-called standard version has not automatically meant that prior versions have thrown in the towel. Secondly, the proposed 'standard' version really does seem to have made a number of errors itself. Indeed, in some respects, it seems more deficient than the earlier IBM version. Hence not everything that I say about SQL will be necessarily valid for you. But then, I have already pointed out that not everything that I say about INGRES is necessarily valid about INGRES either. No one has the resources (or the time) to test every conceivable version of INGRES (or SQL) in order to ensure that every eventuality is covered. Clearly I regret this: it would be delightful to produce the *vade mecum*. Unfortunately, the idiosyncracies of the computer world make this impossible. This is why I have tried to emphasize principles rather than specific practice. If you know the principles of databases or query languages, you are better equipped to

deal with the practicalities than if you only learnt one specific implementation. It has already been pointed out that this book, while largely written by
using Version 5 of INGRES, has also been checked, in part at least, with
Version 6. As far as SQL is concerned, there is virtually no difference in
one's usage of that query language between the two versions. The Relational
Technology Inc. *INGRES/SQL Reference Manual* produced for INGRES
Release 6.3 in January 1990 indicates that 6.3 will still support all earlier
commands. It does, however, recommend that five commands—ABORT,
BEGIN TRANSACTION, CREATE PERMIT, END TRANSACTION,
and RELOCATE—should be replaced, but our glance at SQL in this chapter
and the following two will not be affected by these changes.

This section is, however, designed as an introduction to the nature of SQL,
not as an apologia for its deficiencies or developments, and there is one
obvious question that needs answering. You already know that that QUEL
was the first query language that INGRES selected as its interface. Why,
then, should I virtually ignore QUEL and concentrate instead on SQL?
There are a number of reasons.

I am not sure that I even know how important the respective reasons are.
Hence I shall introduce as the first a very pragmatic point. IBM adopted
SQL. Emerson, Darnovsky, and Bowman begin the first chapter of their *The
Practical SQL Handbook* with the words 'In the beginning was IBM, and
IBM created SQL.' For many years, anything that IBM adopted was assured
of massive usage. At the time that this chapter is being written, IBM is
coming under increasing criticism for its less than avant-garde stance. It is
also being commercially threatened by a number of companies who refuse to
accept the dominance of Big Blue. Hence, by the time you read this, the
dominance of IBM may well be at an end. However, this is not the case at
the moment. IBM may not have a stranglehold, but it does have a massive
influence. The sheer fact that IBM adopted SQL has greatly helped to ensure
that SQL has become the 'standard' query language. Furthermore, the
reasons as to why IBM did invent SQL illustrates the symbiotic nature of
INGRES and a query language to which I referred earlier. During the first
decade of relational database development (1970–80), progress was often
hampered by the slowness and difficulty of managing those databases. It was
the emergence of SQL and other query languages that helped greatly to
overcome this bottleneck.

Despite the differing versions of SQL, it is a very portable tool. If you are
able and content to confine yourself to the basic SQL commands, you can
run it on practically anything. Hence, if you were using SQL on a IBM
mainframe and wanted to move to an Olivetti PC, you should have virtually
no relearning to do. While this is a clear advantage of SQL, it is equally
clearly a very limited advantage. If you really were using SQL on an IBM
mainframe, you would almost certainly have SQL indissolubly linked with
report generators, graphic tools, and a whole host of sophisticated facilities.

As a consequence, you would have lost the portability of the language. None the less, the fact that databases like INGRES, Oracle and Informix have all made themselves SQL compatible is in itself a tribute to the increasingly universality of SQL.

Not only is SQL portable between differing configurations of hardware, it is an ideal bridge between a whole range of programming languages and the DMBS itself. Indeed, the increasing standardization of SQL only increases this facility. Whatever language you are programming in—schoolboy BASIC, Ministry of Defence Ada or polytechnic PROLOG—you can use SQL as the buffer between that language and the DBMS you are employing. SQL may be no better than QUEL, but, unlike QUEL, it has taken off, and, snowball-like, is increasing its user-availability constantly.

Finally, and Elizabeth Lynch in her splendid 1990 book *Understanding SQL* puts this as the first of her SQL benefits, SQL is itself designed along relational lines. Carolyn and Jack Hursch are making the same point in the first chapter of their *SQL: The Structured Query Language* (TAB, 1988) when they write as follows:

> The fact that the developers knew ahead of time what SQL should be and what it would be required to do gave it a strong theoretical foundation. This is probably a first in computer language development because most computer languages in use today are the result of a basic idea supplemented by a great deal of ad hoc patching to meet problems as they arise.

Fabian Pascal, in an article in the magazine *Byte* for September 1989, firmly states that 'It is the relational nature of SQL that has propelled it as the language of choice for connectivity.' Mark L. Van Name and Bill Catchings in another article in the same issue of *Byte* reaffirm that 'SQL is clearly the database server language of choice today.'

Alas this does not mean that SQL is entirely problem free—the number of differing varieties of the language being one obvious factor—but it does mean that SQL is considerably more logically implemented than many other languages. We must also view with care Elizabeth Lynch's claim that SQL is designed along relational lines. Unfortunately, nothing these days would advertise itself without claiming to be modelled along relational lines, but the phrase has manifold meanings. You may recall that virtually at the end of Chapter 2 I referred to E. F. Codd's 1970 paper, 'A Relational Model of Data for Large Shared Data Banks'. It was that paper which laid down the relational model. Understandably, Codd has developed this original thesis somewhat since, but the 12 criteria he laid down are still accepted by most as being the valid determinations as to whether or not a database, query language, or what have you can be validly described as being relational. I have skirted this central issue up to now, but it will be useful to know what those 12 criteria are. I shall attempt to outline them as clearly as possible, though many of these criteria we have already encountered in our progress, so the itemization should be less taxing than one might fear.

1. As you know, a database is a lump of data. In a relational database, all that data is organized as values in tables. Hence all the data concerned is organized into rows and columns, thus providing one with the advantages of familiarity and flexibility.
2. Each and every value in the database can be retrieved or selected by specifying the relevant table name, the primary key value, and the column name. SQL does not always observe this rule with sufficient rigour, though it can be forced to do so by using the command word UNIQUE.
3. Null values (which are a different species from just leaving a value blank or representing a value with a zero) can be supported in the same systematic way as normal values. SQL does not always observe this rule very consistently.
4. There is no difference between handling data one encounters in the database itself and data stored in the so-called system tables. The same tactics can be used for them both. Just to make the position clear, there are two types of tables in a relational database. There is the type that we have created for SOS or that Scotland Yard has created for storing data about criminal offences. Such tables are known as *user tables*. The DBMS, however, also keeps tables containing information about the user tables. These are known as *system tables* or even, sometimes, as the *system catalogue*. Indeed, these system tables, when given additional database management functions, are called a *data dictionary*, the subject of our 13th chapter. The important point to understand at the moment, however, is that a relational system should handle the contents of the user tables and the system tables in exactly the same way. The new ANSI standard seems to ignore this element completely, though in practice all implementations of SQL do seem to support the rule fully.
5. A relational system must have a sublanguage (SQL for instance) which can cope with data definition, view definition (more about views in the penultimate chapter of the book), data manipulation, integrity constraints, authorization, and transaction boundaries. The last two functions might not be immediately comprehensible at the moment. They simply refer to who is authorized to handle the data and to recovery procedures should there be a power failure or other disaster.
6. Everything in the database should be updatable, provided that it is logically possible to so update it. In other words, the DBMS has to have the ability to detect whether or not a proposed update is valid. By and large, this rule is normally implemented perfectly adequately.
7. A relation within a database should be capable of being inserted, updated, or deleted as a single command.

8. Even if the data in the database itself happens to be moved around for whatever reason, this should make no difference to the operations performed upon that data. You, the user, should be able to ignore where the data is upon which you need to work. ANSI SQL and all other implementations fulfil this ruling.

9. Application programs and the activities that you perform at the terminal should remain unimpaired whatever changes are made to the tables in the database. In practice, this does not affect SQL usage at all, since it is the DBMS that is responsible for knowing where the data resides.

10. Integrity constraints (designed to secure the consistency of the database) should only be made within the database itself, not within the application programs using that database.

11. The data sublanguage should be able to operate within a distributed database environment without affecting the efficiency of the application programs. In fact, of course, this rule is merely a logical extension of rule 8, though it receives no mention in the ANSI specification. One expects that the ruling will come to be observed (it would be lunatic not to so enforce it), but there has been, as yet, little experience with distributed SQL databases for any firm evidence to be provided.

12. If you are only examining one single record, you should not be able to amend or alter that individual record in any way that violates the overall rules imposed by the relational language that you are using.

These then, in outline, are the relational rules. I have only commented in passing as to how fully SQL conforms to those rules. Suffice it to say here that SQL does fully satisfy five of Codd's criteria and partially satisfies another three. This is a better adherence to the Codd criteria than many other products can offer, and work is being done to increase SQL's compliance to relational rules. Hence, if you are working with a relational database like INGRES, it is obviously beneficial to handle a query language that shares the same mode of representing data structures.

These four factors—IBM acceptance, portability, user-accessibility, and relational structure—demonstrate why anyone using a relational database is virtually bound to use SQL.

The rest of what I wish to say has already been covered in the three preceding sections of this chapter. SQL will allow you to manipulate the data within a database. It will select data for you, delete data, and join data. It can allow you to set up indexes to speed up data retrieval. It will even create a database for you. As we have already seen, all that you need to do with SQL is create a *statement* by using two or more SQL command words. Thus you can enter

SELECT town FROM store;

or

SELECT role FROM emp_store WHERE role = 'Manager';

You do not need to use upper case for the SQL commands; I have only done so for the sake of clarity. You do, in most SQL implementations, need to end a statement with a semicolon, though even that is no longer universally true. And that is all there is to it. SQL has about 30 command words, but SELECT is far the most frequent. Hence, in the next chapter, we shall take a closer look at this specific command. In so doing we will gain a knowledge of SQL that will be sufficient for most normal circumstances.

11

Select with SQL

Although a section on the use of SELECT in SQL has already been written, I think that it well worth returning to that keyword now. First of all, it is such a frequent and versatile operation that our glance at it in Chapter 5 did not do much more than brush the surface. For instance, Rick F. van der Lans, in his *Introduction to SQL* (Addison-Wesley, 1988), devotes 111 pages to the SELECT operation alone. Secondly, although this book is not intended as a tutor in SQL, it is important for the INGRES user to have a reasonable command of that query language. Hence by looking once again at SELECT, we can gain an understanding of the structure of SQL and its mode of operation, an understanding that will greatly facilitate our usage of other SQL commands and give us an awareness of the very nature of query languages in general. After all, QUEL, for instance, is very similar to SQL. If you understand how SQL operates, you will find it very easy to learn QUEL also. To give an analogy, anyone who has ever learnt Latin finds it incredibly easy to pick up Italian. So it is with SQL and QUEL.

Inevitably there is going to be a certain amount of repetition in this chapter apropos the material given in Chapter 5. I shall try to keep that to a minimum, and anyway the context here is a different one. Furthermore, I entirely agree with Emerson, Darnovsky, and Bowman when they begin the fourth chapter of their *The Practical SQL Handbook* (Addison-Wesley, 1989) with the following words:

> In many ways, the SELECT statement is the real heart of SQL. It lets you find and view your data in a variety of ways. You use it to answer questions based on your data—how many where, what kind of, even what if. Once you become comfortable with its sometimes dauntingly complex syntax, you'll be amazed at what the SELECT statement can do.

Just so. In addition, devoting a specific chapter to SELECT gives me the opportunity to show how SQL is structured, to show how SQL commands depend upon a sequence of instructions. In Chapter 5 I was only concerned to give a run-down of some of the most common queries that users tend to make. In this chapter, however, I shall want to place those queries within a linguistic framework. Hence, even though there will be a little repetition, you will be looking at the SQL commands in a more ordered context. Let us, then, begin.

11.1   The two essentials

Although you may not have become consciously aware of it, a moment's reflection will indicate to you that any SELECT command in SQL demands two parameters. Obviously there has to be the basic SELECT instruction itself:

SELECT...

As you know, the keyword is then followed by the attribute or attributes that you wish to select:

SELECT name, salary

or

SELECT supplier_no, tel_no

Self-evidently, though, such a command is entirely useless by itself. INGRES, through the medium of SQL, cannot be told to select anything without also being told from which source it needs to obtain the data. Consequently, the SELECT command *always* needs to be followed by the FROM instruction. Hence the two commands just given would only be effective if they actually read as follows:

SELECT name, salary
FROM emp_store

or

SELECT supplier_no, tel_no
FROM supplier

INGRES will only select attributes if it is also told from which table those attributes are to be garnered. Hence it is the SELECT and FROM construct that is our basic framework.

Still within this basic framework, we can insist on one or two further conditions being obeyed. If, for instance, we wanted to know in which towns SOS had a store, but were not interested in how many stores they had in any particular town, then we could expand our SELECT statement so that it read

```
SELECT DISTINCT town
```

As a result, we would learn that SOS had a store in London, Swansea, and Liverpool (and 15 other places as well), but we would not learn that SOS had two stores in London, Swansea, and Liverpool. The DISTINCT command excludes all repetitions.

Conversely, we might occasionally need to insist that SQL really did give us every instance of an attribute even if that entailed considerable repetition. In fact, by default, SQL will give us all the mentions of a named attribute unless it is countermanded by DISTINCT. None the less, there can be occasions, particularly in complex and lengthy queries, where it is wise to insist that INGRES gives us every occurrence of an attribute. In such a circumstance, one merely needs to issue the instruction

```
SELECT ALL ...
```

followed, of course, by the appropriate FROM command.

And that is all there is to it. When you next go out shopping, should anyone wander up to you while you are queuing for your artichokes and say to you 'What is the minimum number of commands that must be issued in an SQL Select instruction?', you will immediately be able to reply, 'Two—the SELECT command and the FROM command.' The greengrocer might be so impressed by the rapidity and certainty of your reply, that he gives you the artichokes at a reduced price.

However, as you know, we can build on the SELECT . . . FROM construct a range of further conditions, and it is at these that I now wish to look.

11.2   The WHERE clause

While the SELECT and FROM clauses are essential, most users find the WHERE condition so useful that they come to think of it as virtually essential as well. After all, SELECT and FROM will give you the totality of the rows and domains specified, but nine times out of ten you want to limit those rows and domains by some further condition. If you are living in Leeds, and want to go out for an Indian meal, you do not just frame the request 'SELECT Indian FROM restaurant'; you are much more likely to say 'SELECT Indian FROM restaurant WHERE restaurant is within five miles of my house.' Fortunately, the WHERE clause in SQL will perform this sort of operation with no difficulty:

```
SELECT name, role
FROM emp_store
WHERE emp_store = 'S7';
```

And, not surprisingly, you can extend this WHERE clause:

```
SELECT name, role
FROM emp_store
WHERE emp_store = 'S7' AND 'S11'
```

Indeed, you can use the AND conjunction so that you select from two or more different domains:

```
SELECT name, role
FROM emp_store
WHERE emp_store = 'S7' AND role = 'assistant';
```

Equally, in place of AND, one can use the condition OR. Imagine that you wanted the details of the SOS stores in Sheffield and Cardiff. The SQL instruction issued would be as follows:

```
SELECT store_no, town, address, tel_no
FROM store
WHERE store = 'Sheffield'
OR store = 'Cardiff';
```

In fact, in the example above, one could just have the SELECT line reading as follows:

```
SELECT *
```

The * symbol will be understood as being that you want all the attributes from a given table.

Just imagine, though, that you wanted to issue the command that SQL should give you the name and role from the Employee-Store table of every employee except the manager. You might, of course, do it like this:

```
SELECT name, role
FROM emp_store
WHERE role = 'assistant'
OR      role = 'driver'
OR      role = 'cleaner'
OR      role = 'janitor'
OR      role = 'sales_dir'
OR      role = ...
```

You would rapidly become tired of issuing such commands, because of their length, and would then, after your labours, be unamused to discover that you received no information from your query. One cannot pile up multiple ANDs or multiple ORs. They merely have the effect of cancelling each other out. But you could, of course, do the whole thing much more concisely and obtain the information for which you sought.

```
SELECT name, role
FROM emp_store
WHERE role ! = 'manager';
```

As you can see, it is always wise to remember the comparative symbols that I listed in Chapter 5. In fact, there ought to be two ways of selecting the names and roles of all the SOS employees except managers. You can do it the way given in the example above or you can do it by using the symbol <>. It might be worth checking that your terminal accepts both formats of the not-equal-to qualifier.

The WHERE clause can also be linked with the condition word LIKE. Again an example should illustrate the nature of the query.

```
SELECT town
FROM store
WHERE town LIKE 'B%';
```

In fact, the above query is simply asking what SOS stores exist in towns beginning with the letter B. The % sign stands for an unspecified number of characters, just as the * sign does. It follows, therefore, that you can use the % sign in a variety of ways. You could, for instance, ask for towns ending in the letter 'm':

```
SELECT town
FROM store
WHERE town LIKE '%m';
```

As a result, you would get the answer Birmingham, whereas in the query immediately preceding it, you would have received both Birmingham and Bradford as your answer.

There are a number of these condition words that can be used with WHERE. I shall not attempt to survey them all, but one or two other examples may be helpful. You can, for instance, use BETWEEN in the way shown in the following example:

```
SELECT assistant
FROM emp_store
WHERE hire_date BETWEEN *85 and *91;
```

In a somewhat similar fashion you can use the IN operator. Let us imagine that you wanted to know which managers had been appointed in 1971, 1978, and 1981. Your query would be expressed like this:

```
SELECT name, role, hire_date
FROM emp_store
WHERE role = 'Manager' AND hire_date IN (*71, *78, *81);
```

There are other such operators, words like ANY, ALL, NULL, and EXISTS, but I am sure that you have now seen the basic fashion in which queries are expressed in SQL.

11.3 The GROUP BY clause

In a relational database it is a matter of complete insignificance as to in what order the rows of a table are placed. You, however, in having data presented to you, may well wish to impose a specific order for the presentation of that data. This can be done by means of the GROUP BY instruction.

We will assume that you want a list of the entire employees of SOS, but that you want them grouped by the specific store in which they work. The command to effect this result would be as follows:

```
SELECT *
FROM emp_store
GROUP BY store_no;
```

Again, you might want to know how the different SOS stores had been selecting their suppliers. After all, many products could be obtained from more than one supplier. Was any particular preference being manifested by the different stores? Your query would be as follows:

```
SELECT store_no, supplier_no, product
FROM purchases
GROUP BY supplier_no, store_no;
```

The resulting table would begin with all the sales made by supplier number 1 to store number 1. Obviously we have barely begun to fill our purchases table with data, so it would, at the moment, only give us one entry:

```
Sp1   S1   saucepans
```

In a fully stocked purchases table, however, we might see many lines given over to that first linkage of Sp1 and S1. Then, of course, the table would link the sales made by Sp1 to S2, and so on. Once all the sales made by supplier number 1 had been listed, INGRES would move on to supplier number 2 and list all his sales to the respective SOS stores. At the end you would have a complete breakdown. You could tell, almost at a glance, that supplier number 8 was selling very well to stores in the north of England, but hardly at all to stores in the south. Instead they were getting the same sorts of goods from supplier number 12. That might conceivably be explained on logistic grounds, yet supplier number 3, who was based in Manchester, seemed to be selling very well to the Exeter, Cardiff, and London stores while being virtually ignored by the Leicester, Swansea, and Reading shops.

The UNION . . . SELECT combination is also very useful as it enables you to perform more than one query within a single statement. As always, an example will illustrate this perfectly well. Imagine then that you enter the following statement:

```
SELECT name, role FROM emp_store
   WHERE store_no >S9
```

```
UNION
SELECT name, role FROM emp_store
  WHERE salary >£9700
```

As you will have worked out, the above command will give you the names and roles of all employees in stores 10–18 who earn more than £9700 per annum. I cannot imagine anyone wishing to collect such data, but the technique is, I hope, clear.

You can use UNION in exactly the same way to garner information from more than one table. Hence you could enter the following command:

```
SELECT store_no FROM store
  WHERE town = 'Sheffield'
  UNION
SELECT store_no FROM purchases
  WHERE purchase = 'wheelbarrows';
```

The information given would be even more pointless (unless, of course, you did have some desperate desire to know whether or not Sheffield had bought any wheelbarrows). Do note, however, that the column name or names which follow the SELECT command must be identical. You cannot SELECT store_no FROM store and then, using UNION, go on to SELECT supp_no FROM purchases.

11.4 Matters of precedence

We have seen that, in SQL, it is possible (indeed, essential) to use both logical and arithmetic operators. For instance, when dealing with more than one condition in a WHERE clause, one uses the logical operators AND, OR, and NOT. We have used the first two already, and the last, NOT, is fairly self-evident. Let me, however, just summarize their logical function:

- AND joins two or more conditions but only gives a result when all of the conditions are valid.
- OR also connects two or more conditions but will return a positive result provided any one of the conditions is valid.
- NOT (normally represented by the != sign) will disallow the expression which follows it. Hence, if you wanted to select all the stores except those beginning with 'L', your query would look like this:

```
WHERE town != 'L%'
```

or like this:

```
WHERE NOT town = 'L*'
```

Both expressions should work, though you may find that your system only allows the * operator (or the %).

The arithmetic operators (+ − / *) we have also encountered—doubtless at primary school. It is worth pointing out, however, that SQL allows the arithmetic operators to be used on any numeric column. If you do so use it, the result required will be presented to you on the screen, but the data in the database itself will naturally remain unaltered. Possibly too, if your system provides date functions, then arithmetic operations can be performed on date columns also. Some systems also contain a modulo operation. All this means is that it will give any remainder left as the result of any arithmetic operation. Thus, if you wish to divide 10 by 4, the modulo will be 2 because 4 goes into 10 twice leaving 2 left over. The modulo function is performed by using the % sign.

The title of this subsection is however, 'Matters of Precedence'. What we are primarily concerned to point out is that operations within SQL, like operations in programming or general computer work, take a kind of pecking order. Thus, if you ask, within a single expression, for the addition and multiplication functions to be performed, then the multiplication will be performed before the addition is carried out. Take the following expression:

$$4 + 4 * 2$$

The answer given will be 12 because 4 and 2 are first multiplied, and 4 is then added to the result. If you want the addition to be carried out first, you must surround the 4 + 4 with brackets, because brackets have the highest precedence of all. Consequently, if you do enter (4 + 4) * 2 you will be presented with the result 16 instead of 12.

From this it follows that it is important, if you want to get accurate results, to know the order of precedence in which SQL carries out its operations. The hierarchy is as follows:

1. Brackets.
2. Multiplication and/or division.
3. Subtraction and/or addition.
4. Not.
5. And.
6. Or.

As you can see, the logical operators come below the arithmetic ones. It is clearly important to be aware of this hierarchy when carrying out complex SELECT queries.

And so we end. If, as I mentioned at the beginning, Rich F. van der Lans can devote 111 pages to the SELECT command alone, there is clearly a great deal more that you could learn. Even so, I do feel that we have now covered the basic essentials of this powerful command.

12
Further aspects of SQL

Although I believe that the SELECT command in SQL provides one with the bulk of the information that one needs to know for handling that query language, there are none the less clearly a considerable number of other elements of which one needs to be aware. I have already referred to a number of books devoted to SQL, and they are listed in the Bibliography. One can, therefore, extend one's knowledge of SQL by referring to any or all of those. Even so, if this book is to pretend in any way to being a self-contained introduction to INGRES, it is necessary to devote just a few pages to further aspects of SQL. As we have aready seen, learning about SQL is not a diversion or distraction from learning about INGRES; a database and its query language are indissolubly linked. This chapter will, therefore, highlight other aspects of SQL that enhance one's understanding of INGRES itself.

The previous chapter looked at the SELECT command, a procedure that we first encountered in Chapter 5. Just as it was important to extend our familiarity with that essential command, so is it useful to look again at the JOIN function. When we glanced at this in Chapter 7, we only did so through the in-built screen commands. It will be helpful to see how SQL handles this important function. Secondly, it will be useful to look at subqueries, because the creation of those greatly extends the scope of SQL's power. Finally, since subqueries are only valid within a well-structured context, I would like to continue by looking at the entire logical framework of SQL and, by relating this to the theoretical backcloth of relational databases as a whole, look at how competent INGRES is in fulfilling the demands of relational rigour.

12.1   The JOIN command

Despite the subheading above, there is in fact no JOIN command in SQL at all. Instead, SQL, with a coy diffidence, only allows you to join tables (or sections of tables) by your gently implying that you would like to see such a join. You do so by means of the WHERE clause. Hence your request structure is going to be as follows:

```
SELECT ...
FROM table1, table2 ...
WHERE table1, column1 = table2, column4
```

I hope that the above is very straightforward. First of all, you state what it is that you need to select. Our SOS database is so tiny that it does not illustrate the JOIN command very fully, but just imagine that we wanted to link products supplied to SOS stores with the address of the supplier that had delivered those products. The first line of our instruction will simply specify all the column names of the desired data in the order in which you wanted them to be displayed. Thus our SELECT command could read as follows:

```
SELECT supp_no, supp_name, supp_address, product
```

Notice, however, that though there is no need for us actually to have the supplier number, it has to be specified because it is the only field that links the appropriate tables.

Having specified the columns that you actually want to see, you next indicate from which tables those columns are going to be retrieved, merely separating the tables concerned with a comma. Hence our FROM line would read

```
FROM supplier, products
```

And now you specify the join needed in the WHERE clause by making the one common field in both the above fields explicit:

```
WHERE supplier supp_no = products supp-no;
```

Thus, as you can see, the preconditions for creating a join in SQL are that the FROM clause must contain the name of more than one table and that the WHERE clause provides a valid connective element between those tables. In the example provided above, the connective element has been complete equality in that the names of the respective columns have been identical as well as the contents of those columns being identical. In fact, provided the contents are identical, the columns could have different names. Nor, provided a match is specified between two tables, do you have to display the matching column at all. Hence we could have achieved the join that we have just looked at without the supplier number being displayed. Our instruction would then have read as follows:

```
SELECT supp_name, supp_address, product
FROM supplier, products
WHERE supplier supp_no = products supp_no;
```

Obviously too, there are very different kinds of joins that one can accomplish. We have illustrated the most common type where there is a join on specified columns. You can equally achieve a join where the condition of equality upon which I have so far been insisting does not exist. In such a case, instead of using the equals sign, you substitute it for $>$, $<$, or $<>$, depending upon which condition you want fulfilling. There are, of course, other sophisications on offer, but enough has been done to indicate the nature of the join condition within SQL.

12.2   Subqueries

We are all acquainted with the situation of a question resting upon the response to an earlier question. Such nested queries are the staple fare of discussions:

> Obviously we don't know if the Conservative Government will restore the use of corporal punishment in universities, but if they do, will they insist on the tawse or the whip, which members of the Civil Service will be empowered to inflict corporal punishment, and will staff be able to insist upon a hearing before the University's Disciplinary Committee before sentence is passed?

We all construct queries of this nature (though not, perhaps, on such topics), and it is clearly important for any self-respecting query language to be able to do the same. It is not, in fact, a difficult process, though the SQL expressions containing subqueries do look both ugly and complicated. None the less, subqueries can save considerable effort. Let me illustrate.

Let us imagine that you wanted to find out how many products sold in SOS stores cost exactly the same as a wheelbarrow. You clearly have two operations to perform:

1. Find out the price of a wheelbarrow.
2. Find out all the products that cost the same as the wheelbarrow.

Obviously you could answer the query by making two separate queries. The first SQL instruction would look like this:

```
SELECT purchase, price
FROM purchases
WHERE purchase = 'wheelbarrow';
```

Then, having gained the first necessary piece of information, you could then incorporate it into your second SQL instruction:

```
SELECT purchase
FROM purchases
WHERE price = '10';
```

If, however, you can express the whole thing as one query, it will save time, not because you have less typing to do but because you will not have the break between one operation and the second. All you need to do is just to merge our previous two queries into one:

```
SELECT purchase, price
FROM purchases
WHERE price =
  (SELECT price
   FROM purchases
   WHERE purchase = 'wheelbarrow');
```

Of course, again just for convenience, we have so arranged the universe that SOS only have one type of wheelbarrow at one set price, but it should not be too difficult to see how subqueries could be so nested as to incorporate a whole range of possibilities.

The example given above had a subquery that needed to address the same table as the primary query. It is, of course, perfectly possible to have subqueries that address tables other than the ones cited in the first query. Thus, for instance, you might want to find out how many products bought by SOS cost the same amount as a manager's annual salary. (I am sorry to invent such ludicrous queries, but the smallness of our database is something of a limitation for the formulation of realistic questions.) The resulting instruction would look something like this:

```
SELECT purchase
FROM purchases
WHERE purchase =
  (SELECT salary
   FROM emp_store
   WHERE role = 'Manager');
```

And the basic structure of subqueries should now be clear. Of course, a great deal more can be accomplished by using a whole variety of keywords or keyword phrases. The purpose of these is self-evident:

IN   NOT IN   HAVING   GROUP BY   ANY   ALL   EXISTS

One can also have subqueries that repeat themselves, continuing to ask exactly the same question to an entire sequence of data delivered to it by the primary query. So the use of subqueries can be a valuable aid.

Even though we have only once again skimmed the surface, it is clear that subqueries can only operate in an ordered universe. The theoretical background upon which SQL (and INGRES) is based has to be logically stable enough to cope with multiple subqueries as well as all the other complex commands (and careless errors) to which it will be subjected. Hence looking at a query language is an appropriate time to take a closer look at the entire rationale of relational development.

12.3   Logical foundations

If you think about the entire operation of talking to INGRES with which this part of the book is concerned, you will realize that it is a remarkably complex operation. For it to be done effectively, a great deal (of which you and I are normally unaware) has to be taken for granted. To start with, the database or databases upon which we are operating have to have been sensibly constructed. The database for SOS is so tiny as not to provide a very realistic paradigm, but even in the construction of our tiny database we had to concern ourselves with the matter of normalization. Had we been building a more substantial database, we would have concerned ourselves with entity-relationship modelling, a topic to which whole books have been devoted. Secondly, having constructed the database, we move on to operating upon the data contained therein. As we have seen in this section, such operations are carried out by means of a query language (even though that query language may be encapsulated in on-screen prompts). So far as the user is concerned, the query language (or screen instructions) are all that matters, and so it should be in a non-procedural language. None the less, while a non-procedural language like SQL is a major boon for ease of operation, it does entail gigantic acts of faith. You, the user, just have to trust that the query language is behaving in a proper and correct manner. In other words, you and your intelligence have opted out of the entire operation. Yet what the query language has to do is to submit the queries that you have made to a *query optimizer*, which then analyses your query. It breaks your query down into its component parts, possibly rearranges them so that they will be dealt with in the most efficient manner, and then searches for the most useful indexes to aid it in the solving of the query. Should it not succeed in finding any such indexes, it is then forced to resort to checking the database line by line in order to provide you with the data you need. You will, of course, get your data eventually, but it may be several days or weeks later, depending upon the size of the database.

Such a scenario is rare, of course. Almost invariably, the query optimizer is able to perform its task with admirable efficiency. With how much efficiency depends upon the structure of the database it is searching, upon the effectiveness of the query optimizer itself, and, of course, upon the operating system that forms the entire context within which the procedure is being conducted. And as far as all this is concerned, you personally have about as much influence as an American bison or an Antipodean wombat. In other words, you are irrelevant.

This total irrelevance while operating a relational database has never caused me to lose any sleep. I have found the humble operation of framing the SQL queries in the first place quite sufficient to keep my mind engaged and my soul content. None the less, there seem to have been scores of writers who have been seized with some passionate desire to disturb my tranquility. They have insisted that I cannot possibly understand any relational database or any query language without being instructed in some arcane topics known as relational algebra and relational calculus. Thus the Hursches, in the SQL book to which I have earlier referred, entitle their 10th chapter 'The Relational Algebra and SQL'. In the first 4½-line paragraph, they inform me that SQL owes much to the relational algebra, and in the second paragraph, they begin their explanation:

> Given a finite set of attributes $U = \{A\ A2,\ .\ .\ .,\ Au\}$ with domains dom $(A1)$, a relation scheme is a subset of U. A relational database scheme D over U is a collection of relations schemes, $\{R1, R2,\ .\ .\ .,\ Rd\}$, such that the union of the $R1$ is U. Given a relation scheme R, a tuple, t, over R is a single-valued mapping from the members of R to the domains of the members of R such that . . .

And so it continues. It may be that such impenetrable prose is child's play to someone trained in mathematics. Unfortunately, my own training in mathematics comprised learning the two-times table and not much else. Given the avidity with which universities and polytechnics are now offering conversion courses in information technology to graduates of whatever discipline, it is highly likely that hundreds of others will also view the Hursch prose as constipated gobbledygook. Yet, if you make more than a superficial acquaintanceship with relational databases, you are bound to come across a great deal of this esoteric jargon. Smith and Barnes in their treatment of *Files and Databases* (another book to which I have referred earlier), feel it necessary to explain that there are three levels of DML commands, relational calculus, relational algebra, and tuple-by-tuple processing, and conduct their explanation with only marginally greater clarity than is found in the Hursch book. Even D. S. Bowers, in his 1988 *From Data to Database*, devotes 18 pages to relational algebra and calculus, and, though Bowers is less impenetrable, his explanations still do not thrill the spirit or animate the heart. Yet I lay stress on this simply because it seems to me to be so unnecessary. I am prepared to believe (trusting soul that I am) that relational algebra and calculus are necessary tools for the designer of relational databases and relationally orientated query languages. But few people in business and few undergraduates are ever going to be concerned with such acts of creation. Certainly the readers of this book are unlikely to aspire to such heights. Hence, my argument is, simple users of a DBMS or a query language have absolutely no need whatsoever to concern themselves with such theoretical underpinnings. I note, for instance, that S. Atre, in the 442 pages of his *Database: Structured*

Techniques for Design, Performance and Management (1980), makes no reference to such matters at all. I note, with even more pleasure, that Peter Laurie, in his slim book on databases to which I referred so glowingly in the first chapter of this book, explicitly states that relational calculus 'is another example (so common in the high tech world) of a solution looking for a problem'. Indeed, he relates the appearance of sections on relational calculus in textbooks to an antiquainted historism. Laurie argues that relational calculus had perhaps some relevance when computer systems were tape driven. Now that they are all disk machines, the complications of tape management have become redundant. Unfortunately, the writers of computer textbooks have failed to notice this. It is, Laurie claims, 'as if the captain of the first steamship insisted on tacking to windward as if he were still under sail because it had taken him a lot of time and trouble to learn the art and he was not going to abandon it now just because it was obsolete'. Hence, all the mathematical jargon that I quoted above merely confuses, in Laurie's words again, 'the real issue with masses of difficult and spurious theory'. He sums up by stating that 'It is excellent for setting examination questions, useless to help real computer users.' Yet I devote some relative length to this issue because I recall only too well the personal alarm and despondency that I felt when I first encountered these issues—an alarm and despondency that I have witnessed with sundry undergraduates also. There is, however, no need for such paranoia. When you meet sections on relational algebra and calculus in texts that you are using, just treat such sections as you would a textbook on alchemy.

None the less, we do need to be concerned about the logical validity of the database management system that we are using and the query language that we employ for its interrogation. You will recall that one of the most crucial tenets in the construction of relational tables is that each row within a table must be a unique row. This does not mean that individual values within an attribute column are all different from each other; indeed, many of them can be identical. Take the example of the perennially useful John Smith. In the SOS Bradford store, there are two John Smiths who work in the same department, have the same salary, are members of the same pension scheme, and belong to the same social club. None the less, their respective rows are unique because each row has, as its primary key, the relevant National Insurance Number for the John Smith concerned. And this is all that matters. That primary key renders each row unique. No other row in the entire database is identical to it.

Since the uniqueness of each table row is a vital element of a relational system, we do therefore need a relational database and/or a query language that will enforce the uniqueness of those rows or, failing compulsion, will report on any duplicate rows that do occur. It therefore comes as a considerable regret to discover that no such animal exists. The INGRES database itself will accept whatever you give it. SQL will do what you tell it to do, but it possesses no syntax for designating primary keys, and, as you are aware, it is almost invariably the primary key that enforces the uniqueness of the rows concerned.

This is a serious deficiency, and SQL has been severely criticized for this omission. Fortunately, however, it can be circumvented. First of all, since it is the primary key that normally guarantees the uniqueness of each individual row, you can instruct SQL to ensure that the primary key is never allowed to be a null value. By so doing, you help to ensure the uniqueness of each row. Secondly, you can create a unique index for each table. This does not prevent you from entering a duplicate row into your database, but it does ensure that any duplication is picked up by the index, which will refuse to allow you to perform an INSERT or UPDATE command in such circumstances. Ironically, the ANSI standard allows each user to specify any column or columns as being unique (though you would also have to link it with a not null command). Clearly this would be the most sensible procedure. If you specify a column upon creation as UNIQUE, you thereby ensure that no duplicate entries can possibly be made. Alas, most actual implementations only enforce the uniqueness criterion with respect to indices. One hopes—and expects?— that suppliers will eventually get round to implementing uniqueness in the creation of data tables, but at the moment this is certainly an instance of where the ANSI standard is better than the reality. Were you to be in the position of buying an SQL for your company's relational database, this is one item that you should certainly check beforehand in the documentation provided for your proposed SQL purchase. It is, after all, lunatic that uniqueness, obviously a property of the table concerned, is only enforced in the subsequent index.

12.4   SQL commands

Finally, and very much as an appendix to this chapter, let me give a brief selection of SQL commands. The purpose of many of them is self-evident, and where this is the case, no additional comment has been made. Only for commands that are possibly obscure has a brief gloss been provided. Nor, as I have implied, is this anything like a full list of SQL commands. It is, though, a list of the most frequently used ones, and is likely to see you through many hours of INGRES work without your feeling the need to call upon any others.

COMMIT prevents one from aborting a transaction.
COPY copies data from/into a table from/into a file.
CREATE INDEX
CREATE INTEGRITY for example, one could create an integrity restraint on employee salary so that it was $\geqslant 6000$.

CREATE PROCEDURE accepts a named (or created) procedure as part of the database.

CREATE TABLE

CREATE VIEW a view is a virtual table. They are discussed in Chapter 20.

DECLARE only used in a database procedure definition to declare a list of local variables for use in the procedure.

DELETE

DROP destroys one or more tables, indexes, or views.

DROP INTEGRITY

DROP PROCEDURE

GRANT grants privileges on a table, view, or procedure.

HELP

IF-THEN-ELSE

INSERT

MESSAGE to return a message number, text, or both to the executing application. Can only be issued from inside a procedure.

MODIFY changes storage structure or location

RETURN

ROLLBACK aborts part of the current transaction

SAVE

SELECT

UPDATE

13
The data dictionary

A data dictionary is really nothing more than a catalogue. Just as a dictionary—the sort of book that you and I use to discover what 'recondite' really means or how to spell 'corollary'—is just a catalogue of words, so a data dictionary is just a list of the data used in a database. Hence, as is often said, a data dictionary is data about data.

Just as the utility of a dictionary is fairly self-evident, so is a data dictionary. A database is composed of tables. When there are 34 of them, will you be able to remember the names of them all? Even more, will you stand any chance of recalling the column headings for each table? Clearly not.

There is, however, an important distinction to be made from the outset. INGRES has its own data dictionary. Let us imagine that one issues the following command:

SELECT Bradford
FROM store

In order to carry out this command, INGRES goes to its own data dictionary, looks up the table Store and from it discovers where the store in Bradford is kept on the disk. It then goes to the location indicated, retrieves the requested information, and displays it on the screen. Clearly without its own data dictionary, INGRES could not perform the retrieval, updating, deleting, and joining operations that we have so far encountered. This is not, though, a great deal of explicit help to you or I if we ourselves want to know what the current salary of a sales director is, or want to discover which suppliers have provided plant-pots to SOS stores, or even just want to know how the Purchases table is constructed. The fact that INGRES consults its own data dictionary is indispensable, but we would like to be able to consult it as well.

Fortunately, this is not difficult. The INGRES data dictionary is a database all of its own, and, like all databases in the relational universe, it is made up of tables. We can consult those tables just as easily as we can consult the ones we have constructed for our own SOS database. In other words, just as we have been talking to INGRES by using SQL, so we can persuade INGRES to talk to us by getting it to display its own data dictionary.

This, then, is the broad purpose of this chapter: to learn how to use the INGRES data dictionary. None the less, we need to pause before plunging into this activity. I have indicated that the necessity of a data dictionary is self-evident. So it is, but an enormous number of self-evident things only actually become so when their 'self-evidentness' is pointed out. Let us, therefore, begin at the beginning: what is the purpose of a data dictionary?

In this book *Data Dictionary: Implementation, Use and Maintenance* (Prentice Hall, 1988), Rom Narayan gives a most useful paragraph summarizing the nature of a data dictionary:

> The data dictionary is an automated respository of all definitive information about an organization's data resources. This includes the key data elements that are used in conducting a business enterprise, generating standard names, mnemonics and sizes, and enforcing the use of these standards in all application programs. The data dictionary provides information about the meaning of data elements, system components, and machine configurations where they are located and used. The definitions in the dictionary are meaningful and useful to personnel who are engaged in the systems development life cycle, maintenance of computer systems, and the operational aspects of computer systems.

From this summary, a very considerable number of practical applications for a data dictionary emerge. It is unnecessary to do more than skim the surface here. To do more would unbalance this particular book and, since our own SOS database is so tiny, would be akin to using the hydrogen bomb to defeat the Yorkshire cricket team (particularly when all you need is one accurate bowler and a batsman with two eyes). However, some of the functions of a data dictionary can, at least, be commented upon.

A data dictionary can help to ensure consistency. It is inevitable, for instance, that the attribute 'Town' will occur a number of times in a number of tables. The data dictionary can help you, the user, to ensure that the definition and space required for that attribute are always identical.

A data dictionary can save hours of hunting for a particular data item. You know that the personnel who organize publicity for SOS sales, promotions, charity events, and so on have got a particular title, but you cannot remember what it is. The data dictionary will tell you.

A database is about relations, but, in a large database, those relations can be numerous and complex. A data dictionary can reveal them to you. It can show which programs access a particular data item, which users receive which reports, which programs use a particular subschema, and so on.

If you change the database in any way—and, as the DBA, you are certain to do so—the data dictionary will reveal the result of the change on the logical database, which tables need changing, which relations are modified, and other such conceptual issues.

So, without writing a book about it, we can rest assured that a data dictionary is an invaluable resource. All we need to do is to learn how to use the one provided by INGRES.

Carl Malamud's book, *INGRES: Tools for Building an Information Architecture* (1989), about which I was somewhat dismissive in Chapter 1, does have a most useful chapter on the INGRES data dictionary. I shall not be following entirely its mode of exposition, but it would be a valuable supplement to what I have to say here.

First of all, we must understand that INGRES stores its data in a particular fashion. In fact there are eight alternative methods in which INGRES can store the data with which it is presented:

Heap Btree Cheap Cbtree Hash Isam Chash Cisam

None of these storage structure names will be at all meaningful to you at this moment, and there is no reason why this blissful unawareness should not continue. All that matters for our purposes is to know that each of the above names represents a different way in which data is stored. In some, for instance, duplicate rows are permitted; in others, not so. In some, the data is stored sequentially; in others, it has a tree-like structure. Whatever the method, however, INGRES constructs an index in order to enable it to access the data accurately and rapidly. Hence, when we constructed our SOS database, it was probably stored in a heap structure, and an index (or, more accurately, a series of indexes) was created. Thus there would be one index devoted to the tables contained within the database, one index devoted to the attributes contained within those tables, and even an index for indexing the indexes. None of this, of course, concerns the user of the database, who can happily remain ignorant of what INGRES is doing. None the less, it is the creation of these indexes that allows the data dictionary to be accessed. Take, as an example, the index that INGRES will have created on the attributes contained within the SOS database. You might, for instance, want to know which particular tables contain the attribute Town. To do so, you need to know something about the internal indexes that INGRES has created. The index on attributes will contain one column (attrelid) giving the table name, one column (attname) giving the attribute name, one column (attfrmt) giving the attribute format, one column (attfrml) giving the length of the attribute format, and so on. Hence, if you call up that particular index, you will be able to see which tables do contain the attribute Town. Indeed, you do not need to call up all tables with all the attribute names. Since indexes in INGRES are, like everything else, tables themselves, you can frame a query asking for the specific data that you want:

```
RANGE OF A IS ATTRIBUTE
SELECT ( A. ATTRELID )
WHERE A. ATTNAME = 'town'
```

The first line of this query—RANGE OF A IS ATTRIBUTE—is only present in order to save oneself some writing, as is clear when one looks at the next two lines. Their meaning is fairly self-evident. The query is asking INGRES to select an attribute from all the possible tables whenever that attribute has the name 'Town'. As a consequence, INGRES will present upon the screen a table like the following:

attrelid
store

Obviously, in a full SOS database, the attribute name 'town' would appear in a number of different tables, and each of them would be listed in the data dictionary response to our query.

Equally, if one cannot remember how many columns the Supplier table possesses or what those columns are called, one just enters the query

```
SELECT (A. ATTNAME)
WHERE A. ATTRELID = 'supplier'
```

The result will be as follows:

attname
supp_no
supp_name
address
tel_no

One can also enquire about the indexes themselves. If, for instance, you want to know how many indexes have been constructed on the Purchase Table, one simply asks

```
RANGE OF X IS INDEXES
SELECT ( N = COUNT ( X. IRELIDI WHERE X. IRELIDP = purchases) )
```

IRELIDI is the INGRES name for the name of the index, and IRELIDP stands for the name of the indexed relation.

This, then, is the basic nature and purpose of the INGRES data dictionary. Even if you never use it directly, you ought to know about its existence because it is central to virtually every INGRES transaction. None of the operations at which we have so far looked—creating a database and selecting, updating, and joining tables from that database—could have been accomplished without the presence of the INGRES data dictionary. Let me, therefore, now be more systematic about this data dictionary. If I have managed to convince you that it is a useful tool, it will be convenient to lay out precisely how this data dictionary is constructed.

The INGRES data dictionary consists of 20 system catalogues. Even in a database as small and primitive as our current SOS database, those 20 catalogues are present—storing, codifying, and helping to make our database really useful.

These 20 catalogues can be conveniently divided into three basic categories. There are, first of all, the Base System Catalogs, which provide one with information about the tables in our database. Thus it is in the Base System Catalogs that you will find out about the different columns or domains that each table possesses, about the indexes that have been constructed for those tables, about the levels of protection that have been built into those tables or attributes within the tables. Then, in addition to the Base System Catalogs, there are the Extended System Catalogs. We have, in our exploration of INGRES, so far encountered two important user interfaces to INGRES: Query-By-Form (QBF) and Visual-Forms-Editor (VIFRED). In the next part of this book you will encounter two others: Report-By-Forms (RBF) and Application-By-Forms (ABF). It is in the Extended System Catalogs that you will find information about the implementation of these user interfaces to our database. And finally, there are the Database Catalogs. These give information on database names, about access to those databases, and about the location of those databases.

If this book was designed as a complete compendium to INGRES, there would now follow a description of every catalogue contained within the data dictionary. Not surprisingly, such a catalogue already exists. Produced by Relational Technology Inc., it comprises 19 pages of information like this:

s_catalog   0000001   If set, the table is a system catalog.
s_noupdt   0000002   If set, no updates are allowed.
s_protups   0000004   If set, the 'protect' catalog contains rows that
                        apply to this user table.

As you can see, it constitutes no rival to a Dickens novel. This is not to sneer at the break down of the System Catalogs provided by Relational Technology. It is, in fact, very useful. Should your work or your academic course demand it, you will need to consult this document. But this book is designed as an introduction to INGRES, and I do not see much utility in reproducing such a document here. None the less, it will be useful if you know the basic contents of the data dictionary and some of the basic vocabulary. Indeed, some of that vocabulary has already been introduced when words like 'attrelid', 'attname', and 'irelidi' were used, so it would be good to gain at least a basic awareness of the structure and terminology of the INGRES data dictionary. I must emphasize, however, that what follows is an extremely abridged description.

The Basic System Catalogs comprise eight in number. Two of them you certainly ought to know about. The first is entitled RELATION. This catalogue has one row for every table in the database. It will tell you the table name, the table owner, the number of columns in the table, the storage mode of the table, the number of rows in the table, and a great deal more as well. The second vital catalogue is called ATTRIBUTE, and contains one row for each column of each table in the database. Thus, from this catalogue, you can learn the name of the table in which each particular column appears, the data type of each column, the number of bytes allocated to each column, and whether or not the column in question is a key to the table or part of a key. It was from the Attribute Catalog that the names attrelid and attname that we encountered earlier originated.

Of course, the other tables or catalogues in the Basic System Catalogs are also important. Indeed, I gave an example earlier from the Indexes Catalog. The Tree Catalog, the Protect Catalog, and the Integrities Catalog can also provide one with necessary information. Such data, however, belongs more to the researcher into database design than to someone wanting an introduction to relational databases in general and INGRES in particular.

Nor need we spend long on the second catalogue section, the Extended System Catalogs. The catalogue called QBFMAP is important because it tells you what name to use with QBF when you wish to relate a particular form to a particular table. The catalogue FDFRAMES performs a similar function for VIFRED in that it describes each form defined by VIFRED. REPORTS and ABFAPPL do the same for RBF and ABF respectively.

It is easy to see that this data dictionary function can be very useful. Apart from the simple examples cited above, the data dictionary can save one an enormous amount of time if one is having to access a database without knowing very much (or anything at all) about how that database is constructed. It is not a great deal of use asking questions about how many SOS employees worked overtime last March if one does not know whereabouts that information will be stored. Imagine wanting to borrow Dickens's *Great Expectations* from a library that had no classification system. After searching for five hours, you found the book nestling between Michael Jackson's *System Development* and Charles Osborne's *The Complete Operas of Mozart*. That is what it would be like without a data dictionary. Hence, if you encounter a database of which you know nothing, you simply issue a few queries and are informed what tables exist in that database and what columns those tables contain. With that knowledge, you can then go on to ask meaningful questions. Without the data dictionary, such an operation would be impossible.

The data dictionary also plays a part in securing at least a measure of integrity or consistency within the database. This important aspect is glanced at more fully in the penultimate chapter of this book, but the dictionary performs a service by ensuring that you never call two different tables by the same name. If you attempt to, INGRES will prevent it. With only four tables to our database, the prospect of giving two tables identical names seems remote, but in a large database it is fatally easy. Think how often you use words like 'invoice' or 'order'. Nor, in a large database, does only one person have the ability to create new tables. In such circumstances, it is close to inevitable that Fred in Sheffield will attempt to create a table that has been given the same name by Basil in Bradford. Furthermore, it is sometimes necessary to change the definition of an object within the database. Again, it does not require much imagination to conceive of two people trying simultaneously to alter the definition of the same object. The data dictionary protects itself (and you) against such an occurrence by locking the object in question so that it can only be accessed by one of the two aspirants. Again, particularly in a context like SOS where the structure and content of the database is slightly different in Cardiff from the one in Manchester, and both are different from the one at headquarters, the data dictionary can be used to present a single logical view of them all. You can even use the data dictionary as a reminder. If your company has a system of sending out information on customer accounts to each credit customer every six months, then the data dictionary can be instructed to remind you which customers need to be so informed this week.

As I have already indicated, Carl Malamud has a most useful chapter on data dictionaries in his book. I do not find Malamud entrancing to read, but, if you have understood the material given here, then the 10th chapter of *INGRES: Tools for Building an Information Architecture* would be a useful addition. C. J. Date devotes the seventh chapter of his Volume I *Introduction to Database Systems* to the system catalogue, an entity that he has already explained in Chapter 2 as being synonymous with the data dictionary. Date is specifically concerned with the system catalogue for DB2, but his remarks are, as always, clear and instructive—and, in Chapter 7, very brief. However, Date, Malamud, and myself are all out of date. In Version 6 of INGRES, there are a number of changes to the system catalogue: all catalogue names begin with the ii prefix, object names may now be 24 characters in length, and so on. There are not many changes, and none of them invalidate the remarks made in this chapter except for changes in nomenclature. Hence Date and Malamud would still constitute useful additional material. Whatever follow-up reading you do (or don't), it has, I trust, become evident that the data dictionary is a most valuable element within the INGRES context. Without it, communication, the central concept of this part of the book, would be considerably less easy and less effective.

14
Data communications

In Chapter 3, when talking about the formation of SOS, it was implied that material from one database needs to be transported to another database. Thus, for instance, the database at the Bradford SOS store needs to be accessible by SOS headquarters. Equally, the store at Exeter might need some data that only headquarters possesses. In order, therefore, to use INGRES effectively in a multi-site context, there has to be a facility for transferring data from one site to another. Although this is a vast topic, it did, none the less, seem sensible to give at least a run-down on data communications in this book, particularly since INGRES provides four different levels of distributed processing. In so far as one wants to gain an understanding of the kind of context within which INGRES is likely to be working is concerned, then it would have been absurd to have omitted so important a topic. However, because there is no direct relationship between the theory of data communications and one's actual operation of INGRES, an attempt has been made to make the material presented here as terse as possible.

14.1 Introduction

Data communications is the name given to the transmission of computer data between computer systems and terminals. The trend today is toward *networks* of co-operating computers that can share information. We need to be aware of some terms and what they mean before we can begin looking at this big and important topic.

Teleprocessing is defined by Jerome S. Burstein (*Computers and Information Systems*, 1986, p. 211) as 'processing performed by a computer system at a distance from the user'. Robert and Nancy Stern (*An Introduction to*

Computers and Information Processing, 1982, pp. 178–9) say that 'Teleprocessing refers to the combined use of communication facilities, such as
telephone lines, and data processing equipment to transmit and process data.'
Yet is not a term used at all by French in *Computer Science*, by Behling in
Computers and Information Processing, or the Deitels in *Computers and
Data Processing*. So, in other words, teleprocessing is just an alternative
word for data communications. I only mention the word here in case you
come across it in your reading.

Telecommunications is the transmission of data over distances. Thus
teleprocessing or data communications is what happens; telecommunications
is part of what makes such teleprocessing possible. From this it follows that a
network is a combination of devices linked together for teleprocessing.

14.1.1 HOW DATA COMMUNICATIONS SYSTEMS WORK

Let us take a simple example:

- A person in London wishes to send information to Manchester.
- The person types the information on his or her computer keyboard.
- That information is transformed into bits by the computer.
- Those bits are changed into analogue data by a modem.
- The analogue data is sent along a telephone wire.
- A modem in Manchester turns the analogue data back to digital.
- The VDU displays this data on the screen or a printer prints it.

Thus data communications has taken place. Of course, there can be many
alternatives to this simple system.

1. One does not have to use telephone wires as one's communicating
   medium. Instead one can use coaxial cables, microwaves, communications
   satellites, fibre optics, lasers, or waveguides. All of these are known as
   transmission channels, and will be dealt with individually under that
   heading.
2. Nor does one have to use a modem to modulate between digital and
   analogue signals. Instead one can use an acoustic coupler. Furthermore,
   the modem is likely to be attached to both a concentrator and a front-end
   processor. One may also need to use a multiplexor. All these are dealt
   with under the heading *data communications hardware*.
3. Nor, of course, does the communication have to be as simple as our
   London to Manchester example. There can be quite complex arrangements for distributed data processing by means of *networks*, as can be
   seen under that heading.
4. In data communications, the transmission channels can operate with
   different capacities and in different modes. These are examined under the
   heading of *signal transmission*.

14.2   Transmission channels

14.2.1   TELEPHONE LINES

These consist of pairs of insulated copper wires. Wire pairs have only a limited capacity for transmitting data. A number of wire pairs are bound together; the result is a telephone line. The trouble is that such lines are subject to 'crosstalk', in which messages cross from one wire pair to another. This is a nuisance during phone conversations, but worse for data communications, where it can garble data.

14.2.2   COAXIAL CABLES

These consist of one conducting wire surrounded by an insulator, which is in turn encased in a second conductor. A group of coaxial cables is bound together into bundles. They are a better communications channel than telephone lines: they can transmit signals at a much higher speed, and because they are insulated there is less signal loss than with telephone lines. Also, their broad bandwidths enable them to operate at higher frequencies and to transmit many signals simultaneously. Their major drawback is that they are more expensive than telephone lines, but they are invaluable for high-volume applications.

14.2.3   MICROWAVES

These are super-high-frequency radio waves that can transmit data signals through open space, much as television and radio signals are transmitted. However, stations using microwaves must be within *line of sight* of each other—i.e. no more than 30 miles apart—so that the curve of the earth does not impede the signal. Transmission density is much greater than with coaxial cables.

14.2.4   COMMUNICATIONS SATELLITES

Placed in permanent orbit in space, satellites can be used as a relay station and are much less affected by atmospheric interference than a microwave system. Not even Jason Willspend would contemplate having a satellite in order to communicate between SOS stoes.

14.2.5   FIBRE OPTICS

Fibres of glass can transmit data as light-beam signals. According to the Deitels (*Computers and Data Processing*, 1985, p. 164) 'Fiber optics has established itself as the cable technology of the future.' Because the fibres are hair-thin, they can be highly concentrated. One pound of fibre optics can replace 20 pounds of copper wire, and a single fibre-optic cable is capable of carrying 50 000 individual signals at one time.

14.2.6 LASERS

A laser is a tightly packed and highly controllable light beam of a precisely defined frequency. As light beams are of very high frequency, they can carry thousands of times as much information as microwaves, but, like microwaves, they require a line of sight transmission path and are also expensive.

14.2.7 WAVEGUIDES

Waveguides are round or rectangular metal tubes that act as pathways for very high-frequency radio waves, though the waves will not flow through a pipe with sharp bends. As Behling points out, 'Waveguide technology is just now emerging and its applications for data communications are presently unclear' (*Computers and Information Processing*, 1986, pp. 252–3).

14.3 Data communications hardware

All the transmission channels carry data in either analogue form (i.e. as variable wave patterns) or in digital form (i.e. as binary, or on–off, pulses). Telephone lines carry data in analogue form. Computers, of course, operate only in digital form. Hence, before being carried over a telephone line to another computer, the data has to be converted to analogue form, a process known as modulation. Then, when it arrives at its destination, it has to be converted back from analogue into digital, a process known as demodulation. Normally this process is performed by a *modem*, i.e. a *mo*dulator/*dem*odulator.

A modem transfers data at speeds measured in baud rates. A *baud rate* is the number of times per second that a system, especially a data transmission channel, changes state. In the particular case of a binary channel, the baud rate is equal to the bit rate, i.e.

1 baud = 1 bit per second

For a general channel

1 baud = 1 digit per second
1 baud = 1 symbol per second

or whatever the states of the system represent. The baud rates of a modem range from 300 to 19 000.

Modems are often permanently attached to input/output equipment. Such modems are said to be 'hard-wired'. To accommodate portable terminals a device known as an *acoustic coupler* has been developed. An acoustic coupler is a special type of modem that is attached to a portable terminal. It has two suction cups to hold a telephone handset. The user places the handset on the coupler and dials the telephone number. The coupler then converts the digital signals from the terminal into analogue signals. However, acoustic couplers tend to suffer from static and background noise.

A transmission channel can transmit data at a much faster speed than a terminal can supply the data. Hence it would be useful if one could have a number of terminals sending data at the same time. In this way, the transmission channel could be more fully used. One therefore needs a *multiplexor*.

A multiplexor combines the data signals from a number of terminals into one input flow that can be sent over a single channel. At the receiving end, the data flow is disassembled into its component parts according to a predefined plan.

Alternatively, one could use a *concentrator*. This is a more complex device than a multiplexor as they can be programmed to edit data, compress data, convert between ASCII and EBCDIC, and check for errors, for both incoming and outgoing data.

Both multiplexors and concentrators use two techniques to collect messages and send them to the CPU. *Polling* is the process of continuously checking each terminal to see if there is a message to be sent. *Contention* is somewhat akin to calling a friend on the telephone: if the line is in use, you will get a busy signal and must continue trying until the line is free. The terminal contends for the line in the same way.

Front-end processors also play an important role in the data communications system. These units are usually either special-purpose or programmable minicomputers, and their primary function is to relieve the host computer of a number of communications-control chores.

14.4 Networks

It has become common for computers to communicate with one another over data communications networks—systems with more than one computer and terminal. The Bank of Montreal, for example, operates North America's largest real-time banking computer system. The bank's computer network links 1302 branches throughout Canada by using more than 150 000 miles of telecommunications lines. A teller at any one of the 5000 branch terminals may access any customer's account information in less than 3 seconds. More than 3 million transactions are processed each day. SOS cannot yet rival this sort of transaction frequency.

For this type of operation, one must have an effective network. Not surprisingly, there are a number of different network arrangements.

14.4.1 STAR NETWORK

A central computer is connected to remote peripherals or other computers, which are not connected to each other (see Fig. 14.1). An example of star network could be a number of department stores each linked to headquarters. Such a system would be entirely suitable for SOS.

14.4.2 HIERARCHICAL NETWORK

This has a main computer and, below it in terms of control, are smaller computers arranged somewhat like the roots of a tree (see Fig. 14.2). This type of structure might be used by a large organization that must retain central control of the information system and yet needs to delegate substantial computing power to individual departments within the organization.

14.4.3 RING NETWORK

A ring network has no central computer; all computers within the system are equal and communicate with one another (see Fig. 14.3). A business with widely scattered warehouses, each of which does most of the processing for its own orders, might choose to use a ring network.

14.4.4 BUS NETWORKS

A bus network is essentially a single multidrop line shared by many nodes (see Fig. 14.4). Bus networks are more reliable than stars and rings because a node failure does not affect the other nodes.

14.4.5 COMPLEX NETWORK

We now enter into terminological problems. A complex network might be called a multiple connected network or a distributed network or even a mesh network. All that such labels imply is that the computers or nodes within them can communicate with each other along more than one route, as can be seen from Fig. 14.5.

If there are cross-communication links between all the computers, then it might be referred to as a complete network. Figure 14.6 illustrates the situation.

Although any kind of complex network saves time, it does require a much more elaborate communications control, which increases the complexity of the system. A business that relies on inter-office communications for the sharing of resources and up-to-the-minute information about the activities of any branch location might decide to use a complex network.

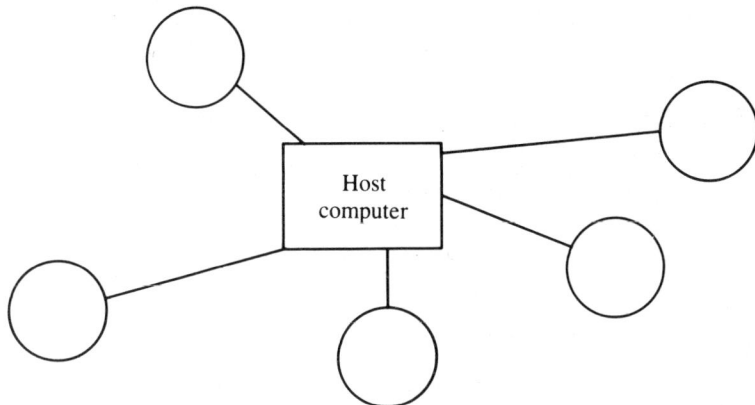

Figure 14.1

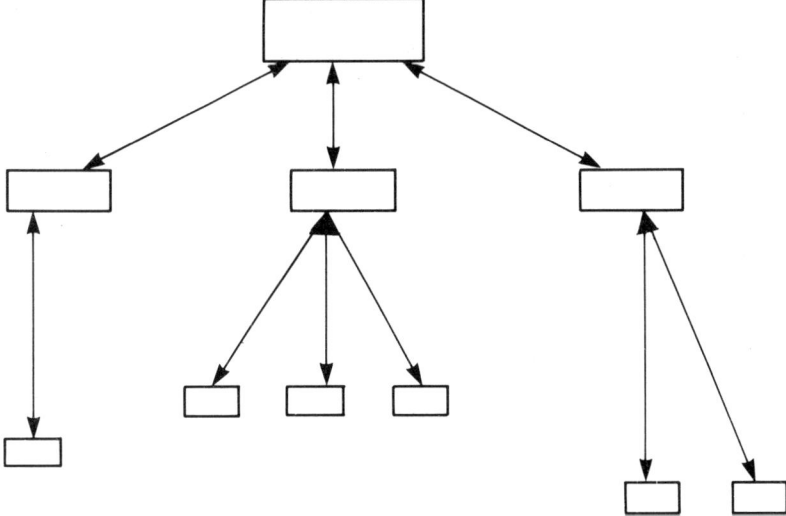

Figure 14.2

14.4.6 LOCAL AREA NETWORK

A newly emerging system is the local area network (LAN), which is a communications network privately owned by the organization using it. Using coaxial cables or fibre optics, it may adopt a star, ring, or complex configuration. Local networks have been developed by many major computer manufacturers:

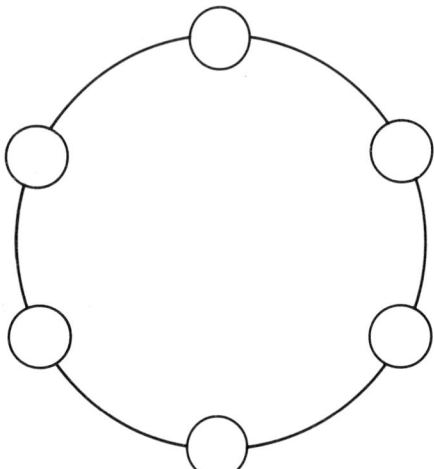

Figure 14.3

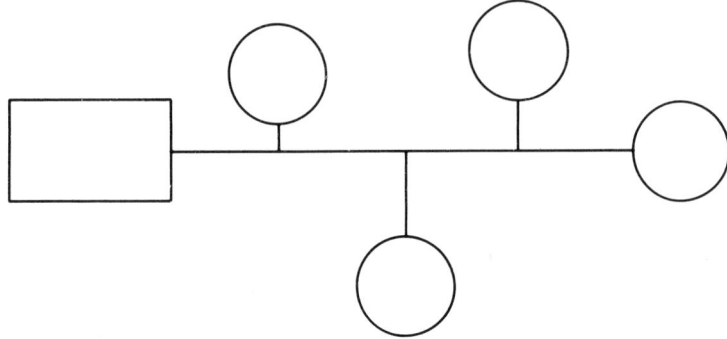

Figure 14.4

Manufacturer	*LAN name*
Xerox	Ethernet
Wang	Wangnet
Zilog	Z-net

The Ethernet is a well-known system. It uses a coaxial copper cable to connect various pieces of information equipment. Information travels over the cable in *packets* of data that are sent from one machine to another. Each packet contains the actual message that is being transmitted as well as information identifying the sending and receiving devices. Error control information is included to help ensure correct transmission.

Ethernet uses the *collision concept* or *contention* to decide which piece of

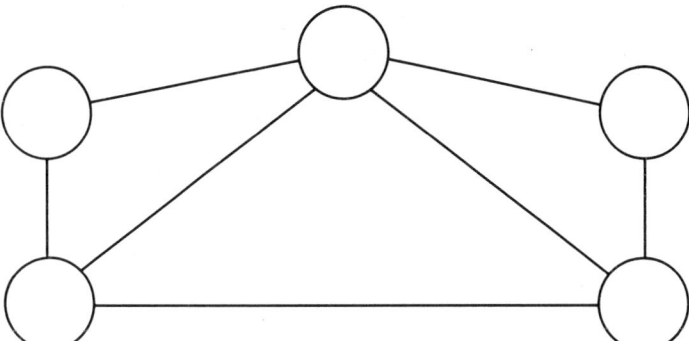

Figure 14.5

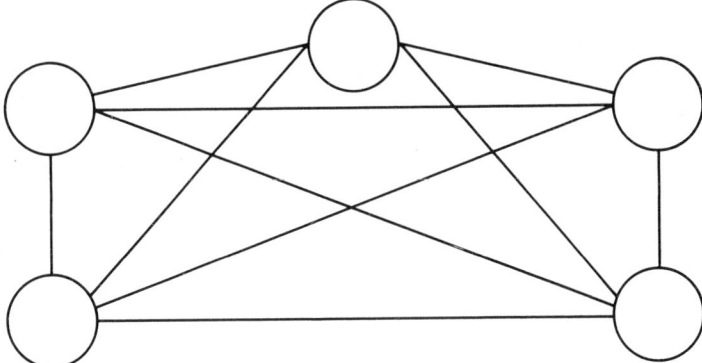

Figure 14.6

office equipment on the network gets to communicate next. When a device is transmitting, all other devices must wait. When the current transmission stops, other devices may attempt transmission. If their transmissions collide (i.e. if several devices attempt to transmit at the same time), all devices stop transmission. Eventually, one of the devices begins transmitting again, no collision occurs, and that device is able to complete its transmission while the other devices wait. This collision concept allows Ethernet to operate without *central network control*, thus making it much easier to add new devices to the network after initial installation.

The contention approach to sharing the network may at first seem inefficient. It is, however, fast (transmitting at 10 million bits per second), reliable and economical. The network operates so quickly and the packets are so short that each transmission lasts less than 1000th of a second, so the number of collisions is small. Because the control is provided by each individual device, the reliability of the network is very high. If an individual device fails, the network keeps functioning. This is called *distributed network control*.

14.4.7   VALUE-ADDED NETWORKS

These provide not only the media that an information system needs, but offer extra services and charge higher rates.

14.5   Signal transmission

We have seen the differing types of hardware employed for transmission channels. We have glanced at some types of control hardware. We have looked at various configurations into which such hardware can be placed. Yet we have not looked at the different types of transmission that can exist:

1. Modes—simplex, half-duplex, duplex.
2. Codes—ASCII, EBCDIC, and so on.
3. Transmission type—asynchronous or synchronous.
4. Bandwidth—baseband or broadband.

14.5.1   MODES

A *simplex transmission*, like a one-way street, allows for transmission in only one direction, as in radio and television.

Half-duplex transmission allows transmission in one direction at a time, which is frequently adequate for links between terminals and a computer.

Duplex transmission allows for simultaneous, bidirectional traffic, like the telephone.

14.5.2   CODES

How does your computer translate the letter A into bits? It might use the ASCII code, in which case it will be 1100 0001, or it might use the EBCDIC code, in which case it will be 1100 0010. There are other codes, but these are the two best known.

14.5.3   TRANSMISSION TYPE

Asynchronous transmission is used with relatively slow devices such as terminals. People type so slowly that characters tend to be transmitted one at a time, with long delays between them. Asynchronous transmission handles individual characters by enclosing their bit patterns between a *start bit* and a *stop bit* to mark the beginning and end of each transmission.

Synchronous transmission is used when high-speed transmission is required and when large groups of characters are normally ready for transmission at once. Synchronous transmission handles characters as one continuous stream of bits; there are no start bits, stop bits, or delays, so line capacity is not wasted. The hardware for synchronous transmission is more costly because it

Table 14.1

Type	Capacity	Application
Wire pairs	Narrow-band to voice grade	User to teleprocessing system
Coaxial cables	Voice grade to wideband	Linking high-speed devices
Microwave systems	Wideband	Long-distance links
Fibre-optic systems	Wideband	Long-distance links

must have precisely timed clocking mechanisms to recognize where each bit and each character begin and end.

14.5.4 BANDWIDTH

Transmission lines may be classified according to the speed at which they carry data. This speed is often called bandwidth. *Narrow-band* or low-speed lines operate at up to 300 bits per second (commonly written as 300 bps or 300 baud). *Voice-band* or medium-speed lines can operate at between 300 and 9600 bps. *Broad-band* or high-speed lines operate faster than 9600 bps. Table 14.1 summarizes the situation.

And, after a somewhat breathless rush, we have covered the basics of this topic. I am sorry that the whole thing read rather like your notes for finals, but you cannot really understand INGRES' implementations of distributed processing without having some standard awareness of the area with which we are dealing. Anyway, at long last, we can look at how INGRES copes within this field.

14.6   Distributed processing with INGRES

As I mentioned earlier, INGRES has four levels of distributed processing support. They are referred to as follows:

1. INGRES/NET.
2. INGRES/NET PC.
3. INGRES/PCLINK.
4. INGRES/STAR.

We can deal with them all in much the same breathless fashion as we attempted to give an overall survey of the entire topic of distributed processing. We are, after all, only concerned here to inform about peaks still to be climbed, not to do the climbing itself.

INGRES/NET allows any number of INGRES sites to be combined into a single network. Those various sites do not even have to have identical configurations or operating systems. Carl Malamud provides an explanation as to how NET operates in his INGRES book (pp. 195–6), but all we really need to know is that NET allows any front end to communicate to any back end over a heterogeneous architecture.

INGRES/NET PC is virtually identical to the above except that the sites running the INGRES front ends can be a PC, thus allowing applications to be developed on a PC and then transported without change to a mainframe or mini. Of course, in time, this facility will become obsolete as mainframes entirely disappear and minis become rarer. For the moment, however, it can be an invaluable service.

INGRES/PCLINK allows a PC to retrieve data (or 'download' it, as some people call it) from a local or remote host that is running INGRES. Clearly such a facility can greatly ease the communication burdens of a company.

INGRES/STAR is the most complex and versatile of them all. Being a fully distributed version, each site can support one or more local INGRES database and INGRES/STAR then allows any collection of tables from these local databases to be defined as a single distributed database. Thus, whereas with INGRES/NET a user must know where his or her server is located and the application can only communicate with a single server, the INGRES/STAR environment makes multiple local or remote databases seem as if they are one. Indeed, this distributed database, which appears to the user as a single entity, can futhermore be linked to other distributed databases (up to a total of 16). As a consequence, the processing ambit of INGRES is massively extended, though, of course, it does make the work of the query optimizer fantastically complex. This should not, however, perturb the user one iota. The whole thing should be transparent—another piece of computer jargon which simply means that the user should not be made aware in any way of the massive processing that a query optimizer has to do in order to process a query. Malamud gives a good and relatively clear discussion of INGRES/STAR in pp. 199–207 of his book if you want further information, and Date, as always, gives an eminently judicious survey of distributed processing in his *Guide to INGRES*.

And with this, we have finished. For most of this book we have been operating in the cosy, but mythical, world of being at our terminal with our INGRES database close at hand and our SQL as an integral part of our configuration. In the real world, this is almost never the case. Even in our invented SOS world, it is not the case. If INGRES, as a relational database, was unable to cope with data communications in the broadest sense, it would not be a viable option for any company or any academic institution. I have tried in this chapter to give just a little of the vocabulary and the knowledge required to begin understanding distributed processing. It has, I hope, become clear that INGRES is eminently capable of operating within that world.

15
Words, Words, Words

In entitling this part of the book 'INGRES and Communication', we knew that we were asking for trouble. To ask a computer scientist to talk about communication is like asking a priest to talk about life or a philosopher to talk about meaning.

You have already seen that this third part of the book contains chapters on matters as diverse as query languages, data integrity and data transmission. Yet what general concept embraces all of these elements? It is surely the concept of communication.

By means of a query language, you communicate with your database. Indeed, you create it, destroy it, or alter it in any one of a number of ways. In other words, you both define it and manipulate it.

The data dictionary communicates with you. It tells you a vast number of things about the database that you have created, things that would take you hours or days to discover for yourself.

Data communications is concerned with moving the information you have compiled to another site—possibly a site thousands of miles away, possibly just to the next room.

It is self-evident that communication is the entire *raison d'être* of a relational database. No one buys INGRES because it provides an entertaining means of spending the winter evenings. Instead of going out to the cinema or to play bingo, one can stay at home and play with INGRES. Not even I, who enjoys playing with INGRES, regards this as a very convincing hypothesis. Instead, INGRES is bought by people or organizations who need to maximize their communication abilities. The chapters in this part have been concerned to show how this can be done. It is, however, useful in conclusion to see how these various communication facilities are physically handled within INGRES.

We have already gathered that a computer system comprises a front end and a back end. Let us look just a fraction more closely at these, because in so doing, we can see how the communication complex is handled.

INGRES itself, the relational database, comprises the back end. Thus, when we talk about any of the DBMS functions, including full support for SQL (or QUEL), we are referring to the back end. All the query processing that one performs within a database is the function of the back end. Hence, when you input a query to INGRES, the back end first parses it (i.e. checks it to make sure that it contains no errors), then possibly modifies it in order to take account of any overriding constraints imposed by security or integrity factors, then works out the most efficient way of dealing with that query, and, having done so, finally executes it.

The INGRES front end is manifested, for the user, by means of the screen, because the front end provides us with all of the facilities for handling our database. It is what you see upon your screen. Thus QBF, VIFRED, and other facilities like Reports and Applications that we have yet to discover, are dealt with by the front end. Indeed, SQL itself is part of the front-end complex, though it provides us with less handholding than something like QBF.

It is obvious, then, that another form of communication takes place within INGRES: that vital communication between the front end and the back end. We tell the front end that we want to create a table. The front end passes the message on to the back end, which, having checked the validity of our request, then tells the front end to put up before us the relevant screen. It is the degree and level of communication between the front end and the back end that determines the efficiency of the entire DBMS. All our attempts to talk to INGRES, to get INGRES to talk to us, and to pass on the results of those conversations to others, depend upon the system structure handling it. It is because that system structure, exemplified by means of tables and forms, is so effective, that INGRES is the preferred relational database of so many companies and so many educational institutions.

Let us place this situation in some sort of historical context. Once upon a time, as all the best fairy stories begin, there were two ways of dealing with a database. You could have the database stored on a mainframe or a mini. You, however, would be sat at a terminal, normally a dumb terminal. The central computer—mainframe or mini—would do everything for you, all the database and application processing. You, at your dumb terminal, and possibly dozens of others also at their respective dumb terminals, would merely receive the products of the request that had been made. Alternatively, the database could be stored on a stand-alone microcomputer. You would, thereby, be in complete charge of everything: database requests, front-end applications, screen input/output. You would not, however, be able to share your work with anybody—unless, or course, you let them take turns with you at the same terminal. The current situation, however, is a kind of amalgam of these two earlier systems. Your database server holds a copy of the database, just as the mainframe or mini would once have done. That copy of the database is also, as before, made available to any authorized user. However, the database server no longer runs the actual database applications or other front-end programs. They are your responsibility at your terminal, no longer a dumb one. Thus, while you are still a client of the server, just as you would earlier have been a client of the mainframe or minicomputer that held the database, you are no longer a passive client.

The resulting increase in communicating facilities has brought with it corresponding constraints. Within a distributed database system, certain operating systems—MS-DOS, for example—can easily become a bottleneck because of their small main memory. SQL, as a query language, needs to become more fully relational. A database server does prevent the database user from having all the independence that was possible on the stand-alone micro. As always, the swings and roundabouts vie for supremacy. None the less, as achievements like INGRES/STAR clearly demonstrate, the world of relational databases is a world of massively more effective communications.

In the next section, we have a look at some even more sophisticated means of communication that INGRES renders available, at least more sophisticated in terms of catering to your individual requirements. As always, however, do have a look at the 10 questions that follow on the next page.

Questions on Part Three

1. Between what two objects is a query language the interface?
2. What is an 'embedded' language?
3. Distinguish between a data definition language and a data manipulative language.
4. How could you, in SQL, ensure that an addition operation was done before a multiplication operation within the same expression?
5. How would you ask the System Catalog which tables had the attribute 'Role' within them?
6. In order to send data from one place to another, one needs a communicating medium or transmission channel, like a telephone wire. Can you name six other transmission channels?
7. What is baud rate?
8. What is the name given to the most complex INGRES facility for data communications?
9. How would you enter SQL if your cursor was resting alongside the system prompt?
10. Within a data dictionary, what information is given by the Base System Catalogs?

Answers

1. The user and the DBMS.
2. An embedded language is a language that is empowered to operate within and alongside another language. Thus SQL can be 'embedded' with FORTRAN (or any other programming language).
3. Query languages perform both of these functions: defining the structure

of the language (DDL) and selecting, updating, joining, destroying, or, in other words, manipulating data (DML).

4. By enclosing the addition operation in brackets.
5. RANGE OF A IS ATTRIBUTE
   SELECT (A. ATTRELID)
   WHERE A. ATTNAME = 'Role';
6. Coaxial cables, microwaves, communications satellites, fibre optics, lasers, waveguides.
7. The number of times per second that a system, especially a data transmission channel, changes state.
8. INGRES/STAR.
9. Type 'isql sos'.
10. Information about the tables in the database, their structure, domains, indexes, etc.

PART FOUR

More advanced techniques

16
The Visual Forms Editor

We encountered the Visual Forms Editor (VIFRED) in Chapter 3, but it is such an important component of the INGRES matrix that it deserves a fuller examination. In Chapter 3 we were so concerned with building our database that VIFRED was treated as merely an incidental tool in that operation. Returning to VIFRED will also be useful because it will reintroduce us to Query-By-Forms (QBF).

As we have seen, a great deal of INGRES is based upon the form. In other words, when we encounter an INGRES screen, we frequently find that it is broken up into various distinct areas, each area being devoted to an equally distinct piece of information. You will recall the JoinDef Definition Table Entry Form as shown on Fig. 16.1. Return to page 85 if you also want to see the form presented in the VAX/VMS Version 6 context. As you can see, in both cases they are a typical form. And so are they all. Into this form, you have to fill things. In computer jargon, a form is full of fields. In the form on page 160, there is a field for JoinDef Name, fields for Table Names, and fields for Range Variables. You just fill in the relevant fields, and the form is completed. As you also know, each field can have different characteristics imposed upon it. Some of those characteristics can be visual, so that the field blinks on and off or is presented in reverse video. Other characteristics are invisible, like when a field is made a mandatory one or when a field has been provided with some validatory parameters. Whatever level of sophistication you choose to use, you are, however, dealing with a form.

The majority of the forms within INGRES are forms that INGRES itself provides. Neither you nor I designed the Table Entry Form on page 160. It was provided for us by INGRES, or, more specifically, by VIFRED. And here lies the distinction between VIFRED and QBF. The latter is concerned with manipulating the data within a form; VIFRED, however, is concerned

Go   Blank   ChangeDisplay   Joins   Rules   Save   [F1=Help]   [F10=End]   Quit

---

QBF - JoinDef Definition - Table Entry Form

JoinDef Name:

Enter table names and corresponding optional range variables in
the tables below.

Master Tables: Detail Tables:

Table Name	Range Variable

Table Name	Range Variable

Figure 16.1

with the form itself. It is VIFRED that creates, edits, or redefines a form,
and it is this that makes VIFRED so important. At the best of times, forms
are not wildly exciting entities, but there is a wealth of difference between a
well-designed form and one that looks as if it were a cure for insomnia. One
may not look at a form with the same appreciation as one looks at a Cézanne
painting, but a well-designed form can at least engage one's attention. Given
the omnipresence of forms in our culture, it is vital to have a relational
database that gives forms the primacy they need. It is appropriate also that
this section should begin with VIFRED, because VIFRED plays a vital role
in providing specific applications for companies and organizations, the topic
of Chapter 18, and VIFRED can also play an important role in the
construction of a report, the topic of the next chapter.

Let us, first of all, be entirely clear about the function of forms. When one
fills in a form for the Inland Revenue, that form just acts as the medium of
communication between yourself and the tax-man. A form in VIFRED is
exactly the same in that it is the medium of communication between yourself
and the database. For your own sake, however, and even more importantly,
for the sake of others, it is worthwhile to design such forms in a fashion that
aids their accurate completion and that engages the user's attention. To this
end, VIFRED provides a range of options. INSERT allows even the virtually
uninformed user to edit a form. EDIT is more sophisticated, takes longer to
learn, but provides more power. Buttressing them both are the HELP
screens. Indeed, it is possible to learn how to operate VIFRED simply by
accessing the relevant HELP screens; so, if you want to experiment on your
own, you can skip the rest of this chapter. Ideally, of course, you will read
this chapter *and* experiment on your own.

Since forms lie at the centre of VIFRED's existence, I shall devote a section to the structure of a form. Then I will try to show how VIFRED can be used, via INSERT and EDIT, to modify the appearance of a form. This two-part division will introduce us to most of the available facilities of VIFRED.

16.1   The structure of the form

The screen of a computer terminal can normally display the entire width of a form. It frequently, however, cannot display at any one time the entire length of the form in question. Consequently one normally has to use the down-arrow key in order to access the whole of the form. This is rarely any real handicap. However, whatever the size of the form, it only consists of two significant components: fields and trim. Fields we already know about. A field is the space needed for any one data entry. Hence, if our form required the entry of a person's name, the field provided for that entry would have to be able to cope with Jo Nax and with Wilhelmina Prendergast. Trim, however, we have not encountered. It has nothing to do with visits to the hairdressers, though it is concerned with appearance. If a field is just the allocation of space for a data entry, then trim is a technique of presenting those fields in as agreeable and attractive a fashion as possible. Let me illustrate.

The form shown in Fig. 16.2 is a typical SOS form, with one exception. Enclosing each element of the form are some brackets. Where I have used < >, it represents a field. Where I have used [ ], it represents trim. Obviously, neither of these brackets actually appear on the form itself. As you can see, there are three trim elements on the form in Fig. 16.2 and six field sections. The former is the simpler of the two. To start with, they are given. No data entry is involved at all. Thus trim is concerned with headings and the positioning of those headings. Trim is concerned with the ruled off divisions between sections of the form. Trim too will be concerned with any typefaces used in those headings, or any decorative elements also included in the form. And that is that. There is no more to concern us with respect to trim. Data entry elements, however, are more complex.

To start with, there are two displayable subcomponents to a field: there is the name given to the field itself, a name like Telephone Number or Store Departments; and there is the space allowed for that telephone number or those store departments to be inserted. The first element is called the title, and the second is called the data window. Hence our form on the previous page has six titles and six associated data windows, though the space given order to the data windows takes up 19 distinct lines or parts of a line.

Secondly, a field can take any one of six data formats. There are only two used in the form we have looked at: 'c' standing for character, and 'i' specifying an integer. The other data formats are much less common, all of

[STORE DATA]

[——————————————————————————————————————]

    ⟨Town: c ....⟩   ⟨Store Number: ....⟩

   ⟨Address: c ....⟩
          ⟨ ....⟩
          ⟨ ....⟩
          ⟨ ....⟩   ⟨Telephone Number: i...........⟩

   ⟨Manager's Name: c ....⟩

[——————————————————————————————————————]

   ⟨Store Department: c ....⟩
        ⟨.................................⟩
        ⟨.................................⟩
        ⟨.................................⟩
        ⟨.................................⟩
        ⟨.................................⟩
        ⟨.................................⟩
        ⟨.................................⟩
        ⟨.................................⟩
        ⟨.................................⟩
        ⟨.................................⟩

——————————————————————————————————————]

Figure 16.2

them referring to specific scientific ways of representing numeric data. The only one of the remaining four that you are likely to use unless you are a research physicist is 'f', which enables one to display a number containing a decimal point. There are, however, two extensions to data types: date and money. A date is represented by the formate 'cn' where 'c' stands for character and 'n' stands for the number of characters needed. Money is represented by the data format 'fw.d', where 'f' stands for a floating-point number (i.e. one with a decimal point), 'w' represents the maximum field width of that number, and 'd' stands for the number of digits that will follow the decimal point.

Thirdly, a field can be displayable or non-displayable. If, for instance, a member of the SOS staff has to type in his or her password in order to gain access to the Accounts table, it would not be very helpful if that password were then displayed upon the screen for all to see. Consequently, that field will be a non-displayable one, or at least it will be if you so instruct, and it would obviously be sensible so to do.

A field can also have a number of other attributes, most of which we have already encountered. Thus a field may be mandatory or it may be presented in upper case or in reverse video, and so on. Perhaps most importantly of all, a field may have a validation check or checks placed upon it. Thus, for instance, the Store Number field in the form that we designed in this chapter would have a validation check to ensure that it began with the letter S. Note too one small distinction here. 'Store Number' is the field title on our particular form. It is not the same as the field name. That is 'store_no'. The filler-in of the form will see and refer to Store Number; the database itself and programs using that database will refer to the internal name store_no.

We have already learnt how to create a form using VIFRED, so it will surely be simplest quickly to create the form that we have just been looking at, and then use that form to edit within VIFRED. If, however, your memory is as expert as mine, you will not remember how to create such a form. Here then is an instruction list:

1. Access the Form Layout Screen.
2. Choose Create.
3. Position the cursor where you want a trim element to be placed.
4. Choose Trim from the menu.
5. Type the desired trim.
6. Press F2.
7. Now position the cursor where you want a field to be placed.
8. Choose Field from the Menu.
9. Choose Title, Data, or Attributes to specify the field's components.
10. Press F10 to complete the creation of a field.
11. Repeat the above operations as many times as is necessary.
12. Press F3 when the form is complete.

16.2   Editing a form

It has been decided that the form requires some considerable modifications. Jason Willspend has decreed that they must, in future, look like Fig. 16.3. As you can see, the form is now designed to indicate how much business has been performed during the year by each department within the store. Consequently, in order to do the form as Jason Willspend now wants it, we will have to add new items and change the positioning of old items. Although it will take up quite a lot of space to describe how to do this, the process is not complicated and employs many identical operations to creating the form in the first place.

16.2.1   EDITING FIELDS

Clearly there are only three things that one can alter when editing fields: titles, data windows, and attributes. We have given no attributes to the fields, so we need only concern ourselves with editing the titles and windows.

Of the existing titles, only two have changed. Telephone Number has been

<u>*SOS STORES: ESSENTIAL DATA*</u>
                        YEAR: :

        STORE NUMBER: ....   TOWN: ....

Address: ....   Tel. No.: ....
           ....
           ....
           ....

                        §§§§§§§§§§§§§§

Manager's Name: ....

Departments: ....   Turnover: ....
....
....
....
....
....
....
....
....
....
....

§§

Figure 16.3

abbreviated to Tel_No and Store Departments has been shortened to
Departments. Hence you will choose the form that you want to edit on the
Forms Catalog Screen (and there is likely to be only the one, unless you have
been experimenting yourself), place the cursor anywhere on the table field,
and choose Edit. To change the title of a field, position the cursor at the
beginning of the title in question, and type out the amended version. Then
you simply have to press F10, and the effects of your changes will be
displayed.

However, although only two titles have changed, one new title—Turnover—has been added, and the position of one title —Tel_No—has been
changed. It would be too condescending to explain again how to create a new
table field, but we certainly need to know how to move the already changed
title, Tel_No, upwards three lines.

Place the cursor at the beginning of the title and then choose Move from
the menu of VIFRED editing operations. You will then be presented with a
set of further options:

Place Left Centre Right Shift Title Data [F1=Help] [F10=End]

Choose Place or Shift—in this instance it does not matter which—and then place the cursor on the spot where you want title to be repositioned. Should anything go wrong, and it probably will, choose the Undo operation from the menu, and try again.

16.2.2   EDITING TRIM

To edit trim is almost identical. You position the cursor on the element that you wish to modify or change, and type your correction over the original. You will need, though, to blank out the remains of the old trim. To clear out the remainder, just press Control and D simultaneously, and then press F2 to return to the original menu. This ought to be the so-called Write menu:

Help Continue Start Write Exit

Because you wish to save your work, you will need to select the Write option. The data entry form will now appear containing just a single demand, namely that you give the form that you have just created a name. Any name of 12 or fewer letters will suffice; 'store_data' seems appropriate enough. Then, from the options given at the bottom of the screen, choose QBFNames. You will then be presented with yet another form. The on-screen instructions should be clear enough. All that you are concerned with doing is to give your new form, store_data, a parallel name that will link it to QBF. Something like 'storinf' or 'stordat' should do. Then, once this operation is completed, you can exit VIFRED completely by accessing, unsurprisingly, the Exit option.

16.2.3   INSERT

While, in the terse instructions given above, we did consciously use the Edit function, it was never made clear as to how Edit differed from Insert. In looking at this, it will be possible to expand a little on the nature of the preceding instructions.

If you look at the bottom right-hand corner of your screen, you may see the following:

input[INSERT]

If you now press the Control and E keys simultaneously, that message will change to input[EDIT]. You can toggle between them by using the Control/ E combination. (Toggle is another jargon word, though it has more charm than most. As you will have inferred, to toggle something is to swap from one mode to another. It would appear to have no connection with the nautical term defined in the dictionary.)

However, assuming that you are currently in INSERT mode, all that you really need to know are a set of commands that can be used while in that mode. There are five, all of them requiring the use of the Control key in combination with another letter:

- Control-W   Redraw the screen.
- Control-E   Toggle between INSERT and EDIT modes.
- Control-H   Move left in the text.
- Control-L   Move right in the text.
- Control-D   Clear from cursor to end of field.

From time to time, however, you may wish to do more extended editing than the INSERT mode will allow. In such instances, you will, of course, enter the EDIT mode. INSERT, however, is viable for most circumstances, and to explore all the other available facilities—like creating a form for many tables, creating a blank form, copying forms from a database to a text file, and so on—would take us well beyond the introductory stage. Relational Technology produce a specific Visual-Forms-Editor User's Guide (or at least they do, to my knowledge, for those using the UNIX operating system, and I can only assume that their coverage is broader than simply that). I regret that I cannot be sure, but RT never had the courtesy to reply to any of my letters of enquiry. Consequently, if and when you do need to extend your understanding, Relational Technology, or whoever has now replaced RT, will probably be able to supply your needs.

17
Report writing in INGRES

The topic of report writing (and this may be entirely a personal prejudice) rouses in me the sort of enthusiasm that I normally reserve for events like watching grass grow or paint dry. One sees job advertisements that state 'experience in writing reports essential'. There are books about report writing. There are probably, for all I know, pretentious magazines devoted to the minutiae of report writing.

Maybe this obsession with report writing is necessary, though I find it difficult to comprehend. Writing is writing. Everyone of any intelligence knows that you do not write an essay on Kant's categorical imperative in the same style as you write a letter to a friend. Few people begin a letter of application for a job with the words 'Listen, mate, you ain't going to let slip the chance of getting me.' In other words, we all know that style, content, and layout of one's writing varies according to its intended audience and according to its intended purpose. A report, by its nature, is going to be overwhelmingly factually based and analytically presented. It will doubtless consist primarily of tables of data or columns of figures. It will not, as this book does, contain snide comments about the Conservative Party or the Yorkshire cricket team. If, however, you are a competent writer, your report will be clear. If you are a good writer, your report may even be interesting. In none of such matters, however, is INGRES of the slightest relevance. The best relational database in the world cannot help you to write a good report. To do that, you have to rely entirely upon your mind, your own educational training from infant school onwards, your own clarity of thought, and, above all, your own determination.

Since this chapter is longer than most others in this book, it may seem somewhat perverse to begin it with such dismissive comments. As you have already seen, this part of the book is entitled 'More Advanced Techniques'.

There is a pretension, a grandiloquence, about that title that makes me feel somewhat uneasy, though I was unable to think of a suitable alternative. 'More Advanced Techniques' sounds as if you are about to be introduced to the mystery of the Grail. Not so. The topics of Part Four are more advanced because they require even more complex techniques on behalf of INGRES itself, but INGRES remains what it has always been: a tool. It is a very good tool, but you do not normally praise the paint-brush for painting the Mona Lisa. And so it is with report writing. If you write good reports, it will not be because of the help of INGRES. It will be because of you.

Having then put INGRES in its place, let us see what relevance it really does have for report writing. INGRES will give two types of help in writing reports. The first type of help is quick and easy, and hence it is at this type that we glance first.

17.1 Quick reports

To produce a quick and easy INGRES report format requires minimal effort on the part of the user, because INGRES takes an already created table like Store, and produces a default report upon that table. Self-evidently, of course, this default report is simply a presentation of the data in the table concerned, a presentation set out in such a way as to make it easy to absorb and access the information of that table. Clearly some examples will clarify what is meant here.

First of all, in order to activate the INGRES Report-By-Forms facility, you simply choose Tables from the INGRES/MENU screen. As we know, the Table Utility Screen then appears. Assuming that you are in the SOS database, the tables listed on the Table Utility Screen will be as shown in Fig. 17.1. As the text on the screen instructs, you next move the cursor to the particular table that you require, and then go to the menu at the top of the screen and select the operation that you need, in this case, Report. You will then be presented with a further list of options:

Default Block Wrap Column

If you opt for Default, you will be presented with a Report layout that, in the opinion of INGRES, is appropriate for the data contained in the particular table that you have selected. If you select Block, you will be presented with a columnless layout of the data. If you select Wrap, INGRES will ensure that the report presentation is in columns but that, if there are too many columns to be shown in one line across the page, some of those columns will be moved down to the next line. The final option, Column, is the same as Wrap in appearance except that, if there are too many columns for the width of the page, the columns will be truncated.

Having made your selection of Default, Block, Wrap, or Column,

Create Destroy Examine Query-By-Forms Report Find [F1=Help] [F10=End]

INGRES TABLE UTILITY   Database: SOS

Table Name	Owner
Store	pc
emp_store	pc
suppliers	pc
purchases	pc

Position cursor on the name of the table you wish to select, then use the menu to perform the appropriate operation on that table.

Figure 17.1

INGRES will next ask you if you wanted the resulting report printed or displayed on the screen. In order to have the report shown on the screen, you simply press Enter. The first page of the report in question will then appear upon the screen. At the bottom of the screen there will be the instruction

ENTER C, S, HELP OR <RETURN>

If you type 'c', the report will rapidly scroll downwards until it reaches the end. You can then return to the Table Utility Screen and move on to another report or, indeed, any other operation. If you type 's', then the Report will simply stop and you will be returned to the Table Utility Screen. If you type Help, you will be presented with the appropriate Help screen, and if you simply press Return, the next screen of the report (if there is one) will be shown.

In INGRES Version 6, the presentation is somewhat different. The Report Catalog screen looks like Fig. 17.2. If you press 1 for Create, the menu disappears and you are asked to enter the table name to use as the basis for the report. Having done so, you gain a list of options, as in Version 5:

BlockMode(1) ColumnMode(2) WrapMode(3) DefaultMode(4) >

From then on, you just follow the menus, as in Version 5, so there seems little point in reproducing the varying screen formats that appear.

Obviously it will remove any possible ambiguity if examples are given of the various report layouts. I shall choose the Store table to illustrate the various options, but, before doing so, let us see these options within another database. It is highly likely that the version of INGRES that you possess contains within it a specimen database. This database is likely to be called

RBF - Report Catalog

Name	Owner	Short Remark

Place cursor in row and select desired operation from menu.

Create(1)   Destroy(2)   Edit(3)   Rename(4)   MoreInfo(5)   >

Figure 17.2

Demo. I have never mentioned this INGRES facility before because it was important for our purposes to build our own database, but, since this facility exists, we may as well now begin to use it.

If you enter INGRES by typing 'addingres' and then enter the Demo database by typing 'ingres demo', you will, of course, be presented as always with the INGRES/MENU screen. Choose Tables from the menu at the top of the screen, and you will see the resulting Table Utility Screen, as shown in Fig. 17.3. You may find it useful to make your own copy of this database in order to experiment. The site upon which you are doing your work will have an appropriate password for so doing. At the University of East Anglia, for instance, the password is UEAINGDEMO. If you type the relevant

Create Destroy Examine Query-By-Forms Report Find [F1=Help] [F10=End]
_____

INGRES TABLE UTILITY   Database: demo

Table Name	Owner	
budget	pc	Position cursor on the name of the table you wish to select, then use
departments	pc	the menu to perform the appropriate
menuopt	pc	operation on that table.
projects	pc	
protasks	pc	
schedule	pc	
staff	pc	
tasks	pc	

Figure 17.3

password, you will then be asked what name you wish to give your Demo database. I called mine Megan simply because my daughter insisted upon appearing somewhere in this book, but any name will do provided that you do not give a name that has already been used for something else within the system that you are using. Having selected your name, the screen will announce

```
Creating DEMO database MEGAN
This will take a few minutes.
```

The copy of Demo will then be created for you, with, in all probability, a running commentary being flashed unto the screen as it proceeds:

```
Creating DBMS Core System Catalogs . . .
Creating Standard Catalog Interface.
Modifying Frontend System Catalogs.
```

and so on. Then, when it has created the database, it will tell you that it has done so and that it is now engaged in filling the database and that it will take minutes so to do. When this operation has been completed, you will be told that you can now access it by giving the command:

```
ingmenu MEGAN
```

From then on, INGRES will guide you, as always, by means of its menu options.

However, this has been a somewhat parenthetical operation, though it is, by this time, a good idea to have a look at the Demo database that INGRES provides, simply because it will give a more meaningful set of data for us to handle than is possible in our own circumscribed SOS database. I note too that the list of tables provided in the Demo database that I used at UEA was somewhat different from the list provided in the Demo database that my students used at Leicester Polytechnic. Again this is of no real practical significance. I shall, however, return to the Version 5 context for the rest of this chapter. There should be little difficulty in adjusting if you are operating within a Version 6 context.

Let us first see some report formats for the table 'budget' (or whatever table that you choose if 'budget' is not one of your available options). If you place the cursor on the first letter of budget, press F2, then move the cursor to the menu option Report and press Return, you will be shown the four report options. Since Default is the first of these, the cursor is already resting upon that option. Just press Return and you will see the screen shown in Fig. 17.4. I have, in fact, omitted most of the content of the budget table default report, but you can none the less see exactly how that report data is presented.

The next option presented is the Block Report. I mentioned earlier that this option does not present data in columns. Instead it shows its report format as shown in Fig. 17.5.

Report on Table: budget

Project_id	Budget	Year
TextProc	3700,000	1988
Advertise	2760,000	1988
	3760,000	1986
	3760,000	1987
	4760,000	1982
EmployBen	625,000	1981
	625,000	1982
	725,000	1983

Figure 17.4

And with these two examples we can leave the budget table, since the Column and Wrap options are, in this instance, identical to the Default example that we have already seen. Default selected to show the budget data in columns anyway, so we would expect it to be identical to the Column option. Wrap always opts for columns too, and in this case there were not sufficient columns for there to be any necessity for wrapping.

If we next select the Staff table from the Demo database, we see a virtual repeat of what we have witnessed with the Budget table. The Default options chooses columns again as its preferred mode of format; consequently, it is again identical to Column and Wrap (see Fig. 17.6). I have again greatly shortened the report, but you can see clearly how it is set out. The Block format produces no real surprises either (see Fig. 17.7). Clearly, the option that you decide to adopt will be a matter of company policy, personal taste, or economy of paper.

If we now move to our own SOS database and perform the same operation for the Table store, there are one or two interesting differences. This time the Default option decides not to choose a column format, but instead

Report on Table: budget

Project_id:	TextProc:	Budget:	3700,000	Year: 1988
Project_id:	Advertise:	Budget:	2760,000	1988
Project_id:	Advertise:	Budget:	3760,000	1986
Project_id:	Advertise:	Budget:	3760,000	1987
Project_id:	Advertise:	Budget:	4760,000	1982
Project_id:	EmployBen:	Budget:	625,000	1981
Project_id:	EmployBen:	Budget:	625,000	1982
Project_id:	EmployBen:	Budget:	725,000	1983

Figure 17.5

Report on Table: staff

Name	Title	Hourly_rate	Manager
Alcott, Scott	Sr Programmer	50,000	Wolfe, Neal
Applegate, Donald	Analyst	51,000	Wolfe, Neal
Bee, Charles	Sr Programmer	43,000	Fielding, Wallace

Figure 17.6

Report on Table: staff

Name: Alcott, Scott   Title: Sr Programmer
Hourly_rate: 50,000   Manager: Wolfe, Neal

Name: Applegate, Donald   Title: Analyst
Hourly_rate: 51,000   Manager: Wolfe, Neal

Name: Bee, Charles   Title: Sr Programmer
Hourly_rate: 43,000   Manager: Fielding, Wallace

Figure 17.7

Store_no: S1   Town: London
Address: 6–9 Regent Street, W1   Tel_no: 071-793-2943

Store_no: S10   Town: Swansea
Address: 16 Fenton Street, SW5 9PX   Tel_no: 0792-23697

Store_no: S11   Town: Exeter   Tel_no: 0392-79251

Figure 17.8

Report on Table: store

Store_no	Town	Address	Tel_no
S1	London	6–9 Regent Street, W1	071-793-2945
S10	Swansea	16 Fenton Street, SW5 9PX	0792-23697
S11	Exeter	Page Mansion, EX2 7GF	0392-79251
S12	Leeds	Malvolio Crescent, L13 8HU	0532-71335

Figure 17.9

chooses a set-up identical to that of Block (see Fig. 17.8). The Column
option does exactly what one would expect it to do (see Fig. 17.9). And so
the columns continue until, having reached S18, it moves on to list S2 to S9.

The Wrap option, finding that the columns concerned take up too much of

Report on Table: store

Store_no	Town	Address
Tel_no		
S1	London	6–9 Regent Street, W1
071-793-2945		
S10	Swansea	16 Fenton Steet, SW5 9PX
0792-23697		
S11	Exeter	Pago Mansion, EX2 7GF
0392-79251		

Figure 17.10

the width of the paper, does its somewhat inelegant wrapping procedure. I do not understand why this should be the case, since the Column option places all the fields perfectly happily across the width of the page. However, Fig. 17.10 shows how Wrap presents its Report format.

As you can see from the examples given, our quick and easy report facility simply arranges the data in what have been regarded as appropriate ways. This is undoubtedly useful. If you are having to present a report on SOS stores, or whatever, it is distinctly time-saving to access a facility that arranges the data you wish to present. But that is all it will do. It will not write the report for you, or even select the appropriate data for you. All the real decisions are left to you.

Convenient and sensible though the report formats are, however, there will inevitably come the time when you need a different format, one not provided by the Report-By-Forms facility at which we have been looking. INGRES can still be of help. There exists in INGRES a component called Report Writer. This will help you to produce report formats of your own choice, and it is to this that we next turn.

17.2   Report Writer

With the type of quick reports at which we have so far been looking, INGRES does all the significant work. Unfortunately, one often needs to produce a report that demands more than can be provided by the default utilities. For instance, you may well need to include in your report data that comes from several tables. You may need to present that data in a specific order, an order different from the way in which it is stored in its original table. You may need to perform calculations upon columns of figures, calculations that are certainly not an in-built facility of the default options. Hence, while RBF can save you time, it will not do anything very sophisticated. Let us imagine that Jason Willspend wants a report showing the amount spent by each SOS store on salaries, and those salaries compared and contrasted with the turnover accomplished by each department within a store so that he can see which departments within which stores have the greatest profit margin in comparison with their salary expenditure. Such a report cannot be produced by any default operation. Instead, the DBA is going to have to produce some specifications indicating what data is needed, how that data should be presented upon the page and what on-running calculations need to be effected upon that data. In other words, this time it is you who has to design the report, not INGRES.

It should be obvious that the most important aspect of producing such a custom-designed report lies in the design of the report itself. One must work out exactly what data needs to be included in such a report. Then one needs to find out where exactly that data can be found. Is it basically all in one already existing table, or does it require access to several tables? Even if the data already exists in an easily accessible form, is that data sorted in the way one currently requires? What size should the report be—not just in terms of length but in terms of paper size? Above all, perhaps, is this going to be a one-off report or one of a series? As I said at the beginning of this chapter, the efficacy of a report is going to depend a great deal more on you than it is on INGRES.

From now on in this chapter I shall be distressingly vague. Obviously, to produce a good report, you need to feed into INGRES a report specification file. This file will answer all the questions (and others) that I cited in the preceding paragraph. As I have indicated, real thought and effort needs to go into this report specification file. It is a long way from being a trivial operation. If you are employed by a company that uses INGRES, however, you will need to produce a report specification relevant to your own company. If you are studying computer science at university or polytechnic, you will doubtless be set an assignment upon Report Writer. In neither case will you want to spend hours devising, or even copying, a report specification for SOS. Consequently, from now on I shall simply talk in generalizations, trying to indicate the principles of report specification rather than anchoring those principles to the creation of a specific report.

Once again, I shall assume that we are positioned at the INGRES/MENU screen. You will choose, logically enough, the Reports option. This will immediately give you the Reports Catalog screen. If you really did create the Store_No report that we looked at in the preceding section of this chapter, the Reports Catalog screen will list it. Otherwise, the grid will be blank like the one shown in Fig. 17.11. As you know, we wish now to create a report specification file. This being the case, we place the cursor on EditFile and press Enter. We will now be commanded to enter the name of the file that we wish to edit. Of course, we do not want to edit a file at all; we want to create one. Fortunately, INGRES allows this. All that you have to do is to type the name of the new file. In fact, this file name will have to conform to

Go   Editfile   Loadfile   Destroy   Rename   Find   [F1=Help]   [F10=End]

INGRES REPORTS   Database: SOS

Report Name	Owner

Position cursor over the name of the
report you wish to select, then use
the menu to perform the appropriate
operation on that report.

Figure 17.11

the naming conventions of the operating systems that your terminal possesses, but by and large any name of no more than 12 characters will suffice.
It will, of course, help if the name you adopt bears some relation to the
nature of the report that you are preparing. YOGI_BEAR is not an entirely
appropriate name for a report on employee salaries.

Once we have named our report, we can begin entering the specifications.
It is this operation that requires both time and concentration. The latter can
be difficult, because it cannot be pretended that entering report specifications
is a very stimulating job. No doubt surgeons have a feeling of ennui when
they face yet another appendix removal, but their concentration is none the
less imperative. So it is with report specifications.

The Relational Technology Reference Guide is admirably clear upon this
topic, even though its comments are split between Chapters 24 and 27. I can,
therefore, do little more than give a slight gloss on that guide.

Let us, as always, be entirely clear as to what we are attempting to do. A
report specification file is nothing more (or less) than a series of instructions.
Everything—repeat, everything—that you wish to be manifested in your
report will be detailed in the specification file. How wide you want the
margins of your report; should the pages be numbered; does the header of
each page need a particular logo; all these, and many others, are specified in
the file that is created.

Not surprisingly, report specification commands can be categorized as to
the type of function that they perform. Hence five commands are taken as
being concerned with the set-up of the report:

.data specifies which table in the database contains the data to be used for
    the report.
.name gives a name to the report.

.output enables you to transfer the report you are writing to an output file
other than the screen.

.query allows you to set up an SQL query to be embedded within the report.

.sort allows you to specify the order in which data will be presented.

As you will have noticed, all Report Writer commands begin with a full-stop,
and as you may have guessed, it is frequently these setup commands that are
used at the beginning of the specification file. Thus, if you wanted to produce
a report, as Date does in the 18th chapter of his INGRES book, showing
cities that had suppliers within them, and what specific goods those suppliers
provided, then your specification file could begin as follows:

```
.NAME    CS_REP_SPEC
.QUERY   SELECT CITY      = S.CITY,
                 SUPPLIER  = S.SNO,
                 PART      = SP.PNO
                 QUANTITY  = SP.QTY
         FROM  S, SP
         WHERE S.SNO       = SP.SNO
.SORT    CITY, SUPPLIER, PART
```

Do not worry if the above specification is not fully meaningful; Date in his
book defines the abbreviations that he uses, and I only wanted to cite Date's
example just to give an illustration of the layout within a specification file.
As you can see, it would be impossible to compile a report specification file
unless you already had a basic grounding in SQL, which is one of the reasons
as to why we looked at SQL in the preceding part of this book. The tiny
section of the report specification that I have reproduced above from Date is
only the initial block of report set-up statements. Having defined the content
of the report by using the appropriate Report Setup commands, you next
proceed to detail the report structure, its text positioning, and its page
layout. For each there is the appropriate command. The Relational Technology Reference Guide and Date in his book each give a list of these
commands conveniently split into their separate categories. Unfortunately
there are differences between the two listings, so I have reproduced them
both side by side in Table 17.1. Neither of the lists given, RT's or Date's,
must be regarded as complete and comprehensive, nor are the discrepancies
between them of any importance. I merely listed them side by side so as to
give some impression of the range of facilities for report specification that
Report Writer can implement. Chapter 24 of the Relational Technology
INGRES Reference Guide gives a 45-page listing, with explanatory
examples, of such commands. Even more detailed is the *INGRES Forms and
Menus and Report Writer for the UNIX and VMS Operating Systems* (Release
6, 1989) if you are operating within a Version 6 context. The remainder of
Date's report specification can be found on pp. 297–8 of his book. Rather

Table 17.1 Comparison of Report commands used by Relational Technology and C. J. Date

Relational Technology	C. J. Date
REPORT SETUP	REPORT SETUP
.data	.name
.name	.output
.output	.data
.query	.query
.sort	.sort
REPORT STRUCTURING	REPORT STRUCTURING
.detail	.header
.footer	.footer
.header	.detail
PRINTING	PRINTING
.print	.print
.println	.println
TEXT POSITIONING	TEXT POSITIONING
.center	.tab
.left	.newline
.newline	.center
.right	.left
.tab	.right
	.linestart
	.lineend
PAGE LAYOUT	PAGE LAYOUT
.formfeeds	.pagelength
.leftmargin	.formfeeds
.newpage	.leftmargin
.pagelength	.rightmargin
.rightmargin	.newpage
	.need
DATAFORMATTING	COLUMN CONTROL
.block	.format
.endblock	.position
.format	.width
.position	.block
.underline	.endblock
.width	.top
	.bottom
	.within
	.endwithin
CONDITIONAL	MISCELLANEOUS
.if	.if
	.underline
	.nounderline
	.ulcharacter
	.tformat

than continue to cite a book to which you may not have access, let us now create a report of our own.

First of all, and this is for our own convenience and has no relevance to INGRES at all, we will begin with the title of the report. Since my son was jealous that his sister had obtained a mention in this book and he had been excluded, we will call our sample report by his name:

```
/*  CHRISTOPHER Report  */
```

That heading, as its delimiters, /* and */, indicate, will be ignored by INGRES itself. It is merely a heading for our own convenience. However, the name of the report has to be included in our set-up statements, so our first entry will be:

```
.NAME Christopher
```

We shall, however, be less ambitious than the Date example quoted earlier in that we shall draw data from one table only. Hence the next entry in our report specification must identify the table from which that data is going to be drawn. We can do that by means of the Report Writer statement DATA:

```
.DATA Store
```

We do, though, want to indicate in what sort of order we wish the data to be presented. Not surprisingly, we need the statement .SORT to do so:

```
.SORT store_no, tel_no
```

And that completes our report set-up statements. We next move unto the report layout statements. These will need to begin with report header specifications:

```
.HEADER REPORT
  .NEWLINE2
  .CENTER
  .UNDERLINE
  .PRINT 'Christopher Report'
  .NEWLINE2
```

All the above are used in positioning and printing the title of the report. You can, of course, perform similar operations for the end of each page of the report under the heading of .FOOTER REPORT. Indeed, you will need to for any report exceeding one page in length.

We next move onto the report layout itself. The basic statement here is .DETAIL, under which we specify which particular items of data we want to present in our report:

```
.DETAIL
  .PRINT store_no(c3), tel_no(c14)
  .NEWLINE
```

Obviously there is a great deal more to it than we have indicated here, but you will have gathered the general procedure.

When you have completed your report specification file, you simply tell INGRES to load it into the database—in our case database SOS. During this operation, INGRES will simultaneously check your file and throw it back at you if you have made any semantic mistakes. Assuming, in our current make-believe world, that no mistakes have been made, INGRES will indicate on its Reports Catalog Screen that the file has been accepted. Consequently, you can now produce the report over which you laboured so long.

17.3   Types of report

Let us conclude this chapter very briefly with something that has nothing directly to do with INGRES itself, but that is necessary at least to mention in any chapter on report writing: what types of report exist?

H. D. Clifton, in his *Business Data Systems* (Prentice Hall, 2nd edn 1983) cites seven types:

1. Analyses.
2. Predictions and forecasts.
3. Optimizations.
4. Regular reports.
5. On-demand reports.
6. Exception reports.
7. *Ad hoc* reports.

Robert Behling in his *Computers and Information Processing* only mentions six:

1. Scheduled reports.
2. Exception reports.
3. Enquiry reports.
4. Detailed reports.
5. Summary reports.
6. Archive reports.

As you can see from those two lists, there is as much terminological disparity in the report writing world as there is in the database world. No doubt your own company has its own nomenclature. However, the only thing with which we are primarily concerned here is that, whatever the type of report with which you are concerned may be, INGRES through RBF or Report Writer can provide some very useful short-cuts. It has only been possible to scratch the surface of the topic here because report writing depends so much upon the demands of the company or organization producing the reports.

Neither Date nor Malamud in their books on INGRES present much more than a very superficial survey for exactly the same reason, and though the objectives of all three books are very different, here at least we share a parameter.

18
Application-By-Forms

By this stage you will be well aware that everything in INGRES seems to begin from the INGRES/MENU screen and to be then determined by the varying options and suboptions that can be accessed from that starting-point. Thus everything at which we have so far looked has been conducted within the INGRES evironment. No longer, however, will this be the case. Application-By-Forms (ABF) is a facility to enable one to build something that has an existence of its own, a being that is quite independent of anything within INGRES, even though one does begin from the Menu page.

We have seen that QBF, VIFRED, RBF, and Report Writer are marvellous adjuncts to one's data-processing requirements. None the less, they have their limitations. It does not require a massive amount of imagination to think of a procedure or operation that cannot adequately be handled by the facilities just mentioned. Consequently, what one does is to build the information context that one needs for oneself. This is the function of ABF.

Not surprisingly, to use the word function when talking about ABF is something of an oversimplification. ABF has at least three functions. First of all, while you are constructing the environment you need, you do not need to worry about the location of the differing bits of coding that make up your application. ABF will look after that. As a result, the eventual user has no idea or interest as to where the editing facility that he or she wishes to use is actually placed. ABF will provide that editor whenever it is called upon without the user having to be concerned as to its location. Equally all the source files or object files that the application may require are provided instantly and automatically. This code management system thus allows the user to concentrate upon the logic of the operation without being distracted in any way.

Secondly, when one is building one's application, one can test modules as one builds them, and is thus able to modify one's product dynamically.

Finally, although one is building an application that the in-built facilities of INGRES, its general-purpose user interfaces, cannot handle themselves, you still have the option of using QBF or VIGRAPH (see Chapter 19) or whatever when such a facility is appropriate. Thus ABF acts as a shell within which one can access other subsystems. Indeed, it is possible to use ABF without using ABF at all. I'm sorry, but I could not resist such a apparently paradoxical statement. What it means is that once you have entered ABF you can construct your specific application by using QBF, VIFRED, and/or Report Writer without actually using any of the more sophisticated techniques available under ABF itself. You may, quite validly, wonder why on earth anyone would wish to do this. There are at least two reasons. First of all, when you are using QBF or any of the other general utilities, no one else can operate on the data that you are yourself using with QBF or whatever. If, however, you first enter ABF and then call upon QBF or VIFRED, you do not at the same time lock out anyone else from accessing that same data. Hence entering ABF can be much more considerate and efficient than using the general-purpose user interfaces. Secondly, if you are in ABF, it is easier to access QBF, VIFRED, or whatever than it is if you enter them in the normal way, and, above all, all the operations that you perform in these general-purpose user interfaces are tied together into a unified and consistent application by ABF. This is, after all, what we mean by calling ABF a shell. Many different things can be combined under its umbrella-like canopy.

It is relatively easy to see that, given such qualities, ABF is an excellent means for prototyping. For those new to the word, prototyping implies the rapid building of an application just to see if the general concept is worthwhile. Thus a prototype will have no frills. It will be the basic, unadorned concept. It will doubtless not even have all of its intended functions present. All a prototype is meant to do is indicate whether or not the flow of control within an application is viable. One does not want to spend many hours constructing elaborate menus or coding complex gateways. ABF allows one to see a system in its intermediate stages and thus to make modifications as one goes along. Even when one has completed the intended application, one can still amend it with relative ease. Thus one is relieved of the burden of carrying a mental picture of one's application throughout its genesis. Instead one can see sundry concrete realizations of that application and adapt one's procedure accordingly. ABF is thus a means of programming without having to be concerned with all of the minutiae of such programming.

To summarize then, ABF allows you, the user, to construct your own environment. You define the objects that are needed in the particular application that you require. ABF then goes on to create the program to activate that application. Having done so, you can then place that specially created program where you want it (normally in a central location), and it can then be used by you or any of your staff in exactly the same way that QBF would be used.

So much, then, for introductory material. In order to ease your own navigation through this chapter, I shall split the remaining contents into a number of brief subdivisions, hoping thereby to facilitate further reference on your behalf to specific items. If you are a genuine beginner to INGRES, you will not remember all the data contained in this chapter. I hope, therefore, that the note-form format will aid the task of looking-up such data.

Before doing so, however, I want to indulge in a significant digression. You will already have gathered that ABF is a major extension of the INGRES facilities at which we have so far looked. I have insisted that INGRES is merely a tool. So it is. ABF, however, is a form of creating one's own tool. It therefore places INGRES very much inside the entire systems analysis context, and it is at this context that I want initially to look. This book is not an instruction manual for SQL, but we have needed to pay considerable attention to SQL in order to appreciate the scope of INGRES. This book is not a guide to data communications, but we have needed to look at networks, transmission channels, and so on in order to put distributed INGRES into context. So it is with systems analysis. A company that possesses INGRES will find that its systems analysis procedures will be significantly different from a company that does not, simply because the powers of ABF impinge markedly upon the systems analysis process. We do, therefore, need to give some brief attention to this process.

18.1 The systems analysis life cycle

As H. C. Lucas points out in his *The Analysis, Design and Implementation of Information Systems* (McGraw-Hill, 3rd edn 1985), 'A computer-based information system has a life cycle, just like a living organism or a new project' (p. 81). The reasons for such a life cycle are not difficult to see. One does, after all, need to define all the activities that are going to be carried out during the entire system development project. Naturally, one wants consistency throughout this process; hence a need for agreed stages and terminology. One also wants the ability, throughout the system development, to access its progress and, if necessary, to call a halt to any further development. Thus, when you are developing a system for a company (or for yourself) to facilitate the operations of that company (or you), then it is likely that certain procedures will be essential:

1. You are likely to need a preliminary survey just to get the problem or objective in a meaningful context.
2. Then you are likely to want to carry out some form of feasibility study in

order to see whether or not it will be even worth while embarking on a full-scale systems analysis.

3. Assuming that it is decided that a full systems analysis is needed, you are next going to need to investigate the existing system very fully in order to ascertain its strengths and weaknesses.

4. Having completed your investigation, you can now analyse the system, both the one that exists and the one that is needed, in order to improve upon the one that already exists.

5. Having analysed the situation, you can now design a new one.

6. Having designed a new one, you move on to build and install it.

7. With the new system now installed, all that remains is to maintain it and, from time to time, review its effectiveness.

Such then is a systems analysis life cycle. I have given a basic scenario without any complications. The situation is, of course, a great deal more complex than the logical development pattern that I have laid out above. If you want a fairly straightforward breakdown of some of those complexities, I cannot resist citing an article of mine published in *Computer Education* in February 1990. If you don't, just read on.

From this systems analysis life cycle, it is not difficult to see that ABF could play a very significant part within it. It could certainly help in analysis. Then, through prototyping, it could help in design. Hence, in looking at ABF, we are no longer concerned with handling data; instead, we are concerned with creating the very framework within which data can come to be handled. So let us move on to see the nature of ABF.

18.2   Objects in an ABF application

An ABF application can consist of seven different kinds of entity or object:

1. The application itself is, of course, the overall object within which the remaining six objects are contained. Each application will be labelled with an owner, a creation date, and the further objects that are used within it.

2. A frame is simply a form linked to an associated database entity, i.e. a table or a JoinDef. I know that this might seem like Esperanto, but it is quite simple, particularly since we have already encountered several frames. When you enter QBF, you are met with a frame. In other words, you see in front of you a form and a menu, i.e. a frame. You can, in fact, do a number of things with that form, though the only things that you can do are default operations, i.e. operations that will be performed automatically by INGRES when you select one of the options offered by the menu shown at the top of the screen. As you also know, if you enter VIFRED you are again presented with a form and a menu, only this time you can enter your own parameters, so VIFRED, as we have seen, is more flexible than QBF. None the less, what you are first presented with upon entering

ABF - Applications Catalog

Name	Owner	Short Remark

Place cursor in row and select desired operation from menu.

Create(1) Destroy(2) Edit(3) Rename(4) MoreInfo(5) >

Figure 18.1

VIFRED is a frame. And so it is in ABF. One of the strengths of INGRES is the uniformity of screen construct with which you are presented. It greatly facilitates the learning process.

3. The remaining objects—procedure, form, table, report, graph—are so self-explanatory that it would be insulting to you for us to labour over defining them.

18.3   Starting to build an application

Let us move now into some 'hands-on' experience. We can begin—as always—with the initial Menu screen of INGRES:

INGRES/MENU
Tables Forms JoinDefs Reports Applications Languages Help Quit

Obviously we now want to access Applications. Consequently we move the cursor to Applications and press Return. As a consequence, we will be presented with the top-level frame of ABF, a frame entitled the Applications Catalog (see Fig.18.1). There are more options in the menu—Go, Utilities, Find, Top, Bottom, and so on—but they do not all fit onto the screen. Nor is it a surprise to find the Applications Catalog empty since we have not, as yet, created any applications. However, to do so is almost self-evident. In the example above, you just press the number 1 from the number/function set of keys to the right or, if your menu is at the top of the screen, you do as we have been accustomed to doing, place the cursor on Create and press Return. Whichever version you are working with, you are next presented with the Create an Application screen as shown in Fig. 18.2. The only trouble with having begun the creation of an application is that, when we are presented with the screen, a certain amount of wringing of hands and gnashing of teeth is likely, because it is far from clear as to what to do next. One of the reasons for that, of course, is because we have ignored the

ABF - Create an Application

```
        Name: unspecified              Created: 18-dec-1990 10.56.58
        Owner: g100                    Modified:
        Short Remark:
        Language: SQL Source Directory:
                  DISKB:[OTH, G100]
```

Long Remark:

```
┌──────────────────────────────────────────────────────────────┐
│                                                                │
│                                                                │
│                                                                │
│                                                                │
│                                                                │
│                                                                │
└──────────────────────────────────────────────────────────────┘
```

Create(1)   Forget(PF3)   Help(PF2)

Figure 18.2

remarks made in the systems analysis section. We have not bothered to think through exactly what our application is going to be; instead we merely charged ahead. Let us now do what ought to have been completed earlier: think about the application that we wish to create.

18.4   Creating an application

As you are aware, INGRES is supplied with a variety of help screens, and ABF is no exception to this rule. As I have said before, I do not always find these help screens very helpful, but it is always wise to glance at them when seeking aid. The one given over to guiding us in the creation of an application (see Fig. 18.3) does, despite its two painful grammatical errors, provide some useful information. The menu operations that it proceeds to list on the next page are: Create, Forget, and Help. Obviously, in our situation, you would choose Create, and you would then be presented with the Edit an Application screen. This screen gives you the ability to create procedures, frames, and a fourth-generation language procedure. Hence it would specify, by such means, a new and possibly complex operation for SOS. However, as we have constantly reminded ourselves, and as you may have been only too conscious in working through this text, there are numerous possible variations in INGRES versions and implementations of identical versions. Fortunately, although it will mean our abandonment of SOS, there does exist a sample application which has been prepared for use with the database 'demo'. It would be unnecessarily complicated to work through a specimen application

---

You are looking at the description of an application before it is created.
You can change the description on the form before you create the application.
Application creation follows selection of the Create menu item.

The Name field specifies the name of the application and must be a unique
INGRES name among all the applications in the database. The Language field
specifies the primary language for specifying queries in the application,
and, by default, the query language transaction semantics with which
the application will start up. This can either be QUEL or SQL, but can only
be changed if your installation supports both query languages.

Finally, the Source-Code Directory field specifies the path name of the
directory that is to contain any source specification files for the
application. By default, this will be the directory where you started
ABF. You can change this specification now, or you can change it on the
"ABF-Application Defaults" frame after you have created the application.

The menu operations are:

Figure 18.3

for SOS when there are so many variables that could be different on your
system. However, if your business or your university possesses ABF on its
INGRES system, it will also possess the *INGRES ABF/4GL Reference
Manual*. This manual concludes with an appendix called the ABF Demo
Program, an appendix that shows you how to install, start, delete, and run a
sample application. The reference manual that your office or college possesses will be tailored for the operating system that your system runs on. The
manual resting upon my knee at the moment is for the UNIX and VMS
operating systems, but I do not doubt that there are comparable volumes for
MS-DOS or Pick. Since such a manual is bound to be available to you, it
would be foolish not to make use of it.

There is, however, one condition that the manual itself lays down. 'To
prepare to use the demonstration for the first time,' it states, 'take the
following steps.' The first of those steps is as follows:

1. You should read through and understand the preceding chapters of this
manual.

There are seven preceding chapters, comprising, in all, 500 pages. Hence
Relational Technology certainly do not see mastering ABF as a trivial
exercise. Indeed, the rationale of this chapter is to short-circuit those
500 pages. If you are going to use ABF seriously, you will need to get to
grips with the manual. As manuals go, it is not a bad example, but it is

tedious, not always ideally clear, and completely lacking in any explanation of the purpose and range of ABF. Hence the first three sections of this chapter have been concerned to provide a kind of context within which you can more confidently approach ABF.

19
Further dimensions

Virtually everyone who uses INGRES will need to use VIFRED. The majority of those users are also likely to need to use RBF and/or Report Writer. Hence the existence of Chapters 16 and 17. ABF, however, is an application generator, and consequently is likely only to be used within a company by someone who already possesses a fair amount of data-processing experience. Hence, to some extent, the cursory nature of Chapter 18. None the less, the scope and range of VIFRED, Report Writer, and ABF inevitably suggest further queries and also entail the introduction of further concepts and entities. It is at two of these that I wish to glance in this chapter.

If you glanced at any of the Relational Technology guides to ABF, you will be aware that they refer frequently to INGRES' 4GL. Computing Services at Leicester Polytechnic do in their *Glossary of Computing Terms* point out that 'the main 4GL in use in the Polytechnic is INGRES' and this is also the case elsewhere. Hence it is at fourth-generation languages that I initially look, though only very briefly.

One element that we have totally ignored so far in our consideration of INGRES in particular and relational databases in general is how effective they are in terms of speed of reponse. It is not a great deal of use being in possession of a superbly designed database, if it takes 10 minutes to retrieve any data from that database. Particularly since this part has been concerned with more advanced database operations, it is appropriate to see how a database copes with such complex procedures while still being able to do so within acceptable time limits. Nor is this purely a question of academic curiosity. If one knows something about processing procedures within INGRES, one can frequently do something to speed up the rate at which such procedures are handled. Hence one needs to look at ways of organizing and indexing data so as to facilitate the speed of response that we can achieve with such data.

19.1   4GLs

When I did my M.Sc. in information technology in 1985–6, fourth-generation languages were regarded as the most useful development since the invention of the wheel. They were, we were told, a major step-up from third-generation languages like COBOL or FORTRAN in that a 4GL was entirely non-procedural and could be used with ease by virtually anybody. The validity of the final claim seemed to be a little dubious given the difficulty students on the course had in handling PROLOG, a claimed 4GL.

Since then I have looked from time to time with interest at people's approach to 4GLs. Colin Corder, in his entertaining *Ending the Computer Conspiracy* (McGraw-Hill, 1985), seems to imply that one should be reluctant to swallow all the hype. Elmasri and Navathe in their *Fundamentals of Database Systems* (Benjamin/Cummings, 1989) sourly comment that '4GLs are, however, not the ultimate panacea for data management and for most report generation that they are made out to be.' Robert Behling, in his *Computers and Information Processing* (Kent, 1986) gives them a guarded welcome but remarks that 'they may not be efficient for complex processing'. John Watt, in *Applied Fourth Generation Languages* (John Wiley, 1987) concludes that, out of the 16 claimed 4GLs that he examined, only one really deserved the name. I mentioned above that PROLOG was the 4GL to which I was introduced during my M.Sc. course, yet, interestingly, Ramachandran Bharath, in his *An Introduction to PROLOG*, nowhere ever mentions 4GLs at all. Ellen Thro, in her *The Database Dictionary* (Microtrend, 1990), defines 4GLs as a language *or* set of tools, but fails to expand upon the difference between the two entities, a failure that pervades Watt's entire book. Date, in his *A Guide to INGRES* (Addison-Wesley, 2nd edn 1989) opts out completely by saying that 'we choose not to adopt the 4GL terminology in this book, since it does not seem to have any very precise definition'. So, yet again, we are faced with the terminological inexactitude that seems to be ever-present.

One thing is reasonably clear. Relational databases are often referred to as fourth-generation tools. Hence, any language that one uses to create an application within the context of that relational database must be a 4GL. Indeed, since 4GLs are most commonly used as an interface to a database, it might be simplest to regard them as just one element in a matrix that includes a data dictionary, a report generator, automatic data access, and a screen painter for the rapid reproduction of standard forms. I am sorry that I cannot provide any very firm information upon this topic. The halcyon acclaim with which tutors on my M.Sc. course greeted 4GLs seems to have waned. Instead, 4GLs would appear to have disappeared into some linguistic black hole. I fear that Date is probably right in refusing to discuss them at all, but I did want to give them a mention in case you encountered them in your other reading.

19.2   Storage and access

A database stores data. We have seen that a relational database like INGRES stores data in tables, and that each row within a table is unique. We have also implied that it matters little in what sort of order such data is stored. Since each table is given over to one specific relation, and since each row within that relation is unique and can be joined or compared with any other row in any other table, we have all the facilities we need for the effective handling of such data. Such is indeed the case, but it possibly entails a massive amount of processing. In a database with thousands of rows per table and tens of thousands of possible interrelations, even a rapid processor can take a considerable amount of time to process such queries. Let us then look more closely at relational database organization.

There are three main ways of organizing data within tables. The one that INGRES normally, by default, uses is called the heap method. This is simplicity itself. If you add a new row to your Suppliers table, that row is simply added on to the end of the existing table. Hence your resulting table will be 'organized' quite simply by the order in which rows were inputted. If you wanted to find out what suppliers existed in Yorkshire, the DBMS would have to make a sequential search through the entire table in order to retrieve the relevant rows. In a database as small as our existing SOS database, this provides no problem, but we have been aware for some time that our own database is hardly representative of typical real-world constructs. The Demo database provided by INGRES is fuller and more complex than our own SOS one, but even so is tiny in comparison with those built up by most organizations. There are real virtues to the heap mode of organization. It is, for instance, extremely easy and rapid to make additions to the table. Everything else, however, is likely to be inordinately time consuming. If one needs to extract a single row from a table, a sequential search is going to be needed in order to find that row. Hence retrieval, alteration, and deletion could well be laborious processes. It would, therefore, be convenient if location of the required data could be accomplished in single action instead of the numerous accesses required with heap organization. This can be done by organizing the data in a hash structure. Meaningless though this, at the moment, sounds, it is not difficult to understand the principle of hash organization. It entails taking the primary key of a row, converting it (if necessary) to a numerical value, and then passing the number through an algorithm that returns a value—known as the hash key—representing the physical position of that row on the disk. The disk head can then go immediately to the disk position indicated and retrieve the data needed. Thus one access is needed instead of possibly hundreds.

While hashing sounds a wonderful technique—and one that can be handled by INGRES—there are handicaps. No one has yet devised a hashing algorithm that can guarantee to generate unique hash keys. Consequently the same key might relate to two or more different rows of data. There are, of course, methods of resolving such collisions, but they understandably increase the expense of the operation. 'Open addressing', 'rehashing', 'overflow tables', or whatever technique is employed to avoid collisions may be effective enough, but they increase the cost of the software management.

An alternative to hash organization is to use some form of index mechanism. This not only provides direct access to individual rows, but also provides, unlike hashing, sequential access to sets of rows. The objective is to hold as much of the index as possible in main memory so as to provide fast access to that index and the consequent once-only disk access to obtain the necessary data. The simplest that INGRES provides is the indexed sequential access method (ISAM), and Malamud provides quite a clear explanation of that in the fifth chapter of his book. The two most effective forms of indexing, however, are known respectively as B-tree and B+-tree. The latter is more effective if you are likely to require substantial sequential processing, though INGRES only allows the creation of B-trees. They both, however, have the inevitable disadvantage in that they both take up a great deal of room. Both being what are known as multi-level balanced indexes, one can find, in a fully indexed database, that the indexes take up more space than the database itself. This, of course, is expensive. There is not a lot of point in describing these two types of index here. Most books on database systems will do so— see Chapter 5 of Elizabeth Oxborrow, *Databases and Database Systems* (Chartwell-Bratt, 2nd edn 1989) or Chapter 5 of Elmasri and Navathe, *Fundamentals of Database Systems* (Benjamin/Cummings, 1989), for instance—and the topic is not one that is directly relevant to our purposes. What is relevant is that INGRES allows one to transform a table organized in the heap procedure into one that is hashed or converted to a B-tree. This can be a very important facility, since it may speed up the processing rate very considerably.

In processing a query within a relational database, however, it is not simply data storage and/or indexing that is significant. Most queries in a company or a university assignment are going to entail accessing more than one table. Imagine, for instance, that SOS headquarters want to know which products have been returned to stores as being defective, which suppliers delivered those defective products, and how long it took before an adequate replacement was provided. We did not, of course, build all the necessary tables for answering such a query, but the real SOS—if it existed—would need tables from which such a query could be answered. It is obvious too that such a query would require the examination of very many rows of data from at least three different tables, and the combination of that data into a meaningful answer. The processing load is massive. Even if the database is superbly stored and indexed, there are other functions that have to be performed:

1. The query itself has to be checked in order to ensure that its syntax is correct.
2. The query then has to be broken down into subqueries, identifying each specific stage necessary for the successful execution of that query.
3. Almost invariably there will be a number of different ways in which a query can be processed, so some evaluation process has to be conducted in order to discover which of those ways is the most effective and economic.
4. Finally, the query has to be executed.

You the user can decide upon the storage structure that you want your database to adopt. It is not always an easy decision to make. INGRES, however, provides what I believe to be a unique facility. It allows you to see the path of access chosen by the query optimizer. Nor need this merely satisfy intellectual curiosity. If a query is very slow in its execution, a glance at the Query Execution Plan can sometimes reveal why. The situation can then, perhaps, be improved by constructing another index upon another field within a table. Query execution depends upon a very considerable number of factors, but INGRES is excellent in the ways it provides for the user to maximize its potential to the very best extent.

And so we end. There is a great deal more to INGRES in particular and to relational databases in general than has been covered here, but I do believe that the basics of relational database management have been discussed. Some of the things omitted are mentioned in the final section, and, because of the varying versions of INGRES, my scenario will not always have been the most appropriate one for your particular circumstances. Despite such factors, however, the essentials have, at least, been introduced. Try the test on the next page to see how fully you have managed to absorb this glance at some of the more advanced facilities of INGRES.

Questions on Part Four

1. Distinguish between trim and field when using VIFRED.
2. What do you do when you toggle?
3. Which four modes exist within RBF for presenting data in a report?
4. What sort of instructions are contained within a report specification?
5. What is a feasibility study?
6. Define a frame.
7. What do the acronyms VIFRED, RBF, and ABF stand for?
8. Distinguish between a hashed table and a B-tree table.
9. Why can it be useful to trace the query optimization path?
10. It would aid query processing to have all tables in a database fully indexed. What drawback would such a policy have?

Answers

1. Trim is concerned with the appearance and positioning of text on a form, whereas a field is the actual area allowed for the entry of that text.
2. You alternate between one context and another. Thus you might toggle between inserting text and editing text.
3. Default, block, wrap, column.
4. All the instructions necessary for the layout of your report: margin setting, logo positioning, page numbering, heading and footing conventions, etc.
5. A survey carried out to see whether or not it is worth while computerizing a particular operation or series of operations.
6. A frame is a screen presentation of a form and an associated menu from which you can choose a number of options for handling that form.
7. Visual-Forms-Editor, Report-By-Forms, Application-By-Forms.

8. The former takes the key value for a row and performs a mathematical operation upon that value so as to locate more quickly the row itself. A B-tree structure uses an index to locate the appropriate data.
9. So that we can possibly identify the cause or causes of slow processing.
10. We would end up with the indexes being bigger than the database itself, and with the consequent expense of massive software storage.

PART FIVE

Conclusion

20
Further exploration

As you will have noticed, this chapter is the first in the part entitled 'Conclusion'. It seems somewhat odd to begin a concluding part with a chapter called 'Further Exploration'. When I was a pupil at school I seem to recall imbibing the dictum that any piece of writing should consist of three things:

1. An 'introduction' explaining what you were about to do.
2. A 'body' that went on to do it.
3. A 'conclusion' that triumphantly announced that one had now done that which you had promised in the first place.

This still seems to me to provide a perfectly adequate overall structure. I am, however, going to ignore it. The conclusion to this book will not recap the material of the preceding chapters. Those chapters were, after all, so brief as to mean that any summary would have to be in telegraphese. Furthermore, if you have read those chapters, you will know what they have been about anyway, and will hardly be enchanted by my telling you all over again. Instead, this concluding chapter attempts to indicate the nature of some of the things that this book has not been concerned with. It has been insisted upon throughout this slim volume that the object of the exercise has been to provide an introduction to INGRES, an introduction that tries neither to bore nor to baffle. Obviously only you can judge how far it has succeeded or failed in that respect. In attempting, however, to be genuinely introductory, it has been inevitable that an enormous quantity of material has either been superficially covered or omitted entirely. If this book has whetted your appetite for INGRES, if you now feel moderately confident with the basics of handling a relational database, then it is likely that you would like to progress a little further. It may even be that the nature of your work or your undergraduate studies demands that you progress further. Consequently it seems only courteous to indicate some of the directions in which you could proceed. Hence this conclusion is not a conclusion at all; it is a series of signposts to further exploration. And that, surely, is what an introductory book should provide. Having shown you how to climb the foothills, it needs then to show you the peaks remaining. Clearly this conclusion will make no attempt to climb those peaks. It will not even provide you with the tools for so doing. All it will do is to provide a map showing exactly where those peaks are.

Before showing even the first peak, however, it is wise to indulge in a necessary warning. INGRES, as you know, is a relational database. It has been stated in this book that relational databases are superior to hierarchical, network, or inverted list databases. So they are. It has, however, been assumed that relational databases are the ultimate answer to every maiden's prayer (or, at least, to every DBA's requirements). A moment's thought will suggest that such a view is bound to be naïve. The astonishing thing about computer science has been the rate of its development. You do not have to be massively aged to remember a world that had no computers. You do not even have to be middle-aged to remember a world where a home computer came with a tape-recorder and a tiny amount of memory. Hence, while relational databases may be the 'state of the art' at the moment, the entire brief history of information technology tells us that their reign is unlikely to be long. Indeed, the writing is already on the wall.

As you know, every piece of data within a relational database is part of a table, a static two-dimensional object. One of the supreme advantages of a relational database is that any piece of data in any one of the tables within that database can be accessed from any other point within the database. As a result, reports, financial data, and textual data can all be manipulated with ease. But there are, none the less, considerable limitations. If you want to compare data x with data y, they both have to belong to the same genus. You cannot compare a number with a text. Still less can you compare a text with a graphical image or a number with an oral message. Yet this is precisely what you might wish to do. You might, for instance, have a set of numbers representing the components of a circuit. You may also have a diagram of that same circuit. Naturally you will wish to compare the two. To handle this sort of request, 'object-oriented databases' have been devised. In such a database, the relationships between data items of any type are not based on comparing values but upon comparing 'identities'. Thus our circuit diagram and our component numbers will share the same identity, and the object-oriented database will move from one object with a particular identity to another object with the same identity.

Expressed as I have just expressed it, the whole thing sounds relatively straightforward. It isn't. Because the objects sharing the same identity can be objects with very different natures, each object has to carry packaged with it a code for manipulating that object. You cannot draw an image on the screen in the same way as you would sort a list of numbers. You cannot, in a relational database, ask the database to find all products that contain Part Number 0183 and then to draw upon the screen each of those products. You have to address two tables, one containing Part Numbers and the other containing pictorial facilities. The Part Numbers table cannot understand the command to draw. The Products table cannot understand the command to select Part Number 0183. Hence each table has to have built into it a sort of SQL appropriate to the type of table that it is.

There can be little doubt that future databases will need to support new types of data such as video and sound. Already proponents of object-oriented databases claim that they can do so. Equally, those within the relational camp claim that it can cope superbly by grafting object-oriented features to the front-ends of relational packages. Whichever, if either, turns out to be right, changes are inevitable within the database field.

I am aware that it is a little discomforting to be nearing the end of a book on one particular relational database and then to be told that relational databases may soon be obsolete. There is no need to worry. When I was doing my own M.Sc. in information technology, we were told in ringing tones that COBOL was dead. 4GLs had ensured that no longer would any programs be written in COBOL. Very shortly, COBOL programmers would disappear as the dinosaur had done. Seven years after hearing this confident statement, I note that COBOL is still the most widely used computer language and that COBOL programmers are still being sought with avidity. The same will be true for relational databases. INGRES is not going to disappear in the forseeable future.

Assuming, then, that my prophecy is correct, let us turn to some of the INGRES applications and aspects that we have ignored. I want to look at three: VIGRAPH, views, and security. None of these will mean very much to you now, and you will not learn a great deal about them in the pages that follow, but they are all important aspects of INGRES, aspects of which you at least need to be aware, and possibly aspects in which your work or studies will demand some competence. Hence I shall take each in turn and try to indicate their nature and their importance.

20.1 VIGRAPH

This facility within INGRES will not take long to describe because it is in nature just like the Query-by-Forms and Report-by-Forms facilities that we have already encountered. You will recall that QBF enables you to browse through data interactively. In other words, you can enter, retrieve, and update the data concerned. RBF, you will also recall, allows you to define reports on data. In exactly the same way, VIGRAPH allows you to define graphs by using the data in the database. It is, consequently, of very

considerable utility. You have the data of sales in one of your tables. It is
clearly more meaningful if you can persuade that data to manifest itself in
the form of a graph or a pie-chart. I have never been convinced that a picture
is always worth a thousand words, but there can be no denying the immediacy
of a graph showing sales or a pie-chart showing departmental expenditure.
The presentation of data in such a fashion makes instant comprehension
easy. Hence it also follows that no introduction to INGRES could fail to
devote an early chapter to VIGRAPH. The fact that this introduction to
INGRES has failed to do anything of the kind stems from purely pragmatic
reasons. Part of the audience for whom this book is intended includes
university and polytechnic students. It is, alas, normal for such students to be
presented with an INGRES that has been shorn of VIGRAPH. Consequently
it did seem pointless to devote an entire chapter to a facility that would be,
in all likelihood, unobtainable by a large section of my readership.

None the less, VIGRAPH is very useful. Students are likely to encounter
it when they begin working within an INGRES environment and, of course,
many readers already at work in such a context will have been irritated by
my failure to mention the facility before. As so often, the question is a
question of cost. To use VIGRAPH, you need to have a terminal capable of
handling graphics. The other subsystems like QBF and RBF can run on any
sort of terminal, including the slow, cheap and out-of-date ones normally
found in our centres of academic excellence.

VIGRAPH has a number of in-built facilities. You can display the graph
with accompanying text. You can have your graph displayed in colour. You
can create graphs, pie-charts, or histograms. You can have sections of your
display filled in with what are known as hatch patterns, i.e. a sort of shading.
This can be particularly useful if you are having to display on a monochrome
monitor. And finally, you can even, when editing a graph, legislate as to
how much of the original graph needs to be redrawn. This can be useful
because, if you want to keep quite a lot of the original graph untouched,
telling INGRES that this is the case saves VIGRAPH the trouble of
redrawing the whole thing from stratch, and thus saves a considerable
amount of time.

Clearly I cannot here give detailed instructions for using VIGRAPH. All
that you have to do is to map (or relate) a graph to the relevant table in the
database. Thus you would specify the vertical and horizontal axes that you
needed to use. Hence, if you were wanting to compare various advertising
campaigns that SOS had used over the last couple of years, one axis would
be the advertising campaign, while the other axis could be the budgets
consumed by the respective campaigns. Once you have done that, all that
remains is to customize your preferred graphical representation: graph, pie-
chart, histogram, bar chart, and so on. Within your customization, you would
select sizes, colours, fonts, and the placement of the entities upon the screen.
There is considerable flexibility available, and, because of that, VIGRAPH

represents quite a sophisticated mode of examining data. None the less, no one who is already comfortable with QBF and RBF need have any fears about using VIGRAPH. Furthermore, once you have created your graphs, the members of your department can then use them without their needing to know anything about programming or, for that matter, about computers. Indeed, in creating the graphs in the first place, one does not need to know anything about programming and remarkably little about computers. It is one of the beauties of a relational database that they can virtually be approached as self-contained entities. You can be an expert DBA without knowing anything about systems design, relational calculus, binary arithmetic, or Boolean algebra.

And that is VIGRAPH. Its basic usage has to be in advertising, because there is no better way of distorting the truth than by showing a pretty chart with carefully chosen axes. Peter Laurie in his *Databases* (1985, pp. 79–81), takes an even more jaundiced view of graphs than I do. His acid comments need, however, to be taken in proportion. If you have a boss to impress, a client to be convinced, or even a tutor to please, using VIGRAPH can be invaluable. Should you, by careful selection of your axes, make the sales figures look better than they are or the product you are selling more wonderful than it really is, then the matter is one for you and your conscience. So far as I know, not even INGRES can cope with moral gradations.

20.2   Views

This subsection will also present no difficulties. Indeed, it has been with some difficulty that I have refrained from mentioning views up to this point. If you know what a table is (and if you don't by this point, I would suggest you transferred your attentions to brain surgery, bee-keeping, or journalism), then you know what a view is. A view is a table. To be fully accurate, a view is a virtual table. You may recall that computer scientists use the word 'virtual' in the same way that other people use the words 'mythical', 'imaginary', or 'insubstantial'. Let me explain.

A table, as you know, consists of a series of rows and columns. No row is ever exactly the same as any other row. However, although the user of a database is only interested in the rows and columns that can be presented upon the screen, edited, deleted, selected, or printed, that table does have a physical existence in the database. It is of no concern to the user as to exactly where that particular table is stored on the disk. That is, after all, why one uses a DBMS so that the tables one wishes to examine or modify can be presented to one without one having to specify that the tables in question can be found in disk 4, row 3, sector 7. None the less, that is the reality of the situation. Somewhere on a disk there physically resides the particular table that you want, inertly comprising a series of digital inputs. A view, however, is a table that does not physically exist. It is, instead, a table that you, the user, define for purposes of your own from an already existing table. You might, for instance, want to see a staff list of the SOS store in Reading. The information is contained in the Emp_Store table, but you have no desire to wade through the entire table in order to extract your information. Instead you create a view. The name that you give to your view must not be the same name as that possessed by any existing table. In the instance just mentioned, you would simply enter the command

CREATE VIEW READING

Then, after the view name, you simply have to indicate which of the columns or domains you wish to access. For a staff list of the Reading store you only need Store_No, Name, and Role.

CREATE VIEW READING
AS SELECT store_no, name, role

You will, of course, have noted the use of the command words AS SELECT for this operation. Next you need to indicate from which table or tables the required information has to be drawn:

CREATE VIEW READING
AS SELECT store_no, name, role
FROM emp_store

Last of all you need to indicate that it is only the Reading store that you require. The resulting view will read as follows:

CREATE VIEW READING
AS SELECT store_no, name, role
FROM emp_store
WHERE store_no = 'S8';

This did not really need spelling out; our earlier exploration of SQL makes the creation of a view almost automatic, apart from the use of the keyword AS.

Since creating a view is so straightforward, learning to do so has not advanced our understanding of INGRES one iota. The true utility of views may not, however, be totally apparent. To begin with, views require very little storage space. Since the data that you want to see in a view is already stored in an existing table, the view does not have to store any data at all. All that needs to be stored in the Views Catalog is the name and definition of the view itself. As a consequence, you can create views that you are likely to use quite frequently without using more than marginal amounts of memory. Alternatively, if you want members of your department to have access to some data from a table but not access to it all, a convenient way of ensuring this is to create a view specifically for those members of the department. Furthermore, since a view can be created incorporating domains from more than one table, a view can be a quick and economic method of combining data.

Although a view looks like a table and is created in a way very similar to the creation of a table, it does have some limitations that are not possessed by tables. The most important of those limitations concern its abilities to update. Thus you can only update a view if it has been derived from only one table. Nor, when selecting the columns that you require for your view, can you use DISTINCT. In fact, though we are not concerned with the matter here, you cannot update a view that, in its creation, has used a function or any of the following command words:

DISTINCT GROUP BY HAVING ORDER BY UNION

Nor can you perform an update if the WHERE clause itself contains a correlated subquery. These, however, are areas outside our remit.

There is not much more to say regarding views. Date has a useful section on them in his *Guide to INGRES* (though he uses QUEL vocabulary rather than SQL) and Malamud devotes about four pages to them, though the four pages are divided into two small sections separated by a hundred pages. Elizabeth Lynch has an excellent chapter on creating and using views in her *Understanding SQL*. As always, though, the best way to find out about views is to play with INGRES itself and learn from experience.

20.3 Security

The question of security, unlike VIGRAPH or views, has been referred to a number of times in this book, but never at any length and never with it as the centre of attention. In one sense, however, it is the most important of all questions that INGRES or any other database system can face. As was pointed out earlier, a database has the potential disadvantage of the fact that it places all your eggs in one basket. If the database breaks down, all productive work can cease at once. If someone penetrates your database safeguards, all the secrets of your company are open to outsiders. Hence security is vital from two aspects: random acts of God such as power failures or human idiocy, and deliberate malice or theft. Hence, to be fully effective, INGRES must provide measures, or allow you to provide measures, for coping with these problems.

Let us begin by some clarification at a purely logical level. It is self-evident that the best form of security is prevention. If acts of God are not allowed to interfere or if computer hackers simply cannot break into your system, then you have no problems to solve or disasters to recover from. If, however, despite your preventive measures, some crisis does occur, then you need effective means of detecting exactly what the nature of the crisis is. This is not always as easy as you might at first assume. Then, having detected the problem, you will need ways of recovering from the crisis and resuming business as rapidly as possible. Finally, of course, should recovery be impossible, you will need something to assuage your grief—in other words, insurance. Let us briefly glance at all of these elements.

Since prevention is clearly the ideal state, I shall spell out some measures that strike me as being imperative. I have frequently used words in this book in a somewhat flippant mode—why on earth get solemn over a relational database?—but my preceding sentence was meant. I am going to spell out measures that are *imperative*. They are all of them tedious. For the vast majority of the times you use them, they will have no relevance at all. The whole thing is a time-consuming and boring hindrance. But it must be done. Your data, or your company's data, is valuable. If you allow that data to be destroyed or stolen when you could have prevented it, then you do not deserve the responsible position that you hold or the degree that you are trying to gain. No systems are ever totally secure, but we, as computer users, *must* make our system as secure as we possibly can.

First of all, data can be destroyed or corrupted entirely by accident. I recall when I was the software manager of a company that produced packages for stockbrokers. One day a client rang me up and asked me if there were any techniques for recovering data that had been deleted. I explained that there were indeed such techniques, and asked him why he needed to know. He told me that during that morning, an employee had deleted the entire contents of the company hard disk. In other words, every piece of data that the company possessed, and every procedure, safeguard, and validation that had been built into that data had been destroyed in a few seconds of carelessness. It does not just happen to others; it could happen to you. So, what does one do to safeguard against human carelessness?

The first thing that one can do is to make a copy of *everything* that you create or use. Every time that I wrote a section of this book, I made a copy of it. It would have been no major loss to Western civilization if the entire text had been destroyed upon my typing the very last sentence—but it would have irritated me a great deal. In fact, and I am near the end now, nothing untoward ever happened, so I wasted both time and disks in keeping those copies. I have, however, heard students apologizing for work being late: 'I'm afraid there was a crash, sir.' 'But presumably you had a copy,' came the reply. The answer was invariably 'No'. As the months go by, and you have suffered no acts of God, you will get very tired of copying everything. It wastes time and is very boring. But few professionals will have very much sympathy for you if you lose data irretrievably because you could not be bothered to keep a copy. Of course, in most business contexts, the computer operations department makes copies of everything automatically on a daily basis, often to tape, when all the staff have gone home to have dinner and watch television. It is only on an individual level that making copies is so tiresome, which is why it is so often neglected.

It is not only the loss of data that can be crippling. Obviously if the data put into the system is not correct in the first place, chaos can and normally does ensue. Yet again, though, there is a great deal that can be done to prevent this happening. If a member of your department needs to enter a date into the system, you can impose range checks so that they do not and cannot enter 31 February or 3 March 199. We have already encountered such checks in the validation check that we imposed on Store Number. It is clearly sensible to impose such restraints wherever they can be so imposed. Such checks guard against both carelessness and malice. Date, in the second volume of his *Introduction to Database Systems* (Addison-Wesley, 1983) refers specifically to INGRES in this context, though his references are widely spaced (pp. 66–8 and 155–6) because one occurs in his chapter on integrity and the second in his chapter on security. The two words are far from synonymous. Integrity refers to the means of ensuring that a database is consistent. It is not helpful if, in one file, Sask Yarduit is given his correct National Insurance Number, while in another file, exactly the same number is attributed to Vaunt Cobol. Both integrity and security are therefore concerned with ensuring that the database remains viable. Hence they both have to be one of the major concerns of the DBA. Data is the life-blood of an organization (or a person). All possible means have to be taken to ensure its validity and its security.

One common practice is to ensure that no one is able to access a table or tables unless they input a password into the system. Each person's password is secret. Hence Jack Hopkins can only see the Purchases table if he puts in the password 'Ararat', Colin Spence can only see the Stores table if he submits the password 'Tristan', and so on. In this way, user access can be controlled at many levels. You can arrange for a user to read a table but not to amend or add to that table in any way. You can arrange for a user to see a table but to limit the number of rows that he can consult within that table. You can permit a user to see a table, but ensure that certain domains are missing from the table that he sees. Thus the password not only safeguards any sort of access at all, but can also determine the nature of the access permitted.

Of course, it is perfectly possible for a hacker to by-pass or overcome all such security checks. He or she can, indeed, trick the computer into believing that he or she is the DBMS itself. Even so, all is not lost. If all the data fed into the database is encrypted, the hacker will only discover meaningless entries. You have, in the Suppliers table the following entry:

Sp12   Carton Ltd   Lowood,   BIRMINGHAM B11 9OP   021-385-2274

When our hacker penetrates the system, all he sees is the following:

1916L   030118201514   1215231515040209181309140708011302KI1516
£BACHEBBGD

Of course, if your code was as naïvely simple as the one I have employed above, it would not take very long for your hacker to break it, but you understand the principle. A valid user, of course, will use a 'decrypt' password whenever he or she wants to access data. Hence even the skilful hacker can be denied.

Thus, as you can see, there are a number of techniques that can be employed in order to make your data secure. If you only employ one, you will reduce the chances of a breach. If you employ two, you will diminish the risk geometrically. If you employ three, then it will be a very determined hacker (and a very lucky one) who really succeeds in penetrating your system. Total security cannot be given, but any self-respecting DBA will ensure that neither malice nor accident are given any unnecessary opportunities.

Even so, before we leave the topic of security, one further factor needs to be mentioned. Since the corruption or deletion of data most commonly occurs by accident, one major preventative action that can be taken lies in the training of staff. If staff are well trained, if the importance of data is ever-present in their minds, then far fewer mistakes will be made. The computer is a superb tool; it is human beings who limit its effectiveness. Train the human beings concerned to do the rigorous self-checking that they need to do, and the efficiency of your company will increase fivefold.

Despite all the safeguards, however, corruption or loss will occur. It may not be easy to discover this. A simple misspelling or the transposition of two numbers is easy to do. The computer system then swallows your error, and, since you did not know that you had made an error, it can take months for it to be discovered. Let us, then, set down in a more ordered fashion some of the measures that can be taken to safeguard even against this. Such measures tend to be known as systems controls because they are a part of the routine processing operations. They may, in fact, have been built into the very hardware that you are using, or they may be an integral element of the control programs of your DBMS. Such systems controls fall into a number of possible categories:

- *Batch controls* The computer will keep a record of the number of transactions going into the computer. It will then add up the number of processed results. Clearly the two totals should tally. If they do not, you are immediately aware that something has gone wrong.
- *Editing* We have already mentioned this facility. It is simply concerned with checking the reasonableness of the data submitted to it. Hence it can detect if a date is entered as 31 February. Again, if accounts are being debited and credited, there can be (and should be) checks instituted between the two tables being accessed to ensure that the transactions tally.
- *Parity checks* This is a simple way of helping to ensure that your data is kept in an accurate state. You impose the rule that every piece of data

submitted to your system must have an even number of positively charged bits. Hence your final bit in a byte will be the parity bit. If the data that you have submitted is, let us imagine, 1001100, then the number of positive bits is an odd number (3). The parity bit will consequently be 1. If the data submitted is 1110111, then the parity bit will be 0. Such a system enables you to detect errors in transmitted data.

- *Passwords*   If someone makes multiple attempts to input a password, then the system should lock them out. Two attempts should, perhaps, be the maximum that the system allows.
- *Encryption*   Obviously this too is a system facility.

If, then, you employ all the systems controls listed above, are rigorous in the copying of all data, and train your staff to be careful and considerate computer users, you have done all that can realistically be done.

If the worst comes to the worst and you have lost data that results in your company being closed down or in you yourself not gaining the degree that you feel you deserve, then one commiserates. You can, however, insure against such calamities. It costs money, but if the potential damage is severe enough, then it will be money sensibly spent.

Now do excuse me while I make a copy of this chapter.

21
Benediction

You are now at the end of this book. I have tediously insisted every few pages that there is a great deal more to learn if you ever want to become a black belt in INGRES handling. Most of us, however, don't. All we want is enough understanding and enough knowledge to pass our exams, cope with our work, or impress our boss. This is what I have tried to provide. If you have bought this book, you will be greatly irritated if I haven't. The time is too late for regrets on your part or apologies on mine. I enjoyed writing the book, particularly since two of the jobs I had while so doing were so bizarre as to make *Black Adder* appear normal in comparison. Hence the book became my slender grasp upon reality. I hope that it has helped you face the reality of relational databases in general and INGRES in particular.

You will have noticed that most of the chapters in this book are extremely brief. This was deliberate. Few people have the time really to concentrate on lengthy screeds. Undergraduates have essays to complete by noon tomorrow, and just want a quick breakdown of VIFRED so that they can give the impression of actually knowing what they are writing about.

Business men have no chance to read books at work; hence something where they can manage a whole chapter between Clapham Junction and Victoria is ideal. Consequently, it is entirely fitting that this concluding chapter, with its monastic title of blessing, should be brief as well. Indeed, it has a special need to be brief, since it has, of substance, very little indeed to impart. So let me impart it.

If you have righteously worked your way through this book, doing everything that I told you to do in exactly the way in which I suggested it, the odds are overwhelmingly in favour of your having encountered problems. Possibly this stemmed from my having misinformed you or my not expressing myself with sufficient clarity. More probably (or at least, I hope it is more probable), it stemmed from the variety of systems and the differing implementations of those systems that one can encounter. I devoutly hope that there were very few of these occasions, and that you were able to resolve them, but I fear that a total absence of them is far too much to hope for.

I want, then, to conclude this book with some sort of consolatory message for all those who did encounter problems from time to time. I can do so by quoting the opening words of Colin Corder's entertaining book, *Ending the Computer Conspiracy* (McGraw-Hill, 1985):

> A survey on the use of computers carried out by the British Institute of Management in 1971 concluded with the following advice:
>
>> stop looking at computers and start looking at your business—don't regard the computer as a panacea for the problems of your organisation.
>
> A review of a more recent survey conducted in 1984 on the use of information technology by management concluded:
>
>> for those upon whom the light does not break information technology will allow bad managers to make bad decisions, more quickly and in greater numbers.

Colin Corder began his book with those words; I virtually end mine with them. A DBMS, even one as good as INGRES, is only a tool. You will use that tool wisely or foolishly. I hope that I have helped you to use the tool correctly. Only you can provide the wisdom.

It does, however, seem appropriate in a concluding chapter to return to what is, after all, the central entity of the entire enterprise: a database. Let us, then, end by looking, with our increased knowledge and understanding, as to what capabilities an ideal DBMS should possess.

First of all, in any realistic set-up, a database is going to be called upon by a variety of users for a variety of purposes. A DBMS has, therefore, to allow the simultaneous sharing of data. Given that this is the case, the DBMS has therefore got to handle potential problems associated with the updating of data, so that two concurrent updates do not clash with each other.

Secondly, a DBMS must ensure that the data that it holds maintains its integrity. Thus, for instance, in our tiny SOS database, it must ensure that there is no such thing as a Store Number P972 or a manager earning £7300 p.a.

A DBMS also needs to restrict access to the database, so that unauthorized personnel cannot obtain information to which they have no right. Indeed, there is likely to be a need for levels of authorization so that staff can see sections of a database but be denied other sections.

A database needs to have a very controlled and circumscribed redundancy. Since storing the same data multiple times leads to many problems—wastage of space, duplication of effort, potential inconsistency—a database worthy of the name needs to integrate the views of different users in the most efficient manner possible.

As we have seen, a database is concerned with relationships. The ability of a DBMS to process complex interrelations is clearly an important index of its utility.

Finally, databases crash, through either a hardware or software failure. A DBMS must provide facilities for recovering from such crashes.

Such, then, are the prime criteria by which to evaluate a DBMS. Clearly there are other factors that may also be regarded as significant—flexibility, rapidity of execution, user-friendliness, and so on—but the six factors listed above do seem to be the crucial ones. You will by now be aware that INGRES can fulfil each one of those criteria. Furthermore, you are now in a position to use INGRES so that its manifold facilities are sensibly employed. From that base, you should be able to move on, if you need to, and extend your knowledge and understanding of INGRES, or, alternatively, transfer your understanding to any other relational database with a much shorter learning curve than would otherwise have been needed.

Glossary

While the selection and formulation of the definitions that follow are clearly my own responsibility, I would like to acknowledge the help that I gained in compiling this glossary from the following:

Glossary of Computing Terms, produced by Computing Services of Leicester Polytechnic.

Glossary provided at the end of Carl Malamud, *INGRES: Tools for Building an Information Architecture* (Van Nostrand Reinhold, 1989).

'Appendix B, Glossary of Terms' towards the end of Richard C. Parkinson, *Data Analysis: The Key to Data Base Design* (QED Information Sciences, 1982).

Ellen Thro, *The Database Dictionary* (Microtrend, 1990).

Equally importantly, perhaps, has been the guidance provided by Humpty Dumpty:

> When I use a word, Humpty Dumpty said, in rather a scornful tone, it means just what I choose it to mean—neither more nor less.
>
> Lewis Carroll, *Alice Through the Looking Glass*

ABF Application-By-Forms, an environment within INGRES that allows the development of personal applications.

access to gain entry into a place or to gain the ability to use something. Thus, in computer jargon, one says that one can access the memory when one has the ability to see what is in the computer's memory, or that one can access the system when one has the ability to gain entry into a computer system.

access method   the way in which the computer system retrieves (or stores) an item of data. The method itself will be determined by an algorithm.

acronym   a word made up of the initial letters of other words. Computer science is littered with acronyms like ROM (read only memory), WAN (wide area network) and BIOS (basic input/output system).

Ada   a computer language developed in the late 1970s for the use of the US Department of Defense.

address   each item of data within a computer's memory has an address, in that it occupies a particular location. The word can also be used as a verb—'to address memory'—when its meaning is almost the same as 'access'.

ad hoc   a Latin phrase that is invariably used within computing circles to indicate that something has happened or been developed that was not previously planned. Hence 'Most of our work here is *ad hoc*' is merely a classical way of saying that we never plan anything here.

AI   see artificial intelligence.

algorithm   the formally set out procedure for solving a problem. Thus, if you want to sort a list of names into alphabetical order, you are going to need an algorithm that logically, and economically, details the distinct steps the computer is going to have to perform in order to accomplish the desired result.

analogue data   while digital data comes in separate and distinct items, analogue data is a continuous sequence of constantly variable data.

AND   a logical operator that connects two propositions and produces a new proposition as a result of the truth or falsity of the original pair. Thus, if the two original propositions were both true, then the new proposition is also true, but if either of the original propositions were false, then the new one is also false.

anomalies   when data within a database is not consistent, the database is said to display anomalies.

ANSI   an acronym standing for American National Standards Institute, an organization that establishes standards for computer languages and so on in an attempt to secure a degree of compatability.

append   a query language command to add an item of data to a database, file, or record.

application   a program, or even series of programs, that allows the user to perform some basic function on a computer. Thus a word processor or a spreadsheet are both applications.

application generator   a program used to generate other applications. Thus ABF is an application generator.

architecture   normally this term refers to the way in which the central processing unit (CPU) of a computer is organized. Thus, if you are talking about the architecture of a computer, you are likely to be talking about how its arithmetic/logic unit is organized, how its registers are arranged, and how it times the various operations for which it is responsible. However, the term is also used in reference to a network of computers; one can have a star architecture or a bus architecture.

array an ordered collection of variables of a similar type.

artificial intelligence the ability of computers to perform certain activities so as to give the impression that they are thinking in just the same way as humans think.

ASCII an acronym for American Standard Code for Information Exchange, a code used in most small computers and their networks. It comprises 128 letters, numbers, punctuation marks, and control characters, each consisting of either seven bits (e.g. P = 1010000) and possibly an eighth as a parity bit, or as an eight-bit code (e.g. P = 110100000) known as ASCII-8.

assembler translates a program written in assembly language into machine code. The translation is done line by line.

assembly language a low-level language that is very close to what the computer itself can 'understand'. Indeed, assembly language is only different from machine code in so far as assembly language does use some short cuts in the form of mnemonics like SUB for subtraction.

asynchronous transmission a method of data transmission that transfers data at irregular intervals rather than regularly.

atomic this word can refer to a single value within a table. It is also used to refer to the integral nature of a data transmission. In other words, an atomic transmission must be completed in its entirety before it can be registered as committed within the database. Should such a transaction be halted before completion, the database resumes the condition it had before the transaction even started.

attribute like so many computer words, the meaning of attribute tends to vary according to the context in which it is used. In this book attribute has meant a value within a table. Thus 'Exeter' is an attribute within the table 'Store'. Many writers, however, use the word attribute when talking about the name of a field or column in a table. Thus 'Town' would be called an attribute of the table 'Store'.

back end a term used to denote all the programs in a database system that get data for a user. An application is a front end and it dispatches SQL (q.v.) statements to a back-end data server, which in turn returns rows of data.

backup normally used to refer to a copy of data that can be used should the data upon which you are working suffer from some form of crash. Equally, though, backup can be used to refer to a spare machine that can be used if the normal one requires attention.

bandwidth the range of frequencies over which a particular communications channel can transmit.

BASIC an acronym for Beginner's All-purpose Symbolic Instruction Code, a programming language developed in the 1960s. Despite being disapproved of by most academic programmers, BASIC is the most common of languages on small personal computers.

baud rate   a unit for indicating the speed of data transmission. Approximately, a baud is the transfer of one bit per second. Hence, when a modem (q.v.) is advertised as transmitting at 300 baud or having a baud rate of 2400, it means that the modem will transmit 300 bits or 2400 bits per second.

binary   a number system with a base of 2. Hence binary arithmetic is performed by only using the numbers 0 and 1.

binary tree   a way of storing data in such a fashion that its indexing system allows rapid and frequent updates.

bit   a binary digit that can have only two possible states, off or on.

block   has at least two meanings: (i) a unit of storage that can be treated as a unit for reading and writing operations; (ii) a sequence of statements in a programming language that form a definable subunit.

Boolean operator   a word that signifies a logical procedure. The words are AND, OR, NOT, and EXCLUSIVE-OR, and these logical operators are used within a database to produce specified combinations of data.

b,p.s.   an abbreviation for bits per second.

buffer   the memory area used for the temporary storage of data before it is moved to main memory or some other action is performed upon it.

bug   an error in a program or a malfunction in the hardware, either of which can prevent the successful carrying out of a program or application.

byte   a grouping of eight bits such as to represent a character, i.e. a letter, number, or other symbol.

C   a programming language.

Cambridge Ring   a type of local area network (q.v.).

cardinality   the number of rows that a table contains. The word is only of real use in a situation where you think unnecessary computer jargon will genuinely impress.

Cartesian product   a set containing all the possible rows available from any two given tables.

catalogdb   an INGRES utility used in order to find out what databases are owned by the current user.

channel   a path for data transmission.

characters per second   a method of measuring the speed of computer data transmission. A character comprises 8 bits, plus, normally, a stop and start bit. Hence, approximately, 10 characters per second is equal to 100 baud.

check bit   a binary digit that is added to a binary number in order to act as a check on the accuracy of that number.

coaxial cable   a cable with an insulated copper conductor at its core and an outer conductor of meshed copper wire sheathed in plastic. It is used in some computer networks (e.g. Ethernet).

COBOL a computer language, COmmon Business Oriented Language, which is widely used in business applications.

code a noun used to refer to programs or a verb used to signify the creation of programs.

compatibility when two or more computing entities, like operating systems, printers, modems, software packages, and so on can work together, they are said to be compatible. In the ideal world, every piece of computer equipment would be able to work with any other piece of computer equipment, every programming language could be embedded with any other programming language, and so on. This would be total compatibility. In the real world, however, compatibility is held up as desirable and totally disregarded in practice.

compiler a translator of a high-level language into machine code in such a fashion that the entire program is translated before any processing begins. Notice the difference between a compiler and an assembler (q.v.).

concentrator a more complex type of multiplexor (q.v.) that can edit and compress data from a number of terminals as well as combining it into one input flow.

concurrent access when more than one person can have access to the same section of data.

configuration the combination and arrangement of the component parts of a computer system.

consistency the state of a database when there are absolutely no conflicts between items of data, no duplicate entries, no identical objects being referred to by different names in different parts of the program. Clearly all databases should demonstrate consistency, but system crashes, parallel processing, and general availability do make it very difficult to ensure the maintenance of consistency.

contention the situation where two or more application programs try to access the same item of data simultaneously.

copy something you should always do unless you want to risk losing valuable data for ever.

crash the unexpected refusal of a computer or computer system to carry on doing its job. A crash can be caused by problems with hardware, the operating system, the software, or the electricity supply.

cursor an indicator on the screen that shows where a character will be placed if one presses the keyboard.

data a plural noun, now largely used as singular as well, indicating the presence of raw, factual items. Data that has some form of meaningful context is called information.

database an organized set of data.

database administrator (DBA) the person, or set of people, responsible for looking after a database and maintaining its reliability.

database management system   always known as the DBMS, it is a package of software that defines and handles a database. INGRES is an example.

data definition language   a language used to define the data in a database; define in the sense of indicating its data format, its data type, its size, and relationships.

data dictionary   often called a catalogue or system catalogue, the data dictionary is a full list of every entity within a database. Thus a data dictionary will list every table, every attribute, every index, and so on.

data manipulation language   the language used to cause data to be transferred between the application program and its database.

data model   the conceptual representation of data tables and the relationships between them.

data type: the classification of an item of data as a character, an integer, a character string, and so on.

DBMS   see database management system.

debug   the activity of removing bugs.

decryption   the process of decoding some encrypted code.

default   the option that the system will use if one is not specified by the user.

delete   the process of removing data, a process that should only be undertaken with extreme care.

density   the number of bits or tracks stored in a given amount of space.

determinant   an attribute (q.v.) on which another attribute is functionally dependent.

distributed database   a database that is available on more than one computer, and of which differing sections of the database may be stored upon different computers.

DOS   an acronym for disk operating system.

dumb terminal   a terminal that can only send or receive characters to and from a computer in the most basic of ways, i.e. without editing, for instance.

duplex, full   a method of data transmission by which each end can receive and send data simultaneously.

duplex, half   a method of data transmission by which each end can only either send or receive data at any time.

EBCDIC   an acronym for Extended Binary Coded Decimal Interchange Code, a code favoured by IBM comprising 8 bit units and thereby allowing 256 combinations.

edit   to make changes to a program or data file.

encrypt   to put data into code, for the purpose of security.

entity   a very common computer word that generally refers to any distinct object or concept.

entity-relationship   an information modelling tool that breaks an information system up into a series of entities that have relationships with each other.

Ethernet   a form of local area network (q.v.).

fibre optics fibres of glass that can transmit data as light-beam signals.

field the space for holding *one* item of data within a database. Thus, in the SOS database, the space for the holding of Store_no is a field.

flag a signal within a program used to indicate when a specific condition has occurred.

floating point a method of representing either very big or very small numbers that would be impossible to represent in normal digits.

flowchart a diagram of the design and flow of data within a computer system or within a computer program.

form a fundamental entity within INGRES, a form is a screen-based receptacle for information.

FORTRAN a computer third-generation language, normally used in engineering and mathematics.

fourth-generation language often abbreviated as 4GL, it is a non-procedural, English-like language that enables the computer user to gain results without undergoing any very taxing learning curve.

frame has at least three computer definitions, but within INGRES it simply refers to the form and associated menu that one is presented with in QBF, VIFRED, and so on.

front-end so far as a DBMS is concerned, the front end translates user queries into instructions for the application to execute.

functional dependence a one-to-one relationship between two items of data.

gateway the combination of hardware and software used to connect networks together.

hard disk a disk made of aluminium or some other rigid material that is coated with a magnetic material so as to enable it to store information as bits. Used as the data storage in large computers and, increasingly, in small ones as well.

hardware the physical equipment of a computer system: computers, printers, and so on.

hash a storage structure in INGRES and other databases.

header a concept employed in Report Writer for dealing with page breaks.

heap an area of memory that has no formal organization.

hierarchical database a database in which the relationship between data entities forms a tree-like structure.

high-level language a computer language that is far removed from the 0s and 1s that the computer can directly understand. Instead, a high-level language bears at least some resemblance to normal language. Third-generation languages like BASIC, FORTRAN, and Pascal are not as close to everyday language as fourth-generation languages like PROLOG, but they are all high-level languages.

IBM International Business Machines, the largest computer company in the world.

index   a cross-reference of fields within a database so as to provide rapid access to data.

INGRES   the INteractive GRaphics and REtrieval System, is a distributed database management program, available under several operating systems.

integer   any positive or negative whole number.

integrity   the assurance that data will not be modified or erased by unauthorized users.

intelligent terminal   a terminal that, unlike a dumb terminal, can perform some limited processing of data such as formatting or editing before sending that data to the computer.

interface   this word can have a range of associated meanings. Thus something can act as the interface between the computer and another piece of hardware. Equally something that allows the user to handle easily a complicated piece of software can be called the interface between the user and the package. In all cases, the word interface implies a meeting or interaction between two different elements.

interpreter   a translator, line-by-line, of a high-level language into machine code.

I/O   common abbreviation for input/output.

join   the joining together of two or more tables or elements from tables. For a join to be effected, there has to be some common value linking the tables.

justification   a term used to describe the alignment of left and/or right margins of a piece of text.

key   within a table, a key is an attribute or field that has a unique value, so that it can be used to locate a record or row. A primary key has a different value in each row in which it appears.

laser   a tightly packed light beam that can carry information.

load   to transfer data from a tape or disk into main memory.

local area network (LAN)   a computer network limited to one building or site.

log   a record of transactions.

low-level language   a language that the computer can execute directly or with very little translation. Thus machine code is the lowest level of computer languages, and assembly language the next higher grade, though still low level.

machine code   see low-level language.

main memory   that section of a computer, often called primary storage, which holds the data necessary for an application.

menu   a list of options within an application.

metadata   data about data; in other words, the data held in a data dictionary that describes the nature of all the data contained within the database.

micro   an abbreviation for microcomputer, a computer small enough to sit upon a desk or even slip into a pocket or briefcase.

microwaves super-high-frequency radiowaves that can transmit data signals through open space, much as television and radio signals are transmitted.

minicomputer a computer midway in size, power, and complexity between a mainframe and a micro.

modem a device that enables a computer to transmit its data over a telephone line.

MS-DOS a wisely used operating system.

multiplexor a piece of hardware that can combine the data signals from a number of terminals into one input flow that can be sent over a single channel.

multitasking the performance by a computer of a number of different operations simultaneously.

network an arrangement for allowing the transfer of data between computers and terminals.

normalization the process of removing all ambiguities and repetitions from data so that it can be clearly and accurately processed by a computer.

object oriented a type of programming in which the code, instead of referring to atomic data, refers to complex objects.

octal a number system with the base of 8.

op code, operation code the part of a machine code instruction that indicates what type of operation has to be performed.

operating system software that performs the basic procedures for operating a computer. Thus all applications software rests upon the context provided by the operating system.

optical fibres a thin glass or plastic fibre used for carrying data as lightwaves.

output the information produced by a computer and displayed on the screen or sent to the printer.

parameter an item of data passed to a procedure, subroutine, or function.

parity bit the 0 or 1 that is added to an existing byte or bytes so as to make the total number of positive bits odd or even (depending upon the convention adopted). Parity bits are used as a form of error checking.

Pascal a high-level language that is distinguished by its logical structure.

password a personal and secret set of characters used in a multi-computer context so as to check that the user has the right to use the computer or application concerned.

portability the ability of a piece of software to work on differing computer systems.

primary key a key that uniquely identifies an entity in a database, e.g. Store_no in the SOS Store table.

process a series of steps leading to a conclusion.

program a sequence of instructions to be executed by a computer.

prototyping the process of creating a piece of computer hardware or software rapidly so as to gain an overall impression of its viability without having to take the time necessary for creating a perfect product.

QUEL the original query language used in INGRES.

query a request for information from a database user.

query optimization the most efficient and speedy method of dealing with queries.

RDBMS relational database management system.

redundancy data that can be eliminated without any information being lost.

Report-By-Forms Forms-based method of defining INGRES reports.

Report Writer command language-based method of defining reports.

relation an association between data items or groups of data. Often used as a synonym for table.

relational database a database, or collection of data, in which all the data is arranged in tables. These tables, composed of rows and columns, are bound by certain rules to ensure that they are unambiguous and efficient. Such rules include normalization (q.v.), the presence of a primary key (q.v.) and the atomicity of each item of data.

row a horizontal grouping of related data fields. Often called a tuple.

security the preservation of a computer system from damage or unauthorized entry.

software life cycle the process of software development from the initial investigation as to the viability of a computerized solution to the maintenance of a new system.

sort to rearrange items of data into an ascending or descending order.

SQL a structured query language that defines, manipulates, and controls data within a relational database.

syntax rules specifying how to construct valid statements within a programming language.

sysmod an INGRES command used to modify the system catalogue to increase peformance.

system life cycle see software life-cycle.

table a presentation of data in a matrix of columns and rows so that each row is unique and each column represents a different value.

telecommunications the transmission of data over distances.

teleprocessing a synonym for data communications, i.e. the transmission of computer data between the computer system or systems and the respective terminals.

third normal form the level of normalization that is almost invariably sufficient for the effective handling of data.

transmission channel a medium like telephone wires or coaxial cables for carrying data from one point to another.

tuple a row within a table.

union in relational databases, union is the operation that combines all the rows of two separate tables to create one new table.

Unix an operating system.

validation the process of testing a program to ensure that it performs as it was intended to perform.

VAX a family of minicomputers.

view a virtual table.

VMS the acronym for Virtual Memory System, an operating system widely used for VAX minicomputers.

waveguides round or rectangular metal tubes that act as pathways for very high-frequency radio waves.

wild card a symbol—usually *—that can be used where the actual characters are unknown. Hence P* would match Palestrina, Palestine, Postgres, and so on.

window a portion of the screen devoted to a particular task.

word a group of bits that can be handled by a computer as a unit.

Appendix
Summary on how to construct a database

To create a database

To enter the INGRES world you will need to type

addingres

or

access/software = secure_ingres (or insecure_ingres)

at the > or $ prompt. Then, having entered the INGRES context one types

createdb

followed by the name of the database that you are creating, for example:

createdb sos

One can now go on to create the tables of that database.

To create a table

Version 5
   Cursor rests on Tables; press Enter.
   Cursor rests on Create; press Enter.
   Type in name of table; press Enter.
   Fill in column names and data types; press F3.
   Press F10; move cursor to Query-by-Forms; press Enter.
   Move cursor to TableFields; press Enter.
   Fill in data; press F3.

Version 6
   Type INGMENU followed by the name of the database.

Place cursor on Tables; press Enter.
Place cursor on Create; press Enter.
Type in the name of the table and the column names.
Save the table by pressing the numeric key 0.
Press FP3.
Place cursor over Query-by-Forms; press Enter.

The rest is identical to the Version 5 procedure.

Bibliography

It seemed to me to be pretentious and unhelpful to provide a list of every book that I felt had aided me in the preparation of this book. Hence I have limited myself to listing, under appropriate subject headings, only the books that have been referred to in the course of the text. The subject headings are as follows: general books; artificial intelligence; databases; data dictionaries; INGRES; SQL.

General books

Robert Behling, *Computers and Information Processing* (Kent, 1986).
Colin Corder, *Ending the Computer Conspiracy* (McGraw-Hill, 1985).
Jeffrey L. Whitten, Lonnie D. Bentley and Thomas I. M. Ho, *Systems Analysis and Design Methods* (Times Mirror/Mosby College, 1986).

Artificial intelligence

G. L. Simons, *Introducing Artificial Intelligence* (N.C.C. Publications, 1984).

Databases

S. Atre, *Database: Structural Techniques for Design, Performance, and Management* (John Wiley, 1980).
D. S. Bowers, *From Data to Database* (Van Nostrand Reinhold, 1988).
Alfonso F. Cardenas, *Data Base Management Systems* (Allyn and Bacon Inc., 2nd edn, 1985).
C. J. Date, *An Introduction to Database Systems*, Vol. I, 4th edn (Addison-Wesley, 1986).

C. J. Date, *An Introduction to Database Systems*, Vol. II (Addison-Wesley, 1983).

Ramez Elmasri and Shamkant B. Navathe, *Fundamentals of Database Systems* (Benjamin/Cummings, 1989).

Mark L. Gillenson, *Database Step-by-Step* (John Wiley, 2nd edn, 1990).

Rob Healey, *A Relational Database and 4GL in Action* (Savant, 1987).

D. R. Howe, *Data Analysis for Data Base Design* (Edward Arnold, 2nd edn, 1989).

Peter Laurie, *Databases* (Chapman & Hall/Methuen, 1985).

Elizabeth Oxborrow, *Databases and Database Systems* (Chartwell-Bratt, 2nd edn, 1989).

Peter D. Smith and G. Michael Barnes, *Files and Databases: An Introduction* (Addison-Wesley, 1987).

Jeffrey Ullman, *Principles of Data Base Systems* (Computer Science Press, 1982).

Jeffrey Ullman, *Principles of Data Base and Knowledge Base Systems* (W. H. Freeman, 1988).

Patrick Valduriez and Georges Gardarin, *Analysis and Comparison of Relational Database Systems* (Addison-Wesley, 1989).

Data dictionaries

Rom Narayan, *Data Dictionary: Implementing, Use and Maintenance* (Prentice Hall, 1988).

Ellen Thro, *The Database Dictionary* (Microtrend, 1990).

INGRES

C. J. Date, *A Guide to INGRES* (Addison-Wesley, 1987).

Carl Malamud, *INGRES: Tools for Building an Information Architecture* (Van Nostrand Reinhold, 1989).

Peter Matthews, *INGRES User Guide: Visual Programming Tools* (Prentice Hall, 1991).

Relational Technology Inc., *INGRES Reference Guide* (1987).

Michael Stonebreaker (ed.), *The INGRES Papers* (Addison-Wesley, 1985).

SQL

Sandra L. Emerson, Marcy Darnovsky, and Judith S. Bowman, *The Practical SQL Handbook* (Addison-Wesley, 1989).

Carolyn J. Hursch and Jack L. Hursch, *SQL: The Structured Query Language* (TAB, 1988).

Rick F. van der Lans, *Introduction to SQL* (Addison-Wesley, 1988).

Elizabeth Lynch, *Understanding SQL* (Macmillan, 1990).

Index